EMPLOYEE BENEFITS DICTIONARY

An Annotated Compendium of Frequently Used Terms

EMPLOYEE
BENEFITS
DICTIONARY

An Annotated Compendium of Frequently Used Terms

Virginia L. Briggs
Michael G. Kushner
Michael J. Schinabeck

The Bureau of National Affairs, Inc., Washington, D.C.

Library of Congress Cataloging-in-Publication Data

Briggs, Virginia L.
    Employee benefits dictionary : an annotated compendium of
frequently used terms / Virginia L. Briggs, Michael G. Kushner &
Michael J. Schinabeck.
    p.   cm.
    ISBN 0-87179-709-7
    1. Employee fringe benefits—Dictionaries.   I. Kushner, Michael
G.   II. Schinabeck, Michael J.   III. Title.
HD4928.N6B75   1991   91–39410
331.25′5′03—dc20   CIP

Published by BNA Books
1250 23rd St., NW, Washington, D.C. 20037-1165

Printed in the United States of America
International Standard Book Number: 0–87179–709–7

Preface

Since the Employee Retirement Income Security Act (ERISA) was enacted in 1974, mountains of legislation and regulations have been issued in the employee benefits area. This, in turn, has given rise to a jargon that is peculiar to the field. It is almost impossible for someone new to this area of the law to deal with it effectively without having a working knowledge of its many "terms of art." In addition to the terms derived from official guidance, employee benefits practitioners themselves (lawyers, accountants, actuaries, consultants, human resource and insurance professionals, and others) have added their informal "trade jargon" to the field.

As a result of this jargon, and of the complexity of the field, even for the seasoned professional it may seem to take forever to fully understand certain provisions of the relevant law. As the saying goes, "you have to know a little Greek before you can learn more Greek." Yet most people come to this area knowing none of its specialized terms and concepts or their interrelation with one another. Further, because employee benefits law is a multidisciplinary subject, people from one discipline may be familiar with the terms and concepts in their area, but may be unfamiliar with those of the other disciplines. Yet, the interrelated nature of the subject requires that they understand the basics of the other disciplines to perform their jobs effectively.

In addition to the terminology, the substantive law of employee benefits is itself so complex and derived from so many sources that it is often difficult to locate the relevant authorities needed to perform effective research. Another impediment to performing effective research stems from the fact that employee benefits law is constantly evolving, making practitioners hard-pressed to digest all the changes.

We have designed this book to be both a learning tool (dictionary) and a research expediter. First, it gives you, the employee benefits professional, the conceptual framework for understanding a particular term, so that you can teach yourself more: it gets you started, which is half the battle. The dictionary portion does this by explaining in clear English the meaning of key terms. Second, the book expedites your research: after the definition of each term, we have provided citations to relevant authorities that further explain a term's meaning and application. These include cites to statutes, regulations, rulings, and case law, as well as references to unofficial sources, such as treatises and articles. A word set in small caps within a definition or citation indicates that it is defined elsewhere in the dictionary. In many entries, examples illustrate the effects of various rulings and regulations.

While this book was not designed to provide treatise-level depth, we believe that consulting it before beginning your research can save you hours of time by bringing the issues into sharper focus and providing citations to assist in further research. The book gives you the equivalent of hands-on experience without the mistakes inherent in the learning process; it gives you a feel for the development of employee benefits law as well as for the meaning of particular terms. This, we think you will find, takes a lot of the pain out of research and helps provide you with assurance that you have not overlooked relevant authority.

In sum, it is a considerable challenge to advise clients properly in light of all the complexity and change in the employee benefits area. However, this very complexity and evolution has made the field a uniquely challenging and interesting one in which to work. We believe you will find this tool highly useful in that endeavor.

The authors wish to thank Louise Goines who conceived of this project and nurtured it to fruition and Mary Hughes, our editor, whose many insightful suggestions are included in this book.

Virginia L. Briggs
Michael G. Kushner
Michael J. Schinabeck

Washington, D.C.
November 1991

List of Terms Defined

common control
compensation
complete withdrawal
conduit IRA
constructive receipt
continuation coverage
contribution (to a qualified retirement plan)
contribution rate/contribution percentage
contributory plan
controlled group
conversion
coordination of benefits (COB)
core coverage
cost of living adjustment (COLA)
coverage
covered compensation (for a plan year)
covered employee
covered service
current liability
current value
custodial account

D

death benefits
death benefit exclusion
death benefit only (DBO) plan
deduction/deductibility
deferred compensation
deferred profit-sharing plan
deferred vesting
deficit reduction contribution
defined benefit excess plan
defined benefit plan/defined contribution
  plan
defined contribution excess plan
definitely determinable benefit requirement
de minimis fringe benefit
dependent
dependent care assistance program
determination date
determination letter
disability retirement benefits

disabled
discount factor
discrimination
distress termination

E

early retirement age/earliest retirement age
earned income
educational assistance plan
elapsed time method
elective deferral
eligibility computation period
eligible deferred compensation plan
eligible employee
eligible employer
employee
employee assistance program (EAP)
employee benefits
employee benefit plan
employee contributions
employee-pay-all VEBA
employee pension benefit plan
employee organization
employee stock purchase plan
employee welfare benefit plan
employer
employer-pay-all split-dollar insurance
employer real property
employer security
endowment policy
enrolled actuary
entry date
equity split-dollar life insurance
equivalency
ERISA
ERISA plan
ESOP (employee stock ownership plan)
excess aggregate contributions
excess benefit percentage
excess benefit plan
excess contribution

investment in the contract
investment manager
involuntary termination
IRA (individual retirement arrangement)

J

joint and survivor annuity
joint and survivor annuity with term certain

K

Keogh plan
key employee
key-man insurance

L

Labor-Management Relations Act of 1947 (LMRA)
lapse restriction
late retirement/late retirement age
leased employee
leveraged ESOP
life annuity
life expectancy
life insurance contract
limitation on contributions/benefits (I.R.C. § 415)
line of business
lump-sum distribution

M

mass withdrawal
master plan
matching contribution
maternity- or paternity-related leave of absence
maximum age requirement
maximum benefits
medical care
medical reimbursement plan

Medicare
Medicare carve-out plan
Medicare Catastrophic Coverage Act of 1988 (MCCA)
Medicare supplement plan
Medigap plan
merged plan/merger
minimum accrual
minimum benefit requirement
minimum contribution requirement
minimum funding standard
minimum participation rule
minimum required distribution
mistake of fact/mistake of law
model amendment
model SEP
modified endowment contract
money purchase plan
mortality assumption
MPPAA (Multiemployer Pension Plan Amendment Act of 1980)
multiemployer plan
multiple employer plan
multiple employer welfare arrangement (MEWA)

N

National Association of Insurance Commissioners (NIAC)
net unrealized appreciation (NUA)
no-additional-cost services
noncompliancc period
noncontributory plan
nonelective contribution
nonforfeitable/nonforfeitable benefit
nonkey employee
nonqualified cash or deferred arrangement
nonqualified deferred compensation plan
nonqualified stock options
normal cost
normal retirement age (general definition)

qualifying employer real property
qualifying employer security
qualifying event

R

Rabbi trust
rate making
ratio test
reasonable compensation
recharacterization
reduction in force (RIF)
registration-class of securities
remedial amendment period
required distribution
restricted property
restricted stock option
retired lives reserves (RLR) insurance
retirement plan
revenue procedure
revenue ruling
reverse split-dollar insurance
reversion
rollover
rule of 45 vesting

S

salary reduction arrangement
salary reduction SEP (SARSEP)
seasonal employees
Section 22 amount
Section 89
Section 401(h) account
Section 401(k) plan
self-directed account
self-employed individual
separate lines of business (SLOB)
separation from service
SEPPAA (Single-Employer Pension Plan Amendments Act of 1986)
70 percent test
severance from service

simplified employee pension (SEP)
simplified split-dollar insurance
single-employer plan
single-premium life insurance
Social Security
Social Security retirement age
Social Security supplement
Social Security tax
Social Security taxable wage base
split-dollar life insurance
split funding
spousal consent
spousal IRA
standard termination
statutorily excludable employees
step-rate/step-rate excess plan
stock appreciation rights (SARs)
stock bonus plan
stock option (compensatory)
stop-loss reinsurance
substantial risk of forfeiture
success tax
supplemental benefits
supplemental executive retirement plan (SERP)
supplemental liability
supplemental unemployment benefit plan
suspension of benefits
switchback liability

T

Taft-Hartley Act plan
target benefit plan
taxable income
taxable year
tax-deferred annuity
technical advice memorandum (TAM)
10-or-more employer plan
termination
term life insurance
3 percent rule
thrift plan

top-hat plan
top heavy/top-heavy plan
top-paid group
trusteed plan
trustee-to-trustee transfer
turnover rate/turnover assumption

U

unemployment tax (FUTA)
unfunded deferred compensation plan
unit-benefit excess plan
unit benefit plan
universal life insurance
unrealized appreciation
unrelated business income tax (UBIT)
user fee
utilization review

V

valuation
variable annuity

variable life insurance contract
VEBA (Voluntary Employees' Beneficiary Association)
vesting

W

waived funding deficiency
welfare benefit fund (WBF)
welfare benefit plan
whole life insurance
window plan/window benefit
withdrawal liability (multiemployer plans)
workers' compensation
working condition fringe benefits

Y

year of service

Z

zero balance reimbursement account plan

A

accidental death and dismemberment (AD&D) plan An employee benefit plan that furnishes benefits in the event of a covered individual's death, permanent disfigurement, or permanent loss of, or loss of use of, a member or function of the body. Benefits generally are paid if there is an accidental death or loss of both hands or both eyes. Loss of use or disfigurement is considered permanent when it reasonably may be expected to continue for the life of the individual. AD&D benefits are not considered income replacement since they are not calculated with respect to the time the individual is absent from work or unable to perform duties. Thus, although amounts received by an employee through accident insurance for personal injuries generally are included in the employee's gross income, gross income *does not* include amounts that constitute accidental death and dismemberment payments. The exclusion does not apply to benefits the amount of which are determined by reference to the period the employee is absent from work.

Example: If an employee is absent from work as a result of the loss of an arm, and the employer maintains an AD&D plan under which the employee is to receive $300 for a period not to exceed 50 weeks' absence from work, the exclusion from income does not apply and the amounts must be included in the employee's gross income. This rule does not apply, however, to amounts paid as workers' compensation or amounts paid under such a policy as a result of death (such amounts are treated under I.R.C. § 101).

See WORKERS' COMPENSATION, DEATH BENEFITS.

Statutory and Regulatory Reference: See I.R.C. §§ 101, 104, 105(c), 106; Treas. Reg. §§ 1.105-3 (payments unrelated to absence from work); 1.106-1, 1.162-10 (employer deduction as trade or business expense). Treas. Reg. § 1.79-1(f)(3) (implies that accidental death coverage is excludable under § 106 despite lack of express statutory exclusion). *See also* Prop. Treas. Reg. § 1.125-2, Q&A-4(a)(2) (coverage under an AD&D policy may be a qualified benefit for CAFETERIA PLAN purposes).

Case and Other Interpretive Reference: PLRs 8801015, 8746024 (accidental death coverage excludable under I.R.C. § 106 despite lack of express statutory exclusion).

Treatise Reference: Tax Mgmt. (BNA), No. 389, *Disability and Medical Reimbursement Benefits.*

accrual/benefit accrual The crediting of benefits to an employee by reason of his or her participation in a retirement or welfare plan. Benefit accrual also refers to the rate at which employees earn benefits under a plan. In a qualified defined contribution plan, an employee's accrued benefit is simply his or her account balance at any point in time. In a defined benefit plan, the plan's benefit formula determines an employee's accrued benefit. Usually, in a defined benefit plan, an employee will accrue benefits at a specified rate for each year of service, e.g., one percent of compensation per year of service. Sometimes for purposes of the tax law it is necessary to distinguish which part of an employee's total accrued benefit is attributable to employee contributions and which part is attributable to employer contributions. Where a defined contribution plan maintains separate accounting for employee and employer contributions, making this determination is relatively easy. In a defined benefit plan, the accrued benefit attributable to employee contributions is determined by:

(1) Dividing the total of employee contributions, less withdrawals, by the total of employer contributions, less withdrawals, and

(2) Multiplying the result by the employee's total accrued benefit.

The result is the employee's accrued benefit attributable to employee contributions. Whatever amount of the employee's total benefit remains is the employee's accrued benefit attributable to employer contributions.

There are two sets of accrual rules: the general rules of I.R.C. § 411(b) that apply to defined benefit plans and the top-heavy minimum benefit/contribution requirements of I.R.C. § 416(c) that require TOP-HEAVY PLANS to provide certain minimum accruals to NONKEY EMPLOYEES. The top-heavy rules apply to both defined benefit and defined contribution plans.

The § 411(b) rules applicable to defined benefit plans are designed to prevent such plans from discriminating in favor of highly compensated employees by excessively backloading the rate at which employees earn benefits. Since highly compensated employees generally tend to remain with the employer longer, delaying benefit accrual to the later years can disproportionately benefit the highly paid. This potential usually does not exist in defined contribution plans that generally allocate the employer's annual contribution to the employees' accounts based on a specified percentage of each employee's compensation for the year. The benefit formulas in defined benefit plans, however, tend to be geared to the length of an employee's service with the employer. As a result, to qualify under I.R.C. § 401(a), a defined benefit plan must satisfy one of three § 411(b) accrual rules designed to prevent excessive backloading. A plan cannot qualify by satisfying one rule in one plan year and another in the next; rather, it must satisfy one rule over all plan years with respect to all plan participants. The three rules are: (1) the 3 percent rule; (2) the 133⅓ percent rule; and (3) the fractional rule.

In addition, as mentioned above, under I.R.C. § 416(c), both qualified defined contribution and defined benefit plans must provide a minimum level of ACCRUED BENEFIT to each participating nonkey employee for any PLAN YEAR in which such plans are top-heavy.

See BACKLOADING, FRACTIONAL RULE, KEY EMPLOYEE, 133⅓ PERCENT RULE, 3 PERCENT RULE, TOP-HEAVY, VESTING.

Statutory and Regulatory Reference: ERISA § 204 (regular accrual rules applicable to defined benefit plans); I.R.C. §§ 411(b) and 416(c); Treas. Reg. §§ 1.411(a), 1.416-1, Q&A M-1 to M-17 (special minimum accrual rules for top-heavy plans).

Treatise Reference: See Tax Mgmt. (BNA), No. 351, *Pension Plans—Qualification*, No. 353, *Owner-Dominated Plans—Top-Heavy and H.R.10 Plans*; *see also Employee Benefits Law* 123-25 (1991).

accrual computation period   Under a qualified retirement plan, this is a measuring period used to determine whether a participant has earned a year of service for benefit accrual purposes.

Labor Department regulations require that an ERISA-covered retirement plan specify in its PLAN DOCUMENT a 12-consecutive-month period that will serve as its accrual computation period. If a participant completes 1,000 hours of service or such lesser amount as the plan requires in this period, he or she generally must be credited with at least a partial year of service in determining the ACCRUED BENEFIT.

A qualified retirement plan, if it so provides, may require employees to perform 2,000 hours of service in a 12-month computation period before crediting them with a full year of service for benefit accrual purposes, but the plan that does this must call for at least a partial year of service to be credited to any employee who completes less than 2,000, but more than 1,000, hours of accrual service.

See EQUIVALENCY, HOUR OF SERVICE, YEAR OF SERVICE.

Statutory and Regulatory Reference: I.R.C. § 411(b)(3)(A)-(C); 29 C.F.R. §§ 2530.200b-1(a), 2530.204-2(c)(1) and (2).

Treatise Reference: Tax Mgmt. (BNA), No. 351, *Pension Plans—Qualification.*

accrued benefit   The amount of benefit that a participant in a qualified or non-qualified retirement plan has earned under the plan's terms as of a specified point in time.

ERISA § 3(23) defines "accrued benefit" as:

"(A) in the case of a defined benefit plan, the individual's accrued benefit determined under the plan and, except as provided in [ERISA] § 204(c)(3), expressed in the form of an annual benefit commencing at normal retirement age, or

"(B) in the case of a plan which is an individual account plan, the balance of the individual's account."

ERISA § 3(23) adds that an employee's accrued benefit shall never be less than the benefit attributable to the employee's own accrued contributions.

See ACCRUAL.

Statutory and Regulatory Reference: ERISA § 3(23); I.R.C. § 411(b); Treas. Reg. § 1.411(b)-1 *et seq.*

Treatise Reference: Tax Mgmt. (BNA), No. 351, Pension Plans—Qualification.

accumulated funding deficiency   For a qualified retirement plan subject to the Internal Revenue Code's MINIMUM FUNDING STANDARD, this term is used to describe an excess of charges over credits in the plan's funding standard account. If the plan's sponsoring employer does not remedy this deficiency by making sufficient timely plan contributions, it will be subject to a two-tiered excise tax. In single-employer plans, the first-tier tax equals 10 percent of the deficiency (as opposed to five percent for multiemployer plans). If the deficiency is not corrected within a statutory correction period, the second-tier tax, equal to 100 percent of the deficiency, applies. The correction period begins with the end of the PLAN YEAR in question and ends on the later of: (1) 90 days after the IRS mails the employer a notice of deficiency; or (2) the date on which a Tax Court decision regarding the FUNDING deficiency becomes final.

Unless it determines collection of the tax is in jeopardy, the IRS must notify the Secretary of Labor before it issues a notice of deficiency with respect to the 10 and 100 percent excise taxes. Also, the IRS may waive the 100 percent penalty.

See FUNDING STANDARD ACCOUNT.

Statutory and Regulatory Reference: See I.R.C. §§ 412(a) and 4971; Treas. Reg. § 1.412(c)(1)-1; *see also* ERISA § 302(a).

Treatise Reference: See Tax Mgmt. (BNA), No. 371, *Employee Plans — Deductions, Contributions, and Funding; Employee Benefits Law* 139-40 (1991).

active participant   An individual who, for the calendar year, is eligible to earn a benefit under an employer-sponsored qualified retirement plan.

The Tax Reform Act of 1986 (TRA 1986), Pub. L. No. 99-513, limited the deductibility of individual retirement account (IRA) contributions for such participants. If an employee or his or her spouse actively participates in a qualified retirement plan at sometime during a calendar year, his or her otherwise allowable IRA deduction for the year (generally the lesser of $2,000 or 100 percent of compensation) is reduced according to a formula. The formula is based on the employee's level of adjusted gross income for the year. For single taxpayers the deduction phase-out begins when adjusted gross income for the year reaches $25,000 and reduces the taxpayer's allowable IRA deduction by 20 cents for every dollar of adjusted gross income in excess of $25,000. For married taxpayers filing joint federal income tax returns, the phase-out begins at $40,000 of adjusted gross income, and for married taxpayers filing separately, it begins with the first dollar of adjusted gross income for the year. As is the case for single taxpayers, the allowable deduction for married taxpayers drops by 20 cents for each dollar of adjusted gross income in excess of the applicable threshold dollar amount.

See PARTICIPANT, IRA.

Statutory and Regulatory Reference: Pub. L. No. 99-514; I.R.C. §§ 219(g)(5)-(6); Treas. Reg. § 1.219-1.

Treatise Reference: See Tax Mgmt. (BNA), No. 355, *IRAs and SEPs. See also* I.R.S. Publication No. 590, *Individual Retirement Arrangements (IRAs)* 4 (Rev. 1989).

actual contribution percentage (ACP)
In a qualified retirement plan that calls for employee after-tax or employer matching contributions, this term describes the amount of such contributions made for the year on behalf of highly compensated plan participants (within the meaning of I.R.C. § 414(q)), divided by such employees' annual compensation, or an amount determined in the same manner with respect to nonhighly compensated plan participants.

Once these percentages are determined for both groups, they are applied in testing the plan for DISCRIMINATION as to employee and matching contributions. The ACP for highly compensated employees must not exceed the greater of (1) 125 percent of the ACP for the nonhighly compensated, or (2) 200 percent of the ACP for the nonhighly compensated (but not more than two percentage points above the nonhighly compensated ACP). A plan that fails to pass certain percentage tests in I.R.C. § 401(m) with respect to these types of contributions must make correcting distributions to the highly compensated participants involved in an amount that is sufficient to enable the plan to pass these tests or face disqualification. Other permissible corrective actions may be taken but they must be made within 12 months of the close of the plan year.

See MATCHING CONTRIBUTION.

Statutory and Regulatory Reference: I.R.C. § 401(m); Treas. Reg. § 1.401(m)1-2.

Treatise Reference: Tax Mgmt. (BNA), No. 358, *Cash or Deferred Arrangements*; *Employee Benefits Law* 214-16 (1991).

actual deferral percentage (ADP)   The amount of salary reduction contributions made by an employee to a § 401(k) plan for the year, divided by his or her compensation for that year. Under special nondiscrimination tests for such plans, the ADP of eligible highly compensated employees as determined under I.R.C. § 414(q) (as a group) cannot exceed that of eligible nonhighly compensated employees (also as a group) by more than 125 percent. Alternatively, a plan will pass the test if the ADP of the highly compensated group does not exceed that of the nonhighly compensated group by more than 200 percent, provided the difference between the ADP of the highly compensated group and that of the nonhighly compensated group does not exceed two percentage points. A § 401(k) plan that satisfies the ADP test will also satisfy the § 401(a)(4) general nondiscrimination rules with respect to its cash or deferred arrangement. If a § 401(k) plan fails the ADP test, corrective actions are permitted, including distributing the excess deferrals and making additional plan contributions.

Example: Under a § 401(k) plan, the sponsoring employer's highly compensated employees defer, on average, 5 percent of their compensation for the year, while nonhighly compensated employees, on average, defer 3 percent. The plan will fail the 125 percent test because 5 percent exceeds 3 percent by more than 125 percent. The plan, however, will pass the 200 percent test because 5 percent is less than 200 percent of 3 percent and does not exceed 3 percent by more than two percentage points.

See SECTION 401(K) PLAN.

Statutory and Regulatory Reference: I.R.C. § 401(k)(3)(A); Treas. Reg. § 1.401(k)-1.

Treatise Reference: Tax Mgmt. (BNA), No. 358, *Cash or Deferred Arrangements*; *Employee Benefits Law* 212-13 (1991).

actual retirement age   Generally, under a qualified plan, the attained age of an employee at retirement, when such retirement takes place after normal retirement age.

See EARLY RETIREMENT AGE, NORMAL RETIREMENT AGE.

actuarial assumptions   A set of estimates made by a defined benefit plan's actuary to determine the amount of funds the employer may or must contribute to the plan. The term also applies to the estimate used in computing the benefit due from a retirement plan to a participant or beneficiary. Typical assumptions include: (1) the amount of interest plan investments will earn; (2) what percentage of participants will ultimately vest in their benefits; (3) participants' future compensation level; (4) participants' average RETIREMENT AGE; and (5) the LIFE EXPECTANCY of participants and beneficiaries.

Statutory and Regulatory Reference: *See* ERISA § 302(b)(5); I.R.C. §§ 412(b)(5) and (c)(3) (rules for computing the plan's INTEREST ASSUMPTION for FUNDING purposes). Note that I.R.C. § 404(a)(1)(A) requires that the actuarial assumptions used for computing a defined benefit plan's limit on deductible employer contributions must be the same as the ones it uses for purposes of applying the I.R.C. § 412 MINIMUM FUNDING STANDARD. *See also* Treas. Reg. § 1.404(a)-3(b). For for the rules on actuarial assumptions governing a participant or spouse's lump-sum distribution from a qualified plan, *see* ERISA §§ 203(e)(2) and 205(g)(3) and I.R.C. § 411(a)(11). For the rules governing actuarial assumptions in calculating an employer's WITHDRAWAL LIABILITY under a multiemployer pension plan, *see* ERISA § 4213. A qualified defined benefit plan must specify its actuarial assumptions in its PLAN DOCUMENT. *See* I.R.C. § 401(a)(25). The actuarial assumptions under a single-employer or multiple-employer defined benefit plan, in general, must all be reasonable and represent the actuary's best estimate of what will happen in the future. The assumptions used in a multiemployer plan are subject to a lesser standard: they must only be "reasonable in the aggregate." *See also* I.R.C. § 412(c); Treas. Reg. § 1.412(c)(1).

Case and Other Interpretive Reference: Rev. Rul. 78-331, 1978-2 C.B. 158, providing that an assumption that employees under a defined benefit plan retire at the plan's NORMAL RETIREMENT AGE may cause the plan's actuarial assumptions not to be "reasonable in the aggregate" if this does not conform to the actual retirement practices of the employees involved. Note that, for single employer defined benefit plans, the reasonable in the aggregate standard that existed for testing actuarial assumptions at the time the above-referenced ruling was issued has been changed statutorily to a rule that generally requires that all actuarial assumptions be reasonable individually. The reasonable in the aggregate standard, however, continues to apply to multiemployer defined benefit plans. Note also that, in Rev. Rul. 78-403, 1978-2 C.B. 153, the IRS ruled that a qualified defined benefit plan may not provide for the allocation of excess earnings (in effect, an actuarial surplus) to a participant's individual account).

Treatise Reference: See Tax Mgmt. (BNA), No. 371, *Employee Plans—Deductions, Contributions, and Funding. See also* D. McGill & D. Grubbs, Jr., *Fundamentals of Private Pensions* 239 (6th ed. 1989).

actuarial cost method   A recognized actuarial technique used for establishing the annual actuarial cost of pension plan benefits and expenses. This is the ERISA term that is equivalent to the term funding method in I.R.C. § 412.

See FUNDING METHOD.

Statutory and Regulatory Reference: ERISA § 3(31). For the use of actuarial cost methods in applying the minimum FUNDING requirements to defined benefit plans, *see* ERISA § 302(c)(1) and I.R.C. § 412(c)(1).

actuarial equivalent   A benefit under a retirement plan that is estimated to be of substantially the same value as another plan benefit, based on a predetermined set of mathematical assumptions used by the plan's actuary. (Typical assumptions include the interest rate that will be earned on the plan's investments and the projected LIFE EXPECTANCY of the employee or his or her beneficiary). In general, all optional forms of benefit distribution under a qualified retirement plan must be the actuarial equivalent of the normal form of benefit called for under the plan.

Treatise Reference: See generally Tax Mgmt. (BNA), No. 371, *Employee Plans—Deductions, Contributions, and Funding.*

actuarial surplus   Excess assets in a defined benefit plan or a prefunded welfare plan that result from the fact that the plan's experience has, over a period of time, outperformed its projected performance as calculated under the assumptions used by the plan's actuary.

Examples of sources that can produce an actuarial surplus include: (1) the fact that the return earned on the investment of plan assets has exceeded the rate of return that was projected by the plan's actuary; (2) the fact that there was a greater level of employees leaving the company prior to becoming vested in their benefits than was predicted; (3) the fact that plan participants' compensation (upon which their benefits are based) has been lower than was projected; and (4) the fact that, on average, plan participants and beneficiaries have not lived to their full LIFE EXPECTANCY (resulting in the less benefits being paid to them).

In a defined benefit plan, for purposes of the MINIMUM FUNDING STANDARD of I.R.C.

§ 412, such actuarial surplus is reflected as an "experience gain," and is amortized over five years for single- and multiple- employer plans and over 15 years for multiemployer plans.

When a plan's ACTUARIAL ASSUMPTIONS are too optimistic and, over time, the plan's performance falls short of its projected performance, the resulting shortfall is characterized as an "experience loss" for minimum FUNDING purposes. This loss is then amortized in the same manner as EXPERIENCE GAINS described above.

The REVERSION (i.e., the return) of an actuarial surplus to an employer upon the TERMINATION of a qualified defined benefit plan is subject to an excise tax. This tax can be imposed at a rate of either 20 or 50 percent of the amount of the reversion, depending on the circumstances surrounding the plan's termination.

Statutory and Regulatory Reference: I.R.C. §§ 412(b)(3)(B) and 4980; Treas. Reg. § 1.412(c)(1).

actuarial valuation   *See* VALUATION.

actuary   *See* ENROLLED ACTUARY.

AD&D   *See* ACCIDENTAL DEATH AND DISMEMBERMENT PLAN.

ADEA (Age Discrimination in Employment Act)   Enacted in 1967, the ADEA protects the rights of employees between the ages of 40 and 70 regarding hiring, discharging, compensation, and terms, conditions, and privileges of employment. The ADEA prohibits discrimination, making it unlawful for an employer: (1) to fail or refuse to hire or to discharge an individual or otherwise discriminate against an individual with respect to compensation, terms, conditions or privileges of employment because of his or her age; (2) to limit, segregate, or classify

employees in a way that would deprive the individual of employment opportunity or otherwise adversely affect the status as an employee because of the individual's age; or (3) to reduce the wage rate of an employee to comply with the provisions of the ADEA. The ADEA applies to employers affecting interstate commerce that have at least 20 employees on each working day in at least 20 calendar weeks in the current or previous year.

Statutory and Regulatory Reference: See Pub. L. No. 90-202, 29 U.S.C. §§ 621-34; Older Workers Benefit Protection Act, Pub. L. No. 101-433 (Oct. 16, 1990); *see also* 29 C.F.R. § 860.120, 44 Fed. Reg. 30648 (May 25, 1979) (Department of Labor); 29 C.F.R. § 1625.13, 46 Fed. Reg. 47724 (Sept. 19, 1981) (Equal Employment Opportunity Commission (EEOC)).

Case and Other Interpretative Reference: *United Airlines, Inc. v. McMann*, 434 U.S. 192, 1 EB Cases 1556, 16 FEP Cases 146 (1977)(ADEA allowed mandatory retirement before age 65 when in accordance with the requirements of a bona fide retirement plan); *but see* Pub. L. No. 95-256 which raised the mandatory retirement age and effectively overturned *McMann*. *See also Public Employees Retirement System v. Betts*, 492 U.S. 158, 11 EB Cases 1049 (1989) (ADEA exempts all provisions of bona fide employee benefit plans from the ADEA requirements unless the plan is a subterfuge for discrimination in the nonfringe benefit aspects of employment. *Betts* overturned 29 C.F.R. § 1625.10 (EEOC regulation). However, The Older Workers Benefit Protection Act, Pub. L. No. 101-433 (Oct. 16, 1990), legislatively overturned *Betts* by amending the ADEA to specifically provide age discrimination protection in matters involving employee fringe benefits).

Treatise Reference: See J.E. Kalet, *Age Discrimination in Employment Law* (2d ed. 1990); Tax Mgmt. (BNA), No. 363, *Age and*

Sex Discrimination and Employee Benefit Plans.

adequate consideration For purposes of part 4, subtitle B of ERISA:

(1) With respect to a security that has a recognized market, either (a) the security's price on a national securities exchange that is registered under § 6 of the Securities Exchange Act of 1934; or (b) if the security is not traded on such an exchange, a price that is no less favorable to the plan than the security's offering price as established by the current bid and asked prices quoted by persons independent of the issuer and of any PARTY IN INTEREST.

(2) With respect to an asset other than a security described in (1), above, the asset's fair market value determined in good faith by the plan's trustee or NAMED FIDUCIARY under the plan's terms and in accordance with any applicable Labor Department regulations.

See FIDUCIARY/FIDUCIARY DUTY.

Statutory and Regulatory Reference: See ERISA § 3(18).

administrative services only (ASO) plan
See MEDICAL REIMBURSEMENT PLAN.

administrator *See* PLAN ADMINISTRATOR.

advance funding/prefunding The FUNDING of benefits under a retirement or welfare plan before the time that they become payable to plan participants. When specifically permitted by the Internal Revenue Code, employers may fund plan benefits in taxable years that begin before the year that such benefits are scheduled to be paid to participants and their beneficiaries. Within certain limits, the Internal Revenue Code allows the sponsoring employer to deduct its prefunding contributions in the taxable year

in which the funds are contributed, rather than having to wait until the benefits are distributed.

See PREFUNDING OF BENEFITS.

Statutory and Regulatory Reference: I.R.C. §§ 404(a)(1)-(3) and (7); Treas. Reg. § 1.404(a) (qualified retirement plans) and §§ 419 and 419A (certain welfare plans).

Treatise Reference: See Tax Mgmt. (BNA), No. 395, *Section 501(c)(9) and Self-Funded Employee Benefits*.

advisory opinion *See* OPINION LETTER.

affiliated service group A group consisting of two or more companies in a service business that are related through ownership and provide services for one another or in association with third parties. The term is also used to refer to two or more organizations that are deemed to be related to each other by virtue of the fact that they perform management services for one another on a regular and continuing basis. For purposes of qualified retirement plans, all employees of the member employers that comprise an affiliated service group are treated as if they were employed by a single employer.

Statutory and Regulatory Reference: I.R.C. § 414(m); Prop. Treas. Reg. § 1.414(m).

Case and Other Interpretive Reference: Rev. Rul. 81-105, 1981-1 C.B. 256 (rules for determining whether employers constitute an affiliated service group and the effect of such characterization on the employers' qualified retirement plans).

Treatise Reference: See Tax Mgmt. (BNA), No. 351, *Pension Plans—Qualification*.

after-tax contribution An employee contribution made to an employee benefit plan (generally a qualified retirement plan) after the employee has already taken the amount involved into his or her gross income (e.g., as salary) for federal income tax purposes. Qualified retirement plans may permit (or require) employees in certain situations to make such contributions. After-tax contributions to qualified retirement plans are subject to the nondiscrimination rules of I.R.C. § 401(m). From the employee's perspective, the principal benefit of making after-tax contributions to a qualified plan derives from the fact that these amounts will earn a tax-free rate of investment return while they are held in the plan's trust, i.e., until they are distributed.

See ACTUAL CONTRIBUTION PERCENTAGE (ACP) for a discussion of the I.R.C. § 401(M) tests.

Statutory and Regulatory Reference: I.R.C. §§ 401(k) and (m); Treas. Reg. § 1.401(k) and (m).

Treatise Reference: Tax Mgmt. (BNA), No. 358, *Cash or Deferred Arrangements*.

age and service rules   A set of rules for qualified retirement plans that specify the highest minimum age and length-of-service requirements that an employer may impose before being required to admit an employee to participation in the plan. These rules are designed to ensure broad employee participation in qualified retirement plans. In general, the maximum amount of time a qualified plan can require an employee to work before becoming eligible to participate is one YEAR OF SERVICE and the highest age a plan may require a participant to have attained before being admitted is age 21. There are exceptions made for plans maintained by tax-exempt educational institutions and for plans that have an immediate vesting upon participation feature.

Statutory and Regulatory Reference: ERISA § 202; I.R.C. §§ 410(a), (1)(B), and (ii); Treas. Reg. §§ 1.410(a)-3, 1.410(a)-3T.

Treatise Reference: *See* Tax Mgmt. (BNA), No. 351, *Pension Plans – Qualification*, and No. 352, *Profit-Sharing Plans – Qualification*; *see also Employee Benefits Law* 90-104 (1991); D. McGill & D. Grubbs, Jr., *Fundamentals of Private Pensions* 82 (6th ed. 1989).

Age Discrimination in Employment Act (ADEA)   *See* ADEA.

age-related vesting   *See* RULE OF 45 VESTING.

aggregation group   A group of qualified retirement plans which, if maintained by an employer, must (or in certain circumstances, at the employer's option, may) be tested together to determine if they are top-heavy. The top-heavy rules provide for two types of aggregation groups: required and permissive.

An employer *must* combine all plans in a required aggregation group in testing its plans for top-heaviness. It need not (although it may elect to) also aggregate plans within a permissive aggregation group in performing these tests.

If the plans in a required aggregation group, taken as a whole, are top-heavy, then all plans in the required group will be considered top-heavy for the plan year. If the employer's required aggregation group is top-heavy for the plan year, and, if it then counts the plans in its permissive aggregation group, and the total of both required and permissive groups is not top-heavy, then only those individual plans that, standing alone, are top-heavy will be considered top-heavy. In other words, if the permissive aggregation group is not top-heavy, then those plans that were deemed to be top-heavy solely by virtue of the fact that they were part of a top-heavy required aggregation group will not be considered top-heavy.

A required aggregation group consists of: (1) each plan of the employer in which a key employee participates; and (2) each plan of the employer that enables any plan covering a key employee to satisfy the I.R.C. § 401(a)(4) general antidiscrimination rule or the I.R.C. § 410 participation rules.

An employer's permissive aggregation group consists of all other qualified retirement plans that it maintains that fall outside of its required aggregation group if the entire group of plans as so expanded would satisfy I.R.C. §§ 401(a)(4) and 410.

See KEY EMPLOYEE, TOP-HEAVY.

Statutory and Regulatory Reference: I.R.C. §§ 416(f) and (g)(2)(A); Treas. Reg. § 1.416-1, Q&A T-6 through T-11.

allocation formula   In a defined contribution plan, the formula contained in the PLAN DOCUMENT under which employer contributions are divided among plan participants' accounts. Generally, in a qualified defined contribution plan, a formula that allocates employer contributions to employees' accounts based on a uniform percentage of their compensation will not be considered discriminatory, nor will one that allocates a specified dollar amount to the account of each participant. A defined contribution plan may also contain formulas for reallocating benefit forfeitures from the forfeiting employees' accounts to the accounts of the remaining participants. These "reallocation" formulas may be, but need not be, identical to the plan's formula for allocating employer plan contributions among participants' accounts. Both allocation and reallocation formulas, however, must not discriminate within the meaning of I.R.C. § 401(a)(4) either "on paper" (i.e., by virtue of an express provision in the plan document) or "in operation" (i.e., due to an administrative practice of the plan).

Statutory and Regulatory Reference: Treas. Reg. § 1.401-1(b)(ii) (profit-sharing plan must provide definite written formula for allocating contributions among participants' accounts).

Treatise Reference: Tax Mgmt. (BNA), No. 352, *Profit-Sharing Plans — Qualification*.

alternate payee   A person, other than the employee, identified under a QUALIFIED DOMESTIC RELATIONS ORDER (QDRO) to be a recipient of part or all of an employee's benefit under a qualified retirement plan, e.g., the employee's spouse or children.

Statutory and Regulatory Reference: ERISA § 206(d)(3)(K); I.R.C. §§ 401(a)(13) and 414(p); Treas. Reg. § 1.401(a)-13(g).

Treatise Reference: *See* Tax Mgmt. (BNA), No. 370, *Qualified Plans — Taxation of Distributions*; *Employee Benefits Law* 172-74 (1991).

annual addition   In a qualified defined contribution plan, the sum for the year of employer and employee contributions and reallocated forfeitures that are allocated to the account of a plan participant. In a qualified defined contribution plan, the limit on a participant's annual additions for a year is the lesser of 25 percent of compensation or $30,000. Allocations to a participant's account(s) under all qualified defined contribution plans maintained by the employer in the aggregate may not exceed this amount in any year. The dollar figure of the formula is indexed for inflation; however, the $30,000 limit is not to be adjusted until the dollar limit of § 415(b)(1)(B) for defined benefit plans has been adjusted upward for inflation to $120,000. At that time, the two limits will be adjusted in tandem to preserve the 1:4 ratio between the defined contribution and defined benefit limits. A plan(s) that allocates amounts to a participant's account(s) in excess of these limits is subject to disqualification.

See ANNUAL BENEFIT, DEFINED CONTRIBU-TION PLAN, MAXIMUM BENEFITS.

Statutory and Regulatory Reference: *See* I.R.C. § 415(c)(1)(A)-(B); Treas. Reg. § 1.415-6.

Treatise Reference: *See* Tax Mgmt. (BNA), No. 371, *Employee Plans — Deductions, Contributions, and Funding. See also Employee Benefits Law* 120-32 (1991); D. McGill & D. Grubbs, Jr., *Fundamentals of Private Pensions* 119 (6th ed. 1989).

annual benefit   In a defined benefit plan, an amount that may not exceed, during the limitation year, the lesser of $90,000 or 100 percent of the participant's average compensation for his or her high three years (3-YEAR HIGH). The $90,000 is adjusted for inflation annually.

See MAXIMUM BENEFITS.

annuity   A contract for the payment of specified or objectively determinable periodic payments over a specified period of time or over the lifetime of the recipient.

For purposes of I.R.C. §§ 401-04, the term "annuity" also includes a face-amount certificate within the meaning of the Investment Advisors' Act of 1940, but does not include any contract or certificate issued after December 31, 1962, which is transferable, if any person other than the trustee of a qualified plan is the owner of such contract or certificate.

Example: A pension plan calls for benefit payments to an employee after his or her retirement of $10,000 per year for life. This would be considered an annuity. A similar contract purchased outside of a qualified retirement plan from a commercial insurer would also be considered an annuity.

See ANNUITY EXCLUSION RATIO RULE, PRERETIREMENT SURVIVOR ANNUITY,

QUALIFIED JOINT AND SURVIVOR ANNUITY (QJSA).

Statutory and Regulatory Reference: *See* generally I.R.C. §§ 72 and 401(g); Treas. Reg. § 1.72-1 *et seq*. For the provisions relating to the penalty for premature distributions of annuities, *see* I.R.C. § 72(q). For the REQUIRED DISTRIBUTION rules for annuities, *see* I.R.C. § 72(s). *See also* I.R.C. § 72(e)(4)(C) for rules governing the taxation of annuities and I.R.C. § 72(g) for the rules regarding the transfer of annuities. The federal estate tax rules governing the taxation of annuities are set forth in I.R.C. § 2039.

Treatise Reference: *See* Tax Mgmt. (BNA), No. 134, *Annuities*, and No. 370, *Qualified Plans — Taxation of Distributions*. *See also* D. McGill & D. Grubbs, Jr., *Fundamentals of Private Pensions* 137 (6th ed. 1989).

annuity exclusion ratio rule   A federal tax law rule providing that, if an employee receives annuity payments (e.g., under a qualified plan) and part or all of their value is attributable to amounts on which the employee has previously been taxed (i.e., employee after-tax contributions), the employee may exclude a ratable amount of each payment from his or her gross income. Thus, for instance, if an employee was eligible to receive a $100 monthly annuity under a plan, and 30 percent of the amounts in the plan account came from the employee's own after-tax contributions, the employee would only be taxable on $70 of each payment. Once an employee has "recovered" (excluded from income) the entire amount of his or her investment in an annuity, all subsequent payments are fully taxable to the individual, notwithstanding the exclusion ratio rule. Conversely, if an employee dies before "recovering" (excluded from income) his or her entire investment in an annuity, the employee's estate may deduct any unrecovered amount on the individual's final federal income tax return.

Note that the exclusion ratio rule applies to all annuities, whether or not a qualified plan is involved. Where the annuity is not part of a benefit under a qualified plan, the level of the annuity owner's investment in the annuity contract is used instead of amounts on which the employee has previously been taxed.

Statutory and Regulatory Reference: *See* I.R.C. §§ 72(b) and 402(a)(1); Treas. Reg. § 1.402(a)-1, applying the exclusion ratio principles to distributions from qualified plans.

Treatise Reference: *See* Tax Mgmt. (BNA), No. 370, *Qualified Plans — Taxation of Distributions*.

annuity plan   Either a retirement plan in which participants' benefits are funded through annuity contracts or a § 403(b) plan ("tax-deferred annuity" or (TDA)). Section 403(b) plans are special plans that may be established for the employees of certain tax-exempt organizations, such as educational institutions, to allow their employees to save for retirement, generally on a salary reduction basis.

Statutory and Regulatory Reference: *See* I.R.C. § 403(b); Treas. Reg. § 1.403(b)-1. For the rules on when an annuity will be treated as a plan, *see* I.R.C. § 401(f).

Treatise Reference: For a discussion of tax-deferred annuities, *see* Tax Mgmt. (BNA), No. 388, *Tax-Deferred Annuities — Section 403(b)*; *see also Employee Benefits Law* 32; 216-22 (1991).

annuity starting date   The first day of the first period for which an annuity is payable under a qualified retirement plan. If a benefit payable from a qualified retirement plan is not payable in annuity form, its annuity starting date is deemed to be the first day on which all events have occurred that entitle the participant to the benefit.

Example: If an annuity is to be paid to a retiree monthly, and the retiree receives the first payment on November 15, the retiree's annuity starting date is November 1st, the first day of the first (monthly) period in which annuity payments are made. If, however, the annuity payments were to be made once per year and the retiree received the same November 15 payment, the annuity starting date would be January 1st of the year in which the first payment was made because this is the first day of the first (yearly) period in which payments were made.

Statutory and Regulatory Reference: I.R.C. § 417(f)(2)(A); Treas. Reg. § 1.401(a)-11(b)(6).

Treatise Reference: *See* Tax Mgmt. (BNA), No. 370, *Qualified Plans — Taxation of Distributions*.

annuity tables   Tables that set forth mathematical factors to be used in computing the value of an employee's benefit under an annuity or a retirement plan. These tables show, among other things, the projected LIFE EXPECTANCY of employees who have reached a specified age and the projected combined life expectancies of multiple beneficiaries that are used when the annuity provides for survivor benefits to the employee's beneficiary.

See ANNUITY EXCLUSION RATIO RULE.

Statutory and Regulatory Reference: *See* Treas. Reg. § 1.72-9; *see also* I.R.C. § 402(a)(1) and Treas. Reg. § 1.402(a)-1, applying annuity principles to the taxation of benefits under qualified retirement plans.

Treatise Reference: Tax Mgmt. (BNA), No. 370, *Qualified Plans — Taxation of Distributions*.

anti-alienation/assignment of benefits rule   This rule requires, in general, that a qualified retirement plan must provide that participants' benefits may not be assigned to someone other than the employee or otherwise pledged (e.g., to a creditor) while they are held by the plan's trust. The rule is designed to help assure that the assets of a tax-qualified retirement plan will be used to provide retirement income to employees, rather than to serve some other purpose. An exception to the general anti-alienation rule of ERISA exists for payments made under a qualified domestic relations order (QDRO) within the meaning of I.R.C. § 414(p). Another exception exists for voluntary and revocable assignments of up to 10 percent of any benefit payment of a participant, so long as the assignment is not used to pay plan administrative costs. A loan from the plan to a participant or beneficiary will not be considered an assignment or alienation if the Code's PROHIBITED TRANSACTION rules concerning plan loans are met.

See QUALIFIED DOMESTIC RELATIONS ORDER (QDRO).

Statutory and Regulatory Reference: ERISA § 206(d); I.R.C. § 401(a)(13) (general anti-alienation rule); I.R.C. § 401(a)(13)(A) (10 percent exception); and § 401(a)(13)(B) (exception for qualified domestic relations orders); Treas. Reg. § 1.401(a)(13).

Case and Other Interpretive Reference: See Rev. Rul. 89-14, 1989-1 C.B. 111 (use of participant's nonforfeitable benefit as security for a plan loan bearing an unreasonably low rate of interest violated the anti-alienation rule). *See also General Motors v. Buha*, 623 F.2d 455, 2 EB Cases 2375 (6th Cir. 1990) (anti-alienation rule bars state tax levy against pension assets). On the issue of whether qualified retirement plan assets are includable in a bankrupt's estate, *see McLean v. Central States Pension Fund*, 762 F.2d 1204 (4th Cir. 1985); *In re Lichstrahl v. Bankers' Trust*, 750 F.2d 1488 (11th Cir. 1985); *Samore v. Graham*, 726 F.2d 1268 (8th Cir. 1984); *Goff v. Taylor*, 706 F.2d 574 (5th Cir. 1983).

Treatise Reference: See Tax Mgmt. (BNA), No. 370, *Qualified Plans – Taxation of Dis-*

tributions; *see also Employee Benefits Law* 168-71 (1991); D. McGill & D. Grubbs, Jr., *Fundamentals of Private Pensions* 143 (6th ed. 1989).

anti-cutback rule   A rule providing that an employee's ACCRUED BENEFIT under a qualified retirement plan may not be reduced by a plan amendment, other than an amendment that has been approved by the Secretary of Labor freezing benefit accruals only for the most recent PLAN YEAR.

Statutory and Regulatory Reference: I.R.C. § 411(d)(6); Treas. Reg. §§ 1.411(d) and 412(c)(8).

Case and Other Interpretive Reference: See Rev. Rul. 79-325, 1979-2 C.B. 190 (plan amendment retroactively decreasing accrued benefits that does not satisfy the requirements of I.R.C. § 412(c)(8) or ERISA § 302(c)(8) violates the I.R.C. § 411(d)(6) anti-cutback rule); *see also* Rev. Rul. 81-12, 1981-1 C.B. 228 (rules for avoiding a violation of the anti-cutback rule due to certain changes in a defined benefit plan's ACTUARIAL ASSUMPTIONS); Rev. Rul. 85-6, 1985-1 C.B. 133 (proposed TERMINATION of plan that provided an early retirement subsidy must provide that subsidy to participants who satisfied the pretermination requirements for such subsidy to avoid violating the anti-cutback rule).

Treatise Reference: See Tax Mgmt. (BNA), No. 351, *Pension Plans – Qualification*; *see also Employee Benefits Law* 128 (1991).

applicable premium   For purposes of the COBRA continuation coverage rules, the cost to a health plan (for the period of continuation coverage in question) to pay for coverage for a similarly situated active employee or beneficiary with respect to whom a qualifying event has *not* occurred (without regard to whether such cost is paid by the employer or the employee). Note that a change in medical coverage for an active employee also must apply to qualified beneficiaries with continuation coverage.

Example: During the period of Employee A's continuation coverage under COBRA, Employer X's premium on its health insurance is raised by its health insurance carrier. This increase in the premium for active employees also represents an increase in the applicable premium for qualified beneficiaries, and Employee A's premium during the period of continuation coverage will increase to the same extent. Note that the applicable premium for a 12-month determination period must be computed and fixed before the period begins.

See CONTINUATION COVERAGE, QUALIFYING EVENT.

Statutory and Regulatory Reference: ERISA § 604; I.R.C. § 4980B(f). Prop. Treas. Reg. § 1.162-26, Q&As 44-48.

Treatise Reference: Tax Mgmt. (BNA), No. 389, *Disability and Medical Reimbursement Benefits*.

appreciation   The increase in value of an asset over time, regardless of whether such increase is realized or recognized for tax purposes. Thus, if an asset, such as stock, is allocated to an employee's account in a qualified retirement plan, and the stock's value increases over time, it is said to have appreciated, even though the employee will not have to pay income tax on this gain until sometime in the future, e.g., when the stock is distributed from the plan.

Statutory and Regulatory Reference: For the rules governing the taxation of the appreciation on employer securities, *see* I.R.C. §§ 402(a)(1), 402(e)(4)(J) (when such securities are part of a lump-sum distribution) and 402(j). For the rules governing the taxation of the appreciation on employer securities that are acquired under an incentive stock option (ISO), *see* I.R.C. §§ 421-25

and Prop. Treas. Reg. §§ 1.421-7 and 1.422A-1 *et seq*.

See INCENTIVE STOCK OPTION (ISO), NET UNREALIZED APPRECIATION.

Treatise Reference: Tax Mgmt. (BNA), No. 7, *Stock Options (Statutory) — Qualification*.

assignment and alientation of benefits
See ANTI-ALIENATION/ASSIGNMENT OF BENEFITS RULE; *see also* QUALIFIED DOMESTIC RELATIONS ORDER (QDRO).

average annual compensation   Generally, under a qualified retirement plan, the average of the participant's yearly salary, bonuses, and other taxable remuneration as reflected on his or her IRS Form W-2 from the employer for the consecutive-year period specified in the plan during which his or her average taxable remuneration is the highest. This period generally must include at least three years. In determining the relevant measuring period, the plan may specify any 12-month period, if it is applied consistently to all participants. If a participant's entire period of service for the employer is less than the measuring period specified in the plan, average annual compensation may be determined by averaging the employee's annual remuneration during his or her entire period of service for the employer.

Statutory and Regulatory Reference: I.R.C. § 401(l)(5)(C); 1(b)(9); *see also* definition of compensation for qualified plan purposes in I.R.C. §§ 414(s) and 415(c)(3), Treas. Reg. § 1.415-3(c)(3) and Treas. Reg. § 1.414(s)-1.

Treatise Reference: *See* Tax Mgmt. (BNA), No. 356, *Qualified Plans — Integration*

average benefit percentage test   One of three minimum coverage rules (qualified retirement plans must satisfy one), requiring that the plan benefit a broad cross-section of the employer's nonhighly compensated employees. A plan will pass this test if: (1) it benefits employees under a classification that does not discriminate in favor of highly compensated employees (the classification test); and (2) the "average benefit percentage" for nonhighly compensated employees (their plan benefits expressed as a percentage of their compensation) is at least 70 percent of the average benefits percentage for highly compensated employees.

See COVERAGE, HIGHLY COMPENSATED EMPLOYEE, RATIO TEST, AND 70 PERCENT TEST.

Statutory and Regulatory Reference: *See* I.R.C. § 410(b)(2); Treas. Reg. § 1.410(b)-2(b)(3).

Treatise Reference: Tax Mgmt. (BNA), No. 351, *Pension Plans—Qualification*; *Employee Benefits Law* 95-99 (1991).

B

backloading (of benefit accruals) The practice, under a qualified defined benefit plan, of providing participants with a lower rate of benefit accruals in their earlier years of service with the employer, with progressively higher rates in later years. Because Congress felt that backloading benefits would tend to discriminate in favor of highly compensated employees (since these employees tend to remain with an employer longer), the I.R.C. § 411(b) regular minimum accrual rules for defined benefit plans require that a defined benefit plan pass at least one of three minimum accrual rules designed to prevent excessive backloading. The rules are: (1) the 3 percent rule; (2) the 133⅓ percent rule; and (3) the fractional rule.

See ACCRUAL, FRACTIONAL RULE, 133⅓ PERCENT RULE, 3 PERCENT RULE.

Statutory and Regulatory Reference: ERISA § 204; I.R.C. § 411(b); Treas. Reg. § 1.411(b).

Treatise Reference: Tax Mgmt. (BNA), No. 351, *Pension Plans — Qualification.*

backup withholding A set of rules under which the payor of certain benefits (generally, in the ERISA context, a qualified retirement plan) must withhold federal income tax equal to 20 percent of the payment, unless the payee (generally the employee) has on file with the employer his or her correct Social Security number or otherwise elects not to be subject to such withholding.

Statutory and Regulatory Reference: I.R.C. § 3405; Treas. Reg. § 35.3405-1 *et seq.*

Treatise Reference: Tax Mgmt. (BNA), No. 392, *Withholding, Social Security, and Unemployment Taxes on Compensation,* and No. 440, *U.S. Information Reporting and Backup Withholding.*

"bad boy" vesting clause A provision in a qualified retirement plan under which an employee will forfeit his or her ACCRUED BENEFIT derived from employer contributions if the employee commits certain acts (e.g., going to work for a competitor or committing a crime). Bad boy VESTING clauses were more prevalent before ERISA because of the less stringent qualified plan minimum vesting rules that prevailed at that time. Such clauses, however, remain valid under post-ERISA law, provided that the FORFEITURE triggered by such a clause does not result in any employee vesting in his or her plan benefit less rapidly than is required under the applicable qualified plan statutory vesting schedule and is not otherwise contrary to law.

Statutory and Regulatory Reference: ERISA § 203(a); I.R.C. § 411(a); Treas. Reg. § 1.411(a).

Treatise Reference: Tax Mgmt. (BNA), No. 351, *Pension Plans—Qualification*, and No. 352, *Profit-Sharing Plans—Qualification*.

bankruptcy A standard bankruptcy operates to liquidate a business or individual and, subject to specific exemptions, assets of the business/individual (debtor) are collected and, subject to specific priorities, proceeds are distributed to creditors. A bankruptcy is governed by the U.S. Bankruptcy Code. Also governed by this Code are reorganizations under Chapter 11 and Chapter 13 that allow businesses time to see if earnings from future business operations will meet creditors' demands better than the proceeds of a current liquidation. Where an employer is bankrupt under the Bankruptcy Code, claims for up to $2,000 in wages (including vacation, sick leave, and severance pay) earned within 90 days of the filing of a bankruptcy petition are preferred over most other unsecured claims. After the wage claims, priority is given to unsecured claims for contributions to employee benefit plans arising from services within 180 days before the petition is filed and limited to $2,000 times the number of employees in the plan. Note, however, that employees receive an immediate right to vested benefits in qualified plans inasmuch as the terms of the trust must make it impossible to divert corpus or income from the exclusive benefit of employees or their beneficiaries prior to satisfaction of all liabilities to them.

Statutory and Regulatory Reference: Title 11, U.S. Code (Congress empowered through Art. I, § 8, U.S. Constitution). Bankruptcy Reform Act of 1978, Pub. L. No. 95-598; I.R.C. § 401(a)(2) (exclusive benefit provision).

bargain element (of a compensatory stock option) The difference between the FAIR MARKET VALUE of employer stock at the time an employee exercises his or her right to purchase it under a compensatory stock option and the amount the employee, under the option's terms, must pay for the stock. For incentive stock options (ISOs), the bargain element constitutes an "item of adjustment" for purposes of the alternative minimum tax. (The alternative minimum tax is a special tax that can apply in lieu of the regular income tax if the taxpayer's tax benefits from certain accelerated deductions and certain items of income that are not recognized, or are recognized on a deferred basis, exceed specified levels.)

See INCENTIVE STOCK OPTION (ISO), STOCK OPTION.

Statutory and Regulatory Reference: I.R.C. §§ 56(b)(3) and 421-25; Prop. Treas. Reg. § 1.422A-1 *et seq.*

Treatise Reference: Tax Mgmt. (BNA), No. 7, *Stock Options (Statutory)—Qualification*, No. 288 *Alternative Minimum Tax*, and No. 383, *Nonstatutory Stock Options*.

base benefit percentage Under a defined benefit plan that integrates with Social Security by using the "excess" method (i.e., a plan that calls for participants to accrue benefits at a specified level with respect to their compensation up to the plan's integration level and at a higher level on compensation above the integration level), the rate at which a participant accrues employer-derived benefits with respect to a participant's compensation up to and including the applicable integration level. For a defined benefit excess plan to integrate with Social Security, its excess benefit percentage cannot exceed its "base benefit percentage" by more than the "maximum excess allowance."

For defined benefit excess plans, the "maximum excess allowance" (the amount by which the excess benefits percentage exceeds the base benefits percentage) for any year of service taken into account under the plan may not exceed the lesser of:

(1) the base benefit percentage; or

(2) .75 percent.

When computing the maximum excess allowance for total benefits under a defined benefit excess plan, the maximum excess allowance is the lesser of:

(1) the base benefit percentage itself; or

(2) .75 percent times the participant's number of years of service taken into account under the plan, not to exceed 35.

Since only 35 years of service are considered in applying this formula to total benefits (i.e., for all years of an employee's participation), the maximum permitted disparity under the integration rules for total benefits under a defined benefit excess plan is 26.25 percent (35 × .75 percent).

Example 1: Employer X maintains a noncontributory defined benefit plan. It provides a benefit of .5 percent of a participant's average annual compensation for the plan year as exceeds COVERED COMPENSATION for the plan year, times years of service for X. The plan provides no benefits with respect to a participant's average annual compensation up to the covered compensation for the plan year. The plan provides a benefit that exceeds the maximum excess allowance for the plan year because the excess benefit percentage (.5 percent) exceeds the base benefit percentage (0 percent) by more than the base benefit percentage (0 percent).

Example 2: Employer Y maintains a noncontributory defined benefit plan. It provides a benefit of 1 percent of a participant's average annual compensation up to the participant's covered compensation for the plan year, times the participant's years of service for Y. It also provides a benefit equal to 1.75 percent of a participant's average annual compensation for the plan year as exceeds the covered compensation for the year, times the participant's years of service for Y. The plan

contains no limit on the number of years of service that may be taken into account. Under the benefit formula, a participant with 40 years of service will receive a benefit equal to the sum of 40 percent (40 × 1 percent) of his average annual compensation up to covered compensation plus 70 percent ((40 × 1.75 percent) × 40) of average annual compensation in excess of covered compensation. The plan exceeds the maximum excess allowance because the excess benefit percentage, determined on a cumulative basis as 70 percent, exceeds the base benefit percentage, determined on a cumulative basis as 40 percent, by more than the cumulative percentage limit (26.25 percent).

See DEFINED BENEFIT EXCESS PLAN, INTEGRATION LEVEL, INTEGRATION (SOCIAL SECURITY).

Statutory and Regulatory Reference: I.R.C. §§ 401(l)(2)(B)(i) and (3)(A)(ii); Treas. Reg. § 1.401(l)-1(c)(3).

Treatise Reference: Tax Mgmt. (BNA), No. 356, *Qualified Plans — Integration*; *Employee Benefits Law* 117-21 (1991).

base contribution percentage Under a qualified defined contribution plan that is integrated with Social Security, the rate at which employer contributions are allocated to a participant's account with respect to that portion of the participant's annual compensation that does not exceed the plan's integration level. This rate is expressed as a percentage of the participant's compensation.

A qualified defined contribution plan will satisfy the integration rules of I.R.C. §§ 401(a)(5) and 401(l) if its "excess contributions percentage" (the percentage of compensation that is allocated to a participant's account with respect to annual compensation exceeding the plan's integration level) does not exceed the participant's "base contribution percentage" by more than the lesser of:

(1) the base contribution percentage itself; or

(2) the greater of (a) 5.7 percent or (b) the applicable Old Age Insurance tax rate in effect under I.R.C. § 3111(a) (relating to FICA taxes) for the year (currently 4.35 percent).

This maximum permitted disparity is referred to as the "maximum excess allowance." This allowance must also be uniform with respect to all participants if the plan is to satisfy I.R.C. §§ 401(a)(5) and (l).

Example: A defined contribution plan uses the Social Security wage base as its integration level. The Old Age component of the I.R.C. § 3111(a) tax for the year is 4.35 percent. The plan provides for a "base contributions percentage" equal to 5 percent of a participant's annual compensation; on annual compensation in excess of the integration level, the plan calls for the employer to contribute 10.5 percent. The plan will not satisfy the requirements of I.R.C. §§ 401(a)(5) and 401(l) because its excess contributions percentage (10.5 percent) exceeds its base contributions percentage (5 percent) by 5.5 percent (10.5 percent − 5 percent = 5.5 percent). This amount exceeds the maximum allowable disparity of 5 percent (the lesser of (a) 5 percent or (b) the greater of (5.7 percent or 4.35 percent, i.e., 5.7 percent)).

See DEFINED CONTRIBUTION EXCESS PLAN, INTEGRATION LEVEL, INTEGRATION (SOCIAL SECURITY), MAXIMUM EXCESS ALLOWANCE, SOCIAL SECURITY TAXABLE WAGE BASE.

Statutory and Regulatory Reference: I.R.C. §§ 401(l)(2)(B) and (l)(3)(A); Treas. Reg. §§ 1.401(l)-1(c)(4).

Treatise Reference: Tax Mgmt. (BNA), No. 356, *Qualified Plans — Integration*; *Employee Benefits Law* 117-21 (1991).

beneficiary The person designated by the participant or by the terms of an employee benefit plan who is or may become entitled to a benefit thereunder.

See QUALIFIED BENEFICIARIES.

Statutory and Regulatory Reference: ERISA § 3(8).

Treatise Reference: Tax Mgmt. (BNA), No. 370, *Qualified Plans — Taxation of Distributions*.

benefit or contribution formulas *See* ACCRUED BENEFIT, ACCRUAL/BENEFIT ACCRUAL, BACKLOADING, DEFINED BENEFIT PLAN/DEFINED CONTRIBUTION PLAN.

bonus life insurance plan An employer-sponsored insurance arrangement pursuant to which an employee purchases a life insurance policy, and the employer either pays the premiums on the policy directly to the insurer or pays a bonus to the employee who in turn uses it to pay the premium. The employee has taxable income equal to the amount of the bonus or premium payment. This is not a split-dollar life insurance policy since the employer has not retained an interest in the policy. Thus, the employer can deduct the premium payment as an ordinary and necessary business expense. A bonus life insurance plan generally is treated as an employee welfare benefit plan under ERISA.

See SPLIT-DOLLAR LIFE INSURANCE.

Statutory and Regulatory Reference: ERISA § 3(4); I.R.C. §§ 61, 101, 162; Treas. Reg. §§ 1.61-1(a); 1.162-9.

Case and Other Interpretive Reference: Rev. Rul. 58-90, 1958-2 C.B. 88 (for company to take business deduction for premiums paid for policy owned by an executive, (1) premiums payments must constitute compensation to the executive, (2) total amount of compensation paid to the executive must not be unreasonable, and (3) company must not be a beneficiary of the policy, directly or indirectly).

Treatise Reference: Tax Mgmt. (BNA), No. 386, *Insurance Related Compensation*; *Financial Planning*, Para. 425, *Insurance Planning* (1991).

break in service   Generally, under a qualified retirement plan, a 12-consecutive-month computation period (e.g., participation, accrual, or vesting computation period) in which an employee is credited with no more than 500 hours of service. Such a break in service can cause an employee to cease earning benefits or vesting credit under the plan until he or she again completes a year of service. The 500 hour rule is a minimum standard. Qualified plans may prescribe a lesser number of hours before a participant will be charged with a break in service, but cannot require more than 500 hours for a participant to avoid a break.

See COMPUTATION PERIOD, HOUR OF SERVICE, YEAR OF SERVICE. For a rule permitting qualified plans to disregard certain service rendered before a participant incurs five or more consecutive one-year breaks in service, *see* PARITY, RULE OF. For a rule prohibiting qualified plans for disregarding certain breaks in service incurred in connection with the birth or adoption of a child of the participant, *see* MATERNITY - OR PATERNITY - RELATED LEAVE OF ABSENCE.

Statutory and Regulatory Reference: *See* ERISA §§ 202(b) (participation); 203(a)(3) (vesting). *See also* I.R.C. §§ 410(a)(5)(C) and 411(a)(6)(A); Treas. Reg. §§ 1.410(a)-5(c); 1.411(a)-6(c).

Case and Other Interpretive Reference: Rev. Rul. 81-106, 1981-1 C.B. 169 (plan may credit employees with service during a leave of absence provided it does so in a nondiscriminatory manner).

Treatise Reference: *See* Tax Mgmt. (BNA), No. 351, *Pension Plans — Qualification*, and No. 352, *Profit-Sharing Plans — Qualification*; *see also Employee Benefits Law* 88-90 (1991).

buyback rule   In a qualified retirement plan that provides for forfeiture of benefits derived from employer contributions if employees withdraw their employee contributions, this rule allows such employees to return the withdrawn amounts to the plan (with interest in the case of a defined benefit plan) and have their forfeited benefits restored.

A qualified defined benefit plan may require the employee to repay the withdrawal with interest from the date of withdrawal to the date of repayment. This right to repurchase may not be denied: (1) in the case of a withdrawal on account of separation from service, before the earlier of five years after the first date on which the participant is later reemployed by the employer, or the close of the first period of five consecutive one-year breaks in service beginning after the withdrawal; or (2) in the case of any other withdrawal, before five years have passed since the withdrawal. Such interest, compounded annually, may not exceed the rate determined under I.R.C. § 411(c)(2)(C) in effect on the repayment date.

Statutory and Regulatory Reference: I.R.C. § 411(a)(3)(D); Treas. Reg. §§ 1.411(a)-4(b)(4); 1.411(a)-7(d)(2) and (3). Note that, where a plan uses the elapsed time method of crediting service, a one-year period of severance is considered a one-year break in service. *See* Treas. Reg. § 1.411(a)-7(d)(2)(D)(2).

Treatise Reference: Tax Mgmt. (BNA), No. 351, *Pension Plans — Qualification*, and No. 352, *Profit-Sharing Plans — Qualification*.

C

cafeteria plan A written benefit plan provided by an employer with respect to which all participants are employees, and these participants may choose among two or more benefits consisting of cash and qualified benefits. Generally, no amount will be included in the gross income of a cafeteria plan participant solely because he or she may choose among the benefits provided under the plan. This general exclusion from constructive receipt does not apply, however, to a highly compensated participant for any plan year for which the cafeteria plan discriminates in favor of such individuals as to contributions or benefits or as to eligibility to participate. A cafeteria plan generally cannot include any plan that provides for deferred compensation, although an exception exists for the provision of § 401(k) plan benefits in conjunction with a cafeteria plan. The "qualified benefits" permitted to be offered are group-term life insurance, medical, accident, and disability benefits; group legal services; and dependent care assistance. Note that a benefit offered under a cafeteria plan may or may not be taxable depending upon whether the benefit qualifies for an exclusion from gross income under the various Internal Revenue Code sections which regulate that particular benefit.

Example: Although dependent care assistance offered under a cafeteria plan is subject to the cafeteria plan rules under I.R.C. § 125, the exclusion of these benefits from income also will be subject to the rules regarding dependent care assistance plans under I.R.C. § 129.

See ACCIDENTAL DEATH AND DISMEMBERMENT (AD&D) PLAN, DEPENDENT CARE ASSISTANCE PLAN, FLEXIBLE BENEFIT PLAN, FLEXIBLE SPENDING ACCOUNT, GROUP-TERM LIFE INSURANCE, GROUP LEGAL SERVICES (GLSP) PLAN, MEDICAL CARE.

Statutory and Regulatory Reference: I.R.C. §§ 79, 105, 106, 117, 120, 124, 125, 127, 129, and 132; Prop. Treas. Reg. § 1.125-1 and -2.

Treatise Reference: *See* Tax Mgmt. (BNA), No. 397, *Cafeteria Plans*. *See also Employee Benefits Law* 970-92 (1991).

capital gain/capital gain element As originally enacted in ERISA, the portion of a lump-sum distribution from a qualified retirement plan that was attributable to an employee's pre-ERISA (pre-1974) service was taxed as capital gain income. The portion of a lump-sum distribution attributable to post-ERISA (post-1973) service was, (and remains) eligible for favorable tax treatment known as "forward averaging." The Tax Reform Act of 1986 (TRA 1986), Pub. L. No. 99-514, phased out the availability of capital

23

gain treatment for lump-sum distributions, subject to certain transition rules.

See FORWARD AVERAGING.

Statutory and Regulatory Reference: former (pre-Tax Reform Act of 1986) I.R.C. § 402(e).

Treatise Reference: See Tax Mgmt. (BNA), No. 370, *Qualified Plans — Taxation of Distributions*.

carryover of deductions   A rule allowing excess employer contributions for a TAXABLE YEAR to a qualified retirement plan to be deducted in a future taxable year when the employer has not exceeded the applicable deductible limit under I.R.C. § 404(a).

When an employer makes such an EXCESS CONTRIBUTION to a defined benefit plan, it may carry forward the nondeductible amount indefinitely to future years. If the defined benefit plan terminates with unused DEDUCTION carryovers, the employer may take such deductions in the year in which the TERMINATION occurs or thereafter.

Generally, an employer may make annual deductible contributions to a qualified profit-sharing or stock bonus plan of up to 15 percent of the compensation paid or accrued to participants for the year. Contributions in excess of the deductible limits arising in taxable years beginning before 1987 may be carried forward to future years, and deducted in such years, provided the total amount deducted in any such future year cannot exceed 25 percent of compensation paid or accrued to participants in that year. Where the carryover arises in 1987 or thereafter, the 25 percent limit is reduced to 15 percent.

Statutory and Regulatory Reference: *See* I.R.C. § 404(a)(1)(E); Treas. Reg. § 1.404(a)-7 (pension and annuity plan). *See also* I.R.C. § 404(a)(3)(A); Treas. Reg. § 1.404(a)-9 (profit-sharing or stock bonus plan). For the limits on carryovers of deductions for excess contributions to profit-sharing and stock bonus plans arising before 1987, *see* I.R.C. § 404(a)(3)(A)(iv).

Treatise Reference: Tax Mgmt. (BNA), No. 371, *Employee Plans — Deductions, Contributions, and Funding*.

cash balance plan   A defined benefit retirement plan in which hypothetical accounts are set up for each participant. These accounts reflect the vested benefit of the participant. In addition, benefits under a cash balance plan ordinarily vest more quickly than under traditional pension plans.

cash or deferred arrangement (CODA)
See SECTION 401(k) PLAN.

cash-out   The distribution to a participant or beneficiary under a qualified retirement plan of his or her entire benefit, generally upon separation from the employer's service. Qualified retirement plans may under certain circumstances "cash-out" (distribute) an employee's benefit upon his or her TERMINATION of participation. Where this occurs, the employee's account is wiped off the plan's books. The circumstances under which such cash-outs may occur depend upon whether the cash-out was voluntary, i.e., at the employee's election, or involuntary, i.e., without the employee's consent.

A plan may cash-out an employee's benefit upon termination of employment without the employee's consent when the benefit's PRESENT VALUE does not exceed $3,500. Where it exceeds $3,500, the plan must obtain a participant's (and spouse's where the plan is subject to the joint and survivor annuity rules) consent before cashing out the benefit.

See QUALIFIED JOINT AND SURVIVOR ANNUITY (QJSA).

Statutory and Regulatory Reference: See ERISA § 204(d)(1); I.R.C. §§ 411(a)(7) and (11). *See also* Treas. Reg. §§ 1.411(a)-11(c)(3) and 1.417(e)-1(b)(2).

Treatise Reference: Tax Mgmt. (BNA), No. 370, *Qualified Plans — Taxation of Distributions*.

cash value policy   A life insurance policy that consists of term insurance and a cash reserve, such as a whole life policy. The owner of a cash value life insurance policy generally acquires a vested interest in the policy through the cash surrender value. Most state laws require that cash value policies contain a nonforfeiture provision giving the insured a claim on that vested portion at any time during the policy's term.

See WHOLE LIFE INSURANCE, TERM INSURANCE.

Statutory and Regulatory Reference: I.R.C. §§ 101, 7702, 816(b).

Treatise Reference: J. Mamorsky, *Employee Benefits Handbook* (1987).

catch-up election   A rule that allows an employee who makes salary reduction contributions to a I.R.C. § 403(b) plan to make contributions for a year that exceed the usual $9,500 and I.R.C. § 415 annual limits applicable to such plans. The extra contribution that these employees may make for any taxable year is equal to the lesser of: (1) $3,000; (2) $15,000 reduced by amounts not included in the participant's income in previous taxable years under this rule; or (3) the excess of $5,000 times the number of years of service of the employee with the employer over the amount of employer contributions made on the employee's behalf for all previous taxable years.

Statutory and Regulatory Reference: I.R.C. §§ 403(g)(4) and (g)(8); Treas. Reg. § 1.415-6(e)(3)-(6).

Treatise Reference: Tax Mgmt. (BNA), No. 388, *Tax-Deferred Annuities — Section 403(b)*.

church plan   A plan established and maintained by a church or association of churches exempt from taxation under I.R.C. § 401.

Statutory and Regulatory Reference: *See* I.R.C. §§ 410(d)(relating to election by church to have otherwise-inapplicable qualified retirement plan participation, VESTING, FUNDING, and other provisions apply) and 414(e); Treas. Reg. §§ 1.410(d)-1 and 1.414(e); *See also* ERISA § 3(33) (ERISA definition of church plan) and ERISA § 4(b)(2) (exclusion of church plans from ERISA).

Treatise Reference: Tax Mgmt. (BNA), No. 372, *Defined Benefit Plans of Churches and State and Local Governments*; *Employee Benefits Law* 38 (1991).

claims procedure   The procedure in a plan subject to ERISA under which the claims of participants and their beneficiaries for benefits are approved or disapproved. Typically, retirement and welfare plans subject to ERISA use the PLAN ADMINISTRATOR to review claims. An ERISA plan must provide a claims procedure and a procedure for appealing the denial of benefit claims.

Statutory and Regulatory Reference: ERISA § 503(l); 29 C.F.R. § 2560.5031(b).

Case and Other Interpretative Reference: *Grossmuller v. Auto Workers*, 715 F.2d 853, 4 EB Cases 2082 (3d Cir. 1983).

Treatise Reference: Employee Benefits Law 490-95 (1991).

classification test   *See* AVERAGE BENEFIT PERCENTAGE TEST.

class-year plan   Prior to the Tax Reform Act of 1986 (TRA 1986), Pub. L. No. 99-514, a type of qualified defined contribution plan in which each year's employer contribution was considered a separate "class." Under such a plan, employees would be subject to a statutory VESTING schedule that would apply separately to each year's class of contributions (unlike regular qualified retirement plans under which a vesting schedule is applied to an employee's total plan benefit at any point in time). Thus, if an employee participated in a class-year plan that called for vesting in 20 percent annual increments for five years, the employee would, after five years of participation, be 100 percent vested in contributions made during his or her first year of participation, 80 percent in contributions made during his or her second year, and so on. Class-year plans were often used to deter employees from leaving to work for another employer because the plans could be structured so that, until an employee reached NORMAL RETIREMENT AGE, he or she would always be nonvested in some year's contributions (and thus subject to FORFEITURE of those benefits).

Statutory and Regulatory Reference: See Pub. L. No. 99-514, § 1113(f)(4) (repeal of class-year vesting). *See also* ERISA § 203(a)(3)(D)(iv); I.R.C. § 411(a)(3) (D)(iv).

cliff vesting   Under a qualified retirement plan, a schedule for vesting of participants' benefits in which all accrued benefits derived from employer contributions become nonforfeitable after a participant has completed a specified period of service for the employer, but, before the end of that period, such benefits are completely unvested. The maximum amount of time a qualified plan can make participants wait until they become fully vested if the plan uses cliff vesting is five years. If the plan is top-heavy for a PLAN YEAR, however, this is reduced to three years.

See TOP-HEAVY, VESTING, YEAR OF SERVICE.

Statutory and Regulatory Reference: See ERISA § 203(a); I.R.C. § 411(a)(2)(A); Treas. Reg. §§ 1.411(a)-3T(b) (regular vest-

ing rules). *See also* I.R.C. § 416(b)(1)(A) and Treas. Reg. § 1.416-1, Q&A V-1 (top-heavy vesting). *See also* ERISA § 203(c)(1) and I.R.C. § 411(a)(10) (certain changes in vesting schedule). For the definition of "year of service" for vesting purposes, *see* ERISA § 203(b)(2) and I.R.C. § 411(a)(5).

Treatise Reference: Tax Mgmt. (BNA), No. 351, *Pension Plans—Qualification*, No. 352, *Profit-Sharing Plans—Qualification,* and 353, *Owner-Dominated Plans—Top-Heavy and H.R. 10 Plans*.

COB   *See* COORDINATION OF BENEFITS.

COBRA   The Consolidated Omnibus Budget Reconciliation Act of 1985. This term is loosely used to refer to the health care continuation coverage rules created by this Act. The health care continuation rules basically provide that a qualified beneficiary covered under an employer's group health plan who experiences a qualifying event may elect to continue that coverage for a specific period of time which varies depending on the qualifying event. Plans of small employers (those passing the 20-employee test), governmental plans, including state and local agencies not receiving Public Health Service funds, and plans maintained by churches generally are exempt from the COBRA continuation coverage rules.

See CONTINUATION COVERAGE, QUALIFIED BENEFICIARIES, QUALIFYING EVENT.

Statutory and Regulatory Reference: Pub. L. No. 99-272; COBRA § 1001(g); ERISA §§ 601-07; I.R.C. § 4980B; Prop. Treas. Reg. § 1.162-26.

Treatise Reference: Tax Mgmt. (BNA), No. 389, *Disability and Medical Reimbursement Benefit Plans*; *Employee Benefits Law* 989-1004 (1991).

CODA (cash or deferred arrangement) *see* SECTION 401(K) PLAN.

Code *See* INTERNAL REVENUE CODE.

COLA rider A disability insurance policy rider, i.e., a document amending the original policy, whereby the disability benefit payable under the policy is subject to cost-of-living adjustments (COLAs) tied to the consumer price index or some other index measuring inflation. A COLA rider can take effect after disability benefits are in pay status, e.g., one year after disability, or can apply retroactively starting with the date of purchase of the policy, in which event they are known as "automatic increasing benefits."

Treatise Reference: *Insurance and Risk Management For Business and Government*, A Desktop Manual (Washington: BURAFF Publications, The Bureau of National Affairs, Inc., 1989).

collectibles Certain rare objects that have inherent economic value, such as stamps, coins, rugs or antiques, metals, gems, works of art, and alcoholic beverages. The Economic Recovery Tax Act of 1981 (ERTA), Pub. L. No. 97-34, prohibited individual retirement accounts from investing their assets in these objects. This prohibition also extends to self-directed accounts in qualified retirement plans.

See SELF-DIRECTED ACCOUNT.

Statutory and Regulatory Reference: *See* Pub. L. No. 97-34; I.R.C. § 408(m); Prop. Treas. Reg. § 1.408-10. Note that the Technical and Miscellaneous Revenue Act of 1988 (TAMRA), Pub. L. 100-647, amended the rules on collectibles to provide that coins issued under the laws of any state are not considered collectibles if they are held by a person independent of the IRA owner. *See* Pub. L. No. 100-647, § 6057(a), adding I.R.C. § 408(m)(3), effective as to acquisitions made after Nov. 10, 1988.

Treatise Reference: *See* Tax Mgmt. (BNA), No. 355, *IRAs and SEPs*.

collectively bargained plan A retirement or welfare plan that provides for benefits specified in a collective bargaining agreement; such a plan can be sponsored by more than one employer.

See MULTIEMPLOYER PLAN.

Statutory and Regulatory Reference: *See* I.R.C. § 413 and Treas. Reg. § 1.413-1 through -2 (relating to collectively bargained retirement plans); and I.R.C. § 7701(a)(46) (tax definition of collective bargaining agreement).

Treatise Reference: *Employee Benefits Law* 692-712; 841-91 (1991).

combined plan limit (1) *Maximum Deduction Context* A rule that provides, where an employer maintains one or more qualified defined benefit plans and one or more qualified defined contribution plans, the regular limits on the deductibility of contributions to individual plans are superseded by an aggregate limit applicable to contributions to both types of plans. This limit restricts the employer's annual deductible contribution to the greater of (1) 25 percent of compensation paid or accrued during the taxable years to the participants in all plans; or (2) the amount of contributions made to defined benefit plans to the extent that they do not exceed the amount needed to satisfy the MINIMUM FUNDING STANDARD of I.R.C. § 412.

Statutory and Regulatory Reference: I.R.C. § 404(a)(7); Treas. Reg. § 1.404(a)-13.

Case and Other Interpretive Reference: Rev. Rul. 79-5, 1979-1 C.B. 448, providing guidance in computing the combined plan limit where the employer's plans do not have the same limitation years.

(2) *Maximum Benefit Context* A rule providing that, where an employee par-

ticipates in one or more qualified defined benefit plans and one or more qualified defined contribution plans maintained by the same employer, the maximum benefit he or she is usually allowed to earn under each individual plan is superseded by an aggregate limit that applies to his or her benefits under all plans. The limit is calculated by first computing a "combined plan fraction." This number consists of the sum of the "defined benefit plan fraction" and the "defined contribution plan fraction." These two fractions generally measure what percentage of the maximum benefit allowable under each type of plan the employee has actually earned.

The sum of these two fractions cannot exceed 1.0 for any participant for any year. If they do, the IRS may disqualify one or more plans.

Statutory and Regulatory Reference: *See* I.R.C. § 415(e); Treas. Reg. § 1.415-7. For additional restrictions on the combined plan limit that apply to top-heavy plans, *see* I.R.C. § 416(h); Treas. Reg. § 1.416-1, Q&A T-33.

Treatise Reference: Tax Mgmt. (BNA), No. 371, *Employee Plans—Deductions, Contributions, and Funding*.

common control group of unincorporated trades or business where ownership of interests in the businesses are related in such a way that the businesses would be members of a controlled group if they were incorporated.

See CONTROLLED GROUP.

Statutory and Regulatory Reference: I.R.C. § 414(c); Treas. Reg. § 1.414(c).

compensation Remuneration received by an employee from his or her employer that is currently includable in gross income for income tax purposes. For self-employed individuals, compensation is the individual's earned income (pursuant to I.R.C. § 401(c)(2)) determined without regard to any exclusions under I.R.C. § 911 (for U.S. residents living abroad). For participants in defined contribution plans who are permanently and totally disabled within the meaning of I.R.C. § 22(e)(3), who are not considered to be highly compensated employees under the rules of I.R.C. § 414(q), and with respect to whom the employer elects to have a special definition apply, compensation is the amount that the disabled individual would have received for the year if the individual was paid at the rate paid immediately before disability. Also, an employer may elect to include in compensation amounts contributed by the employer pursuant to a salary reduction agreement which are not includable in gross income under I.R.C. §§ 125, 402(a)(8), 402(h), or 403(b). There are also alternative definitions of compensation that can be elected (see the regulations cited below).

Example: A plan could elect to use employees' regular or base salary or wages or it could elect to use regular or base salary or wages, plus overtime and/or bonuses.

Statutory and Regulatory Reference: I.R.C. §§ 22(e)(3), 401(c)(1), 414(s), and 415(c)(3); Treas. Reg. § 1.414(s)-1T.

complete withdrawal Under the Multiemployer Pension Plan Amendments Act of 1980 (MPPAA), Pub. L. No. 96-364, an employer is considered to have completely withdrawn from a multiemployer plan either (1) when there is a permanent cessation of the employer's contribution obligation; or (2) when, despite the fact that the employer still has an obligation to make contributions, e.g., under a collective bargaining agreement, the employer no longer has operations that are covered by the plan. Certain employer asset sales can also be treated as a complete withdrawal (with an exception for certain arm's-length sales). Complete withdrawal of an employer from a multiemployer plan triggers MPPAA's withdrawal liability requirements.

See MASS WITHDRAWAL, MPPAA, MULTI-EMPLOYER PLAN, PARTIAL WITHDRAWAL, WITHDRAWAL LIABILITY.

Statutory and Regulatory Reference: ERISA §§ 4201(a) (withdrawal liability established), 4203(a) (defining complete withdrawal), 4203(b)-(d) (defining withdrawal for construction, entertainment, and trucking industries), and 4204 (excepting bona fide, arm's-length sale of assets).

Case and Other Interpretive Reference: *Teamsters Pension Trust Fund v. Central Michigan Trucking, Inc.*, 857 F.2d 1107, 10 EB Cases 1141 (6th Cir. 1988) (employer that spun off subsidiary not subject to MPPAA withdrawal liability following subsequent withdrawal from plan of former subsidiary; spin off was change in corporate structure and employer's liability did not survive in contingent form after such change). *See also Berkshire Hathaway, Inc. v. Textile Workers Pension Fund*, 874 F.2d 53, 10 EB Cases 2625 (1st Cir. 1989) (multiemployer pension plan cannot assess withdrawal liability against employer that withdrew from fully funded plan).

Treatise Reference: *See* Tax Mgmt. (BNA), No. 357, *Plan Terminations and Mergers*, and No. 359, *Multiemployer Plans — Special Rules*; *see also Employee Benefits Law* 762-65 (1991).

conduit IRA An individual retirement account that is used only as a temporary repository of a rollover distribution from a qualified retirement plan (usually a distribution made upon the employee's separation from the employer's service) until the funds may be rerolled into another qualified plan, usually one maintained by the employee's new employer. Using a conduit IRA can, in effect, have the result of extending the normal 60-day time limit on making tax-free rollovers from one qualified plan to another (i.e., the 60-day limit applies to the length of time from the employee's receipt of the distribution from the first plan until it is rolled into the conduit IRA, and from the time the funds are taken out of the IRA until they are rerolled to the new plan, but not to the length of time between the distribution from the first qualified plan until subsequent rollover into the new qualified plan). Use of a conduit IRA is particularly useful where an employee who receives a distribution from a former employer's plan will not be able to roll over the funds to his or her new employer's plan within the statutory period. Distributions held in a conduit IRA will not, if later recontributed to a qualified plan, lose their eligibility for FORWARD AVERAGING treatment under I.R.C. § 402(e). This would not be the case if such amounts were first contributed to a regular IRA (i.e., one that holds some funds that did not come first from a qualified plan).

See INDIVIDUAL RETIREMENT ARRANGEMENT, ROLLOVER.

Statutory and Regulatory Reference: I.R.C. §§ 402(a)(5)(F) and 408(d)(3)(A)(ii).

Treatise Reference: Tax Mgmt. (BNA), No. 355, *IRAs and SEPs*.

constructive receipt A federal tax law doctrine which provides that income is realized by a taxpayer who uses the cash method of accounting when such income is unconditionally credited or set aside for the taxpayer's benefit, or otherwise is made available for his or her withdrawal or other disposition without substantial limitation or restriction. (Taxpayers on the accrual method of accounting are automatically subject to this standard).

Qualified retirement plans are statutorily exempted from the Internal Revenue Code's constructive receipt rules so that an employee's benefit under such a plan is not considered received until it is distributed.

Nonqualified deferred compensation arrangements, however, are subject to the constructive receipt rules.

Example: If Corporation X credits Employee A, a participant in a nonqualified deferred compensation arrangement sponsored by Corporation X with bonus stock, but the stock is not available to A until some future date, the crediting on the books of Corporation X does not cause A to constructively receive the value of the stock for federal income tax purposes.

Statutory and Regulatory Reference: I.R.C. §§ 83 and 451; Treas. Reg. §§ 1.451-1 *et seq.* and 1.83-1 *et seq.* (nonqualified plans); and § 402(a) (qualified plans). *See* Treas. Reg. §§ 1.402(a)-1, and (b)-1 containing rule in effect before the enactment of the Economic Recovery Tax Act of 1981 (ERTA), Pub. L. No. 97-34, under which constructive receipt principles *did* apply to qualified retirement plan benefits.

Case and Other Interpretive Reference: See Rev. Rul. 72-25, 1972-1 C.B. 127; Rev. Rul. 68-99 1968, 1 C.B. 127. *See also Corliss v. Bowers*, 281 U.S. 376 (1930) (taxpayer will be subject to tax if he or she has unfettered control in determining when such items of income should be paid); and PLR 7714001 (tax consequences of constructive receipt with respect to an unfunded deferred compensation plan).

Treatise Reference: Tax Mgmt. (BNA), No. 358, *Cash or Deferred Arrangements*, and No. 385, *Deferred Compensation Arrangements*.

continuation coverage   Health care coverage provided under the COBRA health care continuation rules. These rules basically provide that a qualified beneficiary covered under an employer's group health plan who experiences a qualifying event may elect to continue that coverage for a specific period of time, which varies depending on the qualifying event. Continuation coverage (1) must consist of coverage identical to that provided under the plan to similarly situated beneficiaries with respect to whom there has not been a qualifying event; (2) must extend for at least the period beginning on the date of a qualifying event and ending not earlier than the 18 to 36 month period specified in the statute (varying depending on the specific qualifying event); (3) must meet the premium requirements, one of which is a requirement that the premium for continuation coverage cannot exceed 102 percent of the "applicable premium" amount; (4) cannot require evidence of insurability; and (5) must provide for a conversion option. The continuation coverage rules do not apply to a plan of an employer whose total number of employees was fewer than 20 on a "typical business day" in the prior calendar year. Governmental and church plans generally are also excepted from the rules.

See APPLICABLE PREMIUM, COBRA, QUALIFIED BENEFICIARIES, QUALIFYING EVENT.

Statutory and Regulatory Reference: ERISA § 602, I.R.C. § 4980B(f); Prop. Treas. Reg. § 1.162-26.

Case and Other Interpretive Reference: See *Martinez v. Dodge Printing Centers, Inc.*, No. 89-k-171 13 EB Cases 1348, 123 B.R. 77 (D. Colo. Jan. 9, 1991), (company that filed for bankruptcy and terminated its workers exempt from notifying employees of continuation coverage rights under COBRA because company fit within the small employer exception); *Communication Workers of America v. NYNEX Corp.*, 898 F.2d 887, 12 EB Cases 1049 (2d Cir. 1990) (striking workers entitled to preliminary injunction barring employer from refusing COBRA continuation coverage to employees who elected it but did not pay premiums even though still within 45 day grace period; irreparable harm shown); *Brock v. Premedica, Inc.*, 904 F.2d 295, 12 EB Cases 2118 (5th Cir. 1990) (group health plan participant covered under her employer's and her spouse's employer's health plan not entitled to COBRA continuation coverage; benefits available only to individuals who would have no coverage and participant still covered under spouse's plan). *But see Oakley v. City of Longmont*, 890 F.2d 1128, 11 EB Cases 2453 (10th Cir. 1989), *cert. denied*, 494 U.S. ___, 58 USLW 3658 (1990) (employer can terminate COBRA coverage of qualified beneficiary who has coverage under another group health plan only if the other coverage was acquired after the qualifying event). *See also Hersh v. National Distributing Co.*, 12 EB Cases 1693 (N.D. Ga. 1988), (employer that accepted former employee's payment of COBRA continuation coverage premium equitably barred from terminating employee's coverage after employee began making claims based on fact that employee was covered under spouse's plan; employer's acceptance of premium with knowledge of dual coverage established promise of continuing coverage on which employee relied); *Kidder v. H&B Marine, Inc.*, 734 F. Supp. 724, 12 EB Cases 1345 (E.D. La. 1990) (liability assessed against employer, group health insurance trust, and affiliated underwriter apportioned according to responsibility for failure to notify covered employees of COBRA continuation coverage).

Treatise Reference: Tax Mgmt. (BNA), No. 389, *Disability and Medical Reimbursement Benefit Plans; Employee Benefits Law* 989-1004 (1991).

contribution (to a qualified retirement plan)   The transfer of funds or property by either an employer or an employee to an employee retirement plan.

One of the principal advantages of establishing a tax-qualified retirement plan is that the employer may, within certain limits, deduct its contributions currently, while participants need not recognize taxable income until they receive a distribution of benefits. The deductibility of a contribution by an employer depends on whether the contribution satisfies two tests. First, it must be an ordinary and necessary business expense.

Second, the contribution must fall within the limits of I.R.C. § 404(a).

Section 404(a) also contains provisions that apply to certain types of nonqualified arrangements and annuity plans. It does not apply, however, to a plan or arrangement that does not involve the deferral of compensation. Further, it does not apply to deductions for contributions under a plan that is solely a dismissal wage or unemployment benefit plan, or a sickness, accident, hospitalization, medical expense, recreation, welfare, or similar benefit plan, or a combination thereof.

Generally, for an employer to deduct contributions to a qualified plan for a taxable year, the plan must have been in existence, i.e., the formalities of plan adoption must have been completed, before the end of the year. Thus, the employer can evaluate its financial position as its taxable year draws to a close and determine if it would be beneficial to establish a qualified plan that will begin operation for that year. Such factors as a healthy profitability picture coupled with the potential of having excess retained corporate earnings (in the case of a corporation) are among those that might convince an employer to establish a plan, in addition to the obvious ones of providing for the retirement needs of employees.

Once it adopts a plan, to be able to deduct contributions for the taxable year to which its the return relates, the employer must make its contribution for the year before the due date (including extensions) of that year's federal income tax return. Corporate tax returns are usually due two and one-half months after the close of the taxable year, with extensions of up to six months automatically available. Where a contribution is made after the close of the taxable year that is intended to relate back to the prior year, the employer must note this fact on its federal income tax return for the year in which the deduction is taken, or the IRS will treat the contribution as if it were attributable to the employer's taxable year in which it was made.

Generally, the employer's contribution to a qualified retirement plan may take any form, for example, cash, securities, or other property. An employer, however, cannot take a current deduction for contributing its unsecured promissory note, even if the employer is on the accrual method of accounting. Further, ERISA's fiduciary duty rules limit the ability of certain qualified plans to hold employer securities or employer real property.

Under general principles of taxation, when a taxpayer extinguishes an obligation by transferring property with a fair market value that exceeds its adjusted basis, the taxpayer must recognize gain to the extent of the difference. This treats the taxpayer in the same manner as one who first sold the property at a gain and then used the proceeds to extinguish the obligation. This rule applies in the qualified plan context where the employer uses such appreciated property as part or all of its qualified plan contribution for a year.

Example: An employer satisfies its $10,000 contribution obligation to a plan for a year by contributing property having an adjusted basis of $6,000 and fair market value of $10,000. The employer will be taxed on the $4,000 of appreciation as if it had first sold the asset for $10,000 and then contributed the proceeds to the plan.

Such a difference between a property's adjusted basis and its fair market value can be the result of many factors. One of the most common would be where the employer's depreciation deductions on property have exceeded the actual diminutions of its value over time.

The converse of this situation, however, does not produce a loss deduction, e.g., where a $6,000 obligation is extinguished with the contribution of property having a $10,000 basis and a $6,000 fair market value. This is because I.R.C. § 267 denies taxpayers deductions for losses incurred in transactions be-

tween related parties (in this case, the employer and the plan's trust). In this situation, it is generally advisable for the employer to first sell the property, recognize the loss, and then make a deductible cash contribution to the plan. This is especially so since, for taxable years beginning after 1986, plan sponsors are subject to a nondeductible 10 percent penalty tax if they make nondeductible contributions to a qualified plan for a taxable year. Note that there also may be situations where the plan will have to sell property that has been contributed to provide sufficient liquidity to pay benefits when they fall due.

For single employer plans, only the employer sponsoring the plan is entitled to an I.R.C. § 404 deduction for contributing to it. This rule, however, does not apply to multiple employer and multiemployer plans. Also, where an affiliated group of corporations maintains a single profit-sharing plan, and a group member is unable to contribute to the plan because it lacks profits, the remaining employers may make such contributions on the nonprofitable member's behalf up to the percentage of that member's employees' compensation that would have been contributed. Where the affiliated group of employers does not file a consolidated return for the taxable year in question, the contributions that may be made up by each remaining employer may not exceed each employer's proportionate share of total employer contributions that were made to the profit-sharing plan for the year in which the "make-up" contribution is made.

See PREFUNDING OF BENEFITS for a discussion of the deductibility of an employer's contributions to fund certain employee welfare benefit plans.

Statutory and Regulatory Reference: I.R.C. § 404(a); Treas. Reg. § 1.404(a)-1 *et seq.*

Treatise Reference: Tax Mgmt. (BNA), No. 371, *Employee Plans — Deductions, Contributions, and Funding.*

contribution base units *See* WITHDRAWAL LIABILITY.

contribution carryover *See* CARRYOVER OF DEDUCTIONS.

contribution rate/contribution percentage The amount of funds or property contributed to a retirement or welfare plan on an employee's behalf for a year, expressed as a percentage of that employee's compensation for the year.

Treatise Reference: Tax Mgmt. (BNA), No. 371, *Employee Plans—Deductions, Contributions, and Funding*; *Employee Benefits Law* 117-23 (1991).

contributory plan A retirement-type plan that requires employees to make contributions as a precondition to becoming eligible to earn benefits. Certain contributory qualified plans are subject to special mathematical nondiscrimination tests with respect to employee contributions made thereto.

See ACTUAL CONTRIBUTION PERCENTAGE.

Statutory and Regulatory Reference: I.R.C. §§ 401(k) and 401(m) for nondiscrimination rules applicable to employee contributions to qualified retirement plans.

Treatise Reference: Tax Mgmt. (BNA), No. 358, *Cash or Deferred Arrangements*.

controlled group Two or more corporations if (a) one is the parent and the others are members of an 80 percent owned group (parent-subsidiary group), (b) the same five or fewer persons own at least 80 percent of the voting power or value of each and there is identical ownership of at least 50 percent of the corporations (brother-sister group), or (c) each is a member of either a parent-subsidiary group or a brother-sister group and at least one is the common parent of a parent-subsidiary group and a member of a brother-sister group. A controlled group of corporations is treated as a single employer in applying certain of the Code's qualified retirement plan rules.

Statutory and Regulatory Reference: ERISA § 3(40)(b); I.R.C. § 414(b)-(c); Treas. Reg. § 1.414(b)-(c).

conversion A right provided to a covered employee or other qualified individuals under an insured group health plan to convert to an individual policy of the insurer upon termination of coverage under the group health plan. COBRA requires an employer to provide to qualified beneficiaries with expiring continuation coverage the option of enrollment under a conversion health plan otherwise generally available under the plan. The conversion generally must be made by an election followed by a premium payment within a limited time frame, such as 31 days after termination of employment, and the individual policy generally is a stripped down version of the group policy with a face amount no higher than the policy being converted. The terms of conversion generally are regulated by state law.

See COBRA, CONTINUATION COVERAGE, GROUP HEALTH PLAN, QUALIFIED BENEFICIARIES.

Statutory and Regulatory Reference: ERISA § 602, I.R.C. § 4980B(f); Treas. Reg. § 1.162-26, Q&A-43.

Treatise Reference: Tax Mgmt. (BNA) *Financial Planning*, Para. 425, *Insurance Planning* (1991).

coordination of benefits (COB) A sequential system of uniform rules set up by insurance companies and insurance regulators to prevent an individual from profiting from duplicative group health care coverage. A determination first is made as to the sequence by which the various plans pay benefits or provide services. The primary plan, i.e., the group health plan that provides first, pays benefits, or provides services as if there were no duplicative coverage. The secondary plan, i.e., the plan that pays benefits or provides services second, pays the difference between the applicable maximum amount (which cannot be more than the total expenses incurred) and the amount that the primary plan paid. A set of rules exists for determining which plan is primary and which secondary, for instance, plans that do not have a COB provision are primary and thus pay first, and plans covering an individual as an employee are primary to plans covering the same individual as a dependent. Also, Medicare is secondary to private medical plans for active employees and their spouses.

Statutory and Regulatory Reference: See Omnibus Budget Reconciliation Act of 1989 (OBRA 1989), Pub. L. No. 101-239, § 6202. For illustrative state statutes, *see* CAL. ADMIN. CODE TIT. 10, § 2232.50 to .60 (1986); DEL. INS. REG. 61 (1988); N.Y. ADMIN. CODE TIT. 11, § 52.23 (Reg. 62) (1987). *See also* Group Coordination of Benefits Model Regulations, National Association of Insurance Commissioners (NAIC) (July 1989).

Treatise Reference: Employee Benefits Law 1035 (1991). *See also Report of the Advisory Committee to the NAIC COB Task Force* (June 1985).

core coverage   Under the COBRA continuation coverage rules, basic health care coverage, as opposed to less crucial fringes, or non-core health care coverage such as vision care, care not required to be performed by a physician, or dental care that is not in connection with an accidental injury (unless these benefits are required under state or local law). Under Treasury regulations, core coverage is all of the coverage that a qualified beneficiary was receiving under the plan immediately before a QUALIFYING EVENT, other than non-core coverage, which is defined as vision and dental benefits. Note

that "core coverage only" generally must be available to electing qualified beneficiaries under COBRA.

See COBRA, CONTINUATION COVERAGE.

Statutory and Regulatory Reference: ERISA §§ 601-07; I.R.C. § 4980B; Treas. Reg. 1.162-26, Q&A-24, 25.

Treatise Reference: Tax Mgmt. (BNA), No. 389, *Disability and Medical Reimbursement Benefit Plans*; *Employee Benefits Law* 989-95 (1991).

cost of living adjustment (COLA)   The adjustment of an employee's benefit under a retirement or welfare plan to take into account increases or decreases in the cost of living, according to some objective index, such as the consumer price index. The term can also refer to the indexation for inflation of certain dollar limits imposed on qualified retirement plans by the Internal Revenue Code.

Statutory and Regulatory Reference: I.R.C. §§ 401(a)(17) and 415(d). For the rules governing certain arrangements to provide for changes in the cost of living under defined benefit plans, *see* I.R.C. § 415(k)(2).

Treatise Reference: *See* Tax Mgmt. (BNA), No. 351, *Pension Plans — Qualification*.

coverage   The admission of employees to participation in a retirement or welfare plan. The term "coverage" also refers to the I.R.C. § 410(b) rules designed to insure that qualified retirement plans benefit a broad cross-section of the employer's nonhighly compensated employees.

"Coverage" is also used to refer to an additional qualification rule added by the Tax Reform Act of 1986 (TRA 1986), Pub. L. No. 99-514, requiring that a plan benefit at least the lesser of 50 employees or 40 percent of all employees of the employer.

See AVERAGE BENEFIT PERCENTAGE TEST, PARTICIPATION, RATIO TEST, 70 PERCENT TEST.

Statutory and Regulatory Reference: I.R.C. §§ 401(a)(26) and 410(b). Prop. Treas. Reg. 1.401(a)(26)-1 *et seq.* and §§ 1.410(b)-1 *et seq.*

Case and Other Interpretive Reference: *See* Rev. Rul. 79-337, 1979-2 C.B. 189 (profit-sharing plan for salaried and clerical employees violates the pre-TRA 1986 minimum coverage rules when it results in the coverage of only I.R.C. § 401(a)(4) PROHIBITED GROUP members); Rev. Rul. 80-351, 1980-2 C.B. 152 (plan that covers only highly compensated employee and secretary does not satisfy pre-TRA 1986 I.R.C. § 410(b) where secretary waives right to participate); Rev. Rul. 80-47, 1980-1 C.B. 83 (plan may restrict participation to employees who elect to make employee contributions and undergo a physical examination for life insurance purposes, provided these provisions do not result in DISCRIMINATION); Rev. Rul. 1981-1 C.B. 216 (plan that limits participation to employees who are not eligible for overtime pay under Fair Labor Standards Act does not satisfy pre-TRA 1986 I.R.C. § 410(b)(1)(B)).

Treatise Reference: *See* Tax Mgmt. (BNA), No. 351, *Pension Plans — Qualification; see also Employee Benefits Law* 19-32; 90-104 (1991); and D. McGill & D. Grubbs, Jr., *Fundamentals of Private Pensions* 82 (6th ed. 1989).

covered compensation (for a plan year) In a qualified defined benefit plan, the compensation of an employee that is taken into account in calculating his or her benefit.

For purposes of the Social Security integration rules for defined benefit plans, IRS regulations provide a specific definition of the term. These regulations define covered compensation as the average of the taxable wage bases in effect under the Social Security Act for a 35-year period ending when an employee reaches Social Security NORMAL RETIREMENT AGE (generally age 65).

See INTEGRATION (SOCIAL SECURITY).

Statutory and Regulatory Reference: I.R.C. § 401(l) and Treas. Reg. § 1.401(l)-1(c)(7).

Treatise Reference: *See* Tax Mgmt. (BNA), No. 356, *Qualified Plans — Integration*; *Employee Benefits Law* 131; 133 (1991).

covered employee For COBRA health care continuation coverage purposes, under ERISA, this term describes an individual who is (or was) provided coverage under a group health plan by virtue of the individual's employment or previous employment with the employer. Under the Internal Revenue Code, for these purposes, it is an individual who is (or was) provided coverage under a group health plan by virtue of the performance of services by the individual for one or more persons maintaining the plan (including an employee as defined in I.R.C. § 401(c)(1), referring to self-employed individuals). Basically, these definitions encompass not only employees within the traditional employee/employer relationship, but also can include independent contractors and partners in a partnership, if the plan also covers common law employees. A retired or former employee covered by a group health plan is a covered employee if the coverage results from his or her previous employment.

Example: Law firm X maintains a group health plan for its common-law employees. If the firm also provides group health coverage for its partners, the partners are covered employees regardless of whether the coverage is provided under the same group health plan as the common law employees. If the partners are the only individuals receiving benefits, they are not covered employees.

See COBRA, CONTINUATION COVERAGE

Statutory and Regulatory Reference: ERISA § 607(2); I.R.C. § 4980B(f)(7); Prop. Treas. Reg. § 1.162-26, Q&A-16(b).

Treatise Reference: See Tax Mgmt. (BNA), No. 389, *Disability and Medical Reimbursement Benefit Plans. See also Employee Benefits Law* 992-93 (1991).

covered service   Service by an employee for an employer that must be counted under the terms of a retirement or welfare plan in determining the employee's right to participate in the plan, the value of his or her benefit, or his or her vested rights in such benefit.

Treatise Reference: See Tax Mgmt. (BNA), No. 351, *Pension Plans — Qualification*, and No. 352, *Profit-Sharing Plans — Qualification*; *see also Employee Benefits Law* 41; 84; 107-09 (1991).

current liability   In the case of a single or multiple employer qualified defined benefit plan, for purposes of the I.R.C. § 412 minimum funding standard, the amount the plan would have to pay as benefits to participants and beneficiaries if it terminated, calculated in accordance with certain rules governing the actuarial assumptions and interest rates that may be used.

See FUNDING STANDARD ACCOUNT.

Statutory and Regulatory Reference: ERISA § 302(d)(7); I.R.C. § 412(f)(7).

Treatise Reference: Tax Mgmt. (BNA), No. 371, *Employee Plans — Deductions, Contributions, and Funding.*

current value   As defined in ERISA § 3(26), fair market value where available and otherwise fair value as determined in good faith by a plan's trustee or named fiduciary under a plan's terms and in accordance with applicable Labor Department regulations, assuming that there is an orderly liquidation at the time the determination is made.

Statutory and Regulatory Reference: ERISA § 3(26).

custodial account   An arrangement in which a bank or other person (such as a stock brokerage firm) holds the assets of a qualified retirement plan. The custodian is required to administer those assets consistent with I.R.C. § 401(a)'s trust requirements and is treated as a trustee with respect to the account. Similar rules apply to custodial accounts used with respect to an individual retirement account. A custodial account can also be used by a § 501(c)(3) tax-exempt organization or a public school to invest § 403(b) plan (tax-sheltered annuity) funds in regulated investment company stock; any amounts used in this way are treated as amounts contributed for an annuity contract for the employee.

Statutory and Regulatory Reference: See ERISA § 403(b)(3)(i); I.R.C. § 401(f) (custodian as trustee — self-employed individual). *See also* ERISA § 403(b)(3)(ii); I.R.C. § 408(h)(individual retirement accounts); I.R.C. § 403(b)(7) (I.R.C. § 501(c)(3) organizations); and Treas. Reg. § 1.401(f)-1.

D

DBO plans *See* DEATH BENEFIT ONLY
(DBO) PLAN

death benefits Benefits payable from a
qualified or nonqualified retirement plan to
an employee's beneficiary due to the death of
an employee.

See INCIDENTAL DEATH BENEFITS.

Statutory and Regulatory Reference: I.R.C.
§ 101.

death benefit exclusion A federal tax
law rule that provides, in general, that an
employee's beneficiaries or his or her estate
need not pay income tax on the first $5,000
paid to them under a life insurance contract
where the payments are made by reason of the
employee's death.

This exclusion is not available when the
employee possessed a NONFORFEITABLE
right to the funds involved while he or she was
still alive (e.g., where the death benefit is
payable out of an employee's vested benefit in
a qualified retirement plan).

The exclusion is also not available for
amounts paid in the form of a LUMP-SUM
DISTRIBUTION from a qualified retirement
plan or a § 403(a) annuity plan. It is also
unavailable for benefits paid from a § 403(b)
tax-deferred annuity contract if they are attributable to employer or deemed employer
contributions on which the employee had not,
at the time of his or her death, paid federal
income tax.

Statutory and Regulatory Reference: I.R.C.
§ 101(b)(1)-(3).

Treatise Reference: See Tax Mgmt. (BNA)
No. 386, *Insurance Related-Compensation.*

death benefit only (DBO) plan An arrangement between an employer and
employee whereby the employer agrees to
pay an annuity or lump-sum death benefit if
the employee dies while employed (and in
some instances while retired). A DBO plan
may be informally funded by insurance, but it
cannot be formally secured or funded. The
death benefit paid to the beneficiary generally
is taxable to the beneficiary as income in
respect of a decedent (under I.R.C. § 691),
subject to the $5,000 death benefit exclusion
from income (under I.R.C. § 101(b)). The
payment generally is deductible by the
employer as an ordinary and necessary business expense due to its nature as compensation with respect to the decedent.

Statutory and Regulatory Reference: I.R.C.
§§ 72, 101(b), 162 and 691.

Case and Other Interpretive Reference:
Dependahl v. Falstaff Brewing Corp., 653 F.2d

1208 (8th Cir.), *cert. denied*, 454 U.S. 968, 2 EB Cases 2392 (1981), illustrates the need to create an unfunded DBO plan; here DBO found to be a funded welfare benefit plan and thus subject to ERISA's prohibited transaction requirements. *See also Essenfeld v. Commissioner*, 311 F.2d 208 (2d Cir. 1962) (employer receives proceeds of supporting DBO policies income tax free on employee's death, but the proceeds are not paid tax-free to survivor, even if paid in a lump sum); and Rev. Rul. 81-31, 1981-1 C.B. 475 (a gift occurs at the executive's death if the DBO plan predesignates the beneficiaries and the executive cannot change the beneficiary).

Treatise Reference: Tax Mgmt. (BNA) No. 386, *Insurance-Related Compensation*.

deductible employee contribution (DEC) *See* QUALIFIED VOLUNTARY EMPLOYEE CONTRIBUTION.

deduction/deductibility
Expenses paid by a cash method taxpayer or incurred by an accrual method taxpayer that may be subtracted in determining the amount of income on which the taxpayer must pay income tax.

The amount of an employer's tax deduction for contributions to a qualified retirement plan is subject to certain percentage limits, depending on the type of plan involved. The deductibility of employer contributions to a qualified defined benefit plan is limited under a formula that is based on the amount needed to satisfy the Internal Revenue Code's MINIMUM FUNDING STANDARD. For a qualified profit-sharing or stock bonus plan, generally, an employer may contribute and deduct up to 15 percent of the compensation paid for the year to its participants. Where the employer maintains *both* one or more qualified pension or annuity plans *and* one or more qualified profit-sharing or stock bonus plans, special combined limits apply. The employer's contributions to health, disability, life insurance, and other employee welfare benefits are generally deductible as ordinary and necessary business expense. I.R.C. §§ 419 and 419A provide special limiting rules for determining the timing and amount of an employer's deduction for contributions to a VEBA (voluntary employees' beneficiary association—a form of welfare benefit arrangement). Under these rules, an employer contribution to a VEBA that is otherwise deductible as an ordinary and necessary business expense is deductible only to the extent that it does not exceed the "qualified cost" of the plan, i.e., the direct cost of providing the benefits for the taxable year, plus certain reserves.

See CARRYOVER OF DEDUCTIONS, COMBINED PLAN LIMIT, CONTRIBUTION, NONQUALIFIED DEFERRED COMPENSATION PLAN, SUBSTANTIAL RISK OF FORFEITURE.

Statutory and Regulatory Reference: *See* I.R.C. § 162. *See also* Treas. Reg. § 1.404(a)-1 (general rule for qualified plans). For the limits applicable to qualified pension or annuity plans, *see* I.R.C. § 404(a)(1)-(2) and Treas. Reg. §§ 1.404(a)-3 to (a)-8. For the limits applicable to qualified plan contributions on behalf of a self-employed individual, *see* I.R.C. § 404(a)(8) and Temp. Treas. Reg. § 1.404(a)(8)-1T. For the rules applicable to qualified profit-sharing or stock bonus plans, *see* I.R.C. § 404(a)(3) and Treas. Reg. §§ 1.404(a)-9 to -10. I.R.C. § 404(a)(7) and Treas. Reg. § 1.404(a)-13 contain the rules for determining allowable deductions where the employer maintains *both* one or more qualified pension plans *and* one or more qualified profit-sharing or stock bonus plans. Note that, in general, an employer may not deduct an amount contributed to a nonqualified deferred compensation plan until the employee on whose behalf the contribution is made has paid income tax on it. Generally, this occurs when the employee has a NONFORFEITABLE right to the amounts involved and may freely transfer such property.

For the rules applicable to nonqualified plans, *see* I.R.C. §§ 83(h) and 404(a)(5). For the rules governing the deductibility of VEBA contributions, *see* I.R.C. §§ 419 and 419A.

Treatise Reference: For the rules applicable to qualified plans, *see* Tax Mgmt. (BNA), No. 371, *Employee Plans — Deductions, Contributions, and Funding; Employee Benefits Law* 147-152; 987-89 (1991).

deferred compensation   Remuneration for services under any employer-sponsored plan or arrangement that an employee will take into income for tax purposes in the future, rather than in the current year. The plan or arrangement can be a qualified pension, profit-sharing, or annuity plan; qualified or nonqualified stock option; a stock purchase plan; or a restricted property arrangement. For purposes of the employer's DEDUCTION for contributions to a nonqualified deferred compensation arrangement, compensation is considered to be deferred if the employee receives compensation or benefits more than a brief period of time after the end of the employer's TAXABLE YEAR in which the services creating the right to such compensation or benefits are performed. For this purpose "a brief period of time" is two and one-half months.

See NONQUALIFIED PLAN, QUALIFIED RETIREMENT PLAN.

Statutory and Regulatory Reference: *See* I.R.C. § 404(a); Treas. Reg. § 1.404(a)-1 *et seq.*; and Treas. Reg. § 1.404(b)-1T, Q&A-2. *See also* I.R.C. § 404(a)(5) (deductions for contributions to nonqualified deferred compensation plans), I.R.C. § 402(b)(2) (taxation of benefits under nonqualified deferred compensation plans to employees), and I.R.C. § 457 (special rules for certain deferred compensation plans for the employees of state and local governments and tax-exempt organizations).

Treatise Reference: Tax Mgmt. (BNA), No. 385, *Deferred Compensation Arrangements*.

deferred profit-sharing plan   An employer-sponsored profit-sharing plan (typically tax-qualified) that delays an employee's right to receive his or her share of employer-derived contributions to a TAXABLE YEAR of the employee that is later than the one in which the profits to which the contribution relates were generated.

See PROFIT-SHARING PLAN.

deferred vesting   Any vesting schedule in which accrued benefits do not fully and immediately become NONFORFEITABLE.

See VESTING.

deficit reduction contribution   An additional amount, over and above the regular minimum funding standard, that the employer must contribute annually to a qualified defined benefit plan subject to the Internal Revenue Code's minimum funding standard to reduce its level of unfunded benefits, if any. The deficit reduction contribution consists of an amount designed to reduce a plan's past unfunded benefit liabilities (the "old unfunded liability amount"), plus an amount needed to reduce its unfunded liability for benefits that are being earned currently (the "unfunded new liability amount)."

See FUNDING STANDARD ACCOUNT, MINIMUM FUNDING STANDARD.

Statutory and Regulatory Reference: ERISA § 302(d)(2); I.R.C. § 412(l)(2).

Treatise Reference: Tax Mgmt. (BNA), No. 371, *Employee Plans — Deductions, Contributions, and Funding*.

defined benefit excess plan   A defined benefit plan that is integrated with Social Security and under which the rate of benefits an employee earns based on compensation above a specified level is greater than the rate an employee earns with respect to compensation below that level.

Example: Under a defined benefit plan, a participant earns an annual benefit equal to 1 percent of the first $30,000 of compensation and 2 percent of compensation in excess of $30,000.

See BASE BENEFITS PERCENTAGE, INTEGRATION (SOCIAL SECURITY), MAXIMUM EXCESS ALLOWANCE.

Statutory and Regulatory Reference: *See* I.R.C. § 401(l)(3)(A); Treas. Reg. § 1.401(l)-1(c)(16)(i).

Treatise Reference: Tax Mgmt. (BNA), No. 356, *Qualified Plans—Integration*; *Employee Benefits Law* 119-21 (1991).

defined benefit plan/defined contribution plan　Qualified retirement plans fall into two basic categories: defined benefit and defined contribution plans. A defined contribution plan is conceptually the easiest to understand.

The name "defined contribution" derives from the fact that the employer's annual contribution obligation is spelled out in the plan document. The plan need not specify that a particular dollar figure or percentage of compensation will be contributed; it need merely provide a method whereby the employer's contribution obligation may be determined with specificity. For example, a profit-sharing plan which provides that the employer's board of directors will vote an annual contribution of between 1 and 15 percent of compensation out of the employer's profits will suffice. (Profit-sharing plans are unique in their ability to provide that the employer's annual contribution obligation will be discretionary. Other types of qualified plans must provide for a specific contribution obligation).

The terms "defined contribution plan" and "individual account plan" are synonymous. A defined contribution plan's trust consists of individual accounts for participating employees. Employer contributions are allocated among employees' accounts according to a formula contained in the plan. The benefit to which any participant is entitled at any given time is that participant's nonforfeitable (vested) portion of his account balance. The account can contain both employer and employee contributions, depending on the plan's terms. Thus, participating in a defined contribution plan is somewhat like maintaining a bank account—an employee's benefit is equal to his or her account balance. The trustee of a defined contribution plan generally invests the plan's assets, although self-direction by participants may be permitted. Any investment return is credited to participants' accounts and they bear the incidence of any investment loss. Amounts credited to participants' accounts that are later forfeited due to the occurrence of some event, such as layoff or other separation from service, either may be reallocated to the accounts of participants remaining in the plan or may be held in suspense until a later plan year. At that time, they may be used to decrease the employer's contribution obligation. The method of allocating contributions, investment gains or losses, and forfeitures depends upon the plan's terms, subject to the general rule that such methods may not discriminate in favor of highly compensated employees.

Examples of defined contribution plans include profit-sharing plans (generally plans designed to enable employees to participate in the employer's profits), stock bonus plans, employee stock ownership plans (ESOPs) and, to some extent, money purchase pension plans (although money purchase plans for funding purposes are treated as defined benefit plans).

Individual retirement arrangements (IRAs) and simplified employee pensions (SEPs) also operate on the defined contribution plan model.

In contrast, defined benefit plans may be said to work "backward." That is, in a defined benefit plan, as the name suggests, the benefit to which an employee will be entitled upon retirement is specified in the plan. For example, a provision that "a participant shall be entitled to a normal retirement benefit of 1 percent of his average career compensation for each year of service with the employer" would constitute a defined benefit plan formula. An annual benefit of $500 per year of service would also qualify.

In a defined benefit plan, it is the employer's annual contribution obligation that may fluctuate from year to year. The employer must contribute annually an amount necessary to make reasonably certain that the benefits promised will be available when employees become eligible to receive them. The annual funding calculation is made by an actuary, who must consider the likely level of forfeitures, the possibility that some employees may leave the plan without earning a benefit, the life expectancies of employees and their beneficiaries, the form of benefit payment, the level of future compensation, and so forth.

Thus, in a defined benefit plan the benefit is spelled out. In a defined contribution plan, all that is specified is how much the employer will contribute. Factors such as the level of forfeitures and the rate of return on the plan's investments determine how large a retirement benefit will be available. Another way of expressing this is that, in a defined contribution plan, the investment risk (of gain or loss) falls on employees, while, in a defined benefit plan, it falls on the employer.

One disadvantage of establishing a defined benefit plan is the cost of retaining a qualified actuary—a cost a defined contribution plan does not have.

One way employers may minimize their risk while maintaining a defined benefit-type plan is to establish a target benefit plan. A target benefit plan essentially works on the defined benefit plan model except that the actuarial assumptions that are in effect when the plan is established are the ones that remain in effect throughout the life of the plan. Thus, the benefit which is defined in the plan document is the one that will be paid if the actuarial assumptions conform to experience. Where there is a variance between assumed and actual experience, it will produce a gain or loss, i.e., a benefit that is higher or lower than the one targeted by the plan document. Where this occurs, gain or loss will be reflected in higher or lower retirement benefits.

A money purchase pension plan follows, in many respects, the defined contribution plan model although, for funding purposes, money purchase plans are treated as defined benefit plans. A money purchase plan is essentially one in which the employer agrees to make annual contributions that are not based on profits. The contributions are divided among participants' accounts according to a formula contained in the plan in the same manner as under a profit-sharing plan. A participant's benefit is the annuity or similar benefit that can be purchased with his account balance upon retirement.

Stock bonus plans are similar to money purchase plans in that they are defined contribution plans where the employer's annual contribution obligation is not based on profits. Stock bonus plans, however, are designed to hold their assets in the form of stock of the sponsoring employer.

See ACTUARIAL ASSUMPTIONS, ACTUARY, DEFINITELY DETERMINABLE BENEFIT REQUIREMENT, ESOP, IRA, MONEY PURCHASE PENSION PLAN, PENSION PLAN, PROFIT-SHAR-

ING PLAN, SEP, STOCK BONUS PLAN, TARGET BENEFIT PLAN.

Statutory and Regulatory Reference: ERISA §§ 3(34)-(35); I.R.C. §§ 414(i)-(j).

Treatise Reference: *See* Tax Mgmt. (BNA), No. 351, *Pension Plans — Qualification*, No. 352, *Profit-Sharing Plans — Qualification*, No. 354, *ESOPs*, and No. 355, *IRAs and SEPs*; *see also Employee Benefits Law*, 24-25; 29-31; 75-83 (1991).

defined contribution excess plan   A defined contribution plan that is integrated with Social Security where the rate at which contributions are allocated to participants' accounts for compensation above the plan's IN-TEGRATION LEVEL exceeds the rate at which they are allocated for compensation up to the integration level. All integrated defined contribution plans must use the excess method.

Example: A defined contribution plan has an integration level of $30,000. It provides that the employer will contribute 7 percent of an employee's annual compensation for the first $30,000 earned and that it will contribute 10 percent on any compensation the employee earns for the year in excess of $30,000.

See BASE CONTRIBUTION PERCENTAGE, IN-TEGRATION (SOCIAL SECURITY).

Statutory and Regulatory Reference: *See generally* I.R.C. § 401(l)(2) for the Social Security integration rules applicable to defined contribution plans. *See also* Treas. Reg. § 1.401(l)-1(c)(16)(ii);

Treatise Reference: Tax Mgmt. (BNA), No. 356, *Qualified Plans — Integration*.

defined contribution plan   *See* DEFINED BENEFIT PLAN/DEFINED CONTRIBUTION PLAN.

definitely determinable benefit requirement   The requirement that a qualified defined benefit plan or money purchase pension plan provide systematically for the payment of benefits that are either spelled out in the PLAN DOCUMENT or readily ascertainable under a formula contained in the plan. Retirement benefits under qualified pension plans are usually based on such factors as the employee's number of years of service with the employer and his or her compensation level. The requirement is satisfied if a plan provides a mathematical formula under which an employee's retirement benefit can be readily calculated.

A defined benefit plan will not be considered to provide definitely determinable benefits if funds arising from forfeitures on TERMINATION of service or otherwise may be used to increase the benefits of employees who remain in the plan.

Example: A defined benefit plan provides that an employee will earn a benefit equal to 2 percent of AVERAGE ANNUAL COMPENSA-TION for each YEAR OF SERVICE performed.

Statutory and Regulatory Reference: Treas. Reg. §§ 1.401-1(a)(4)(b)(1)(i) and -1(b)(1)(i).

Case and Other Interpretive Reference: *See* Rev. Rul. 76-259, 1976-2 C.B. 111 (defined benefit plan that provides benefits that are offset by the employer's contributions to a qualified profit-sharing plan will not fail to satisfy the definitely determinable benefit requirement because the defined benefit plan contains such an offset provision). *See also* Rev. Rul. 78-57, 1978-1 C.B. 116 (examining the circumstances under which a defined benefit plan funded solely by life insurance contracts described in I.R.C. § 412(i) will satisfy the definitely determinable benefit requirement); Rev. Rul. 79-90, 1979-1 C.B. 155 (defined benefit plan, to satisfy definitely determinable benefits requirement, must specify its ACTUARIAL ASSUMPTIONS in its plan document). Note that the requirements of Rev. Rul. 79-90 were later codified in I.R.C. § 401(a)(25).

Treatise Reference: Tax Mgmt. (BNA), No. 351, *Pension Plans – Qualification*; *Employee Benefits Law* 76 (1991).

de minimis fringe benefit Property or services offered by an employer to an employee, the value of which is so small as to make accounting for it unreasonable or administratively impracticable, taking into account the frequency with which similar fringes are provided by the employer to employees. The employee can exclude from income the value of these benefits.

Example: The value of meals provided to employees at an employer-operated eating facility may be excludable as a de minimis fringe if all statutory requirements are met. Also, the value of occasional typing of personal letters by a company secretary, occasional personal use of an employer's copying machine (provided that the employer exercises sufficient control and imposes significant restrictions on the personal use of the machine so that at least 85 percent of its use is for business purposes), occasional cocktail parties or picnics for employees and their guests, traditional holiday gifts of property (not cash) with a low fair market value, occasional theater or sporting event tickets, coffee and doughnuts are other examples of de minimis fringes.

Statutory and Regulatory Reference: I.R.C. § 132(a)(4); Treas. Reg. §§ 1.132-6 and -7.

Treatise Reference: Tax Mgmt. (BNA), No. 394, *Employee Fringe Benefits*; *Employee Benefits Law* 983-85 (1991).

dependent Any of the following individuals over half of whose support was received from the taxpayer: (1) a son or daughter of the taxpayer, or a descendent of either; (2) a stepson or daughter of the taxpayer; a brother, sister, stepbrother or step-sister of the taxpayer; (3) the father or mother of the taxpayer, or an ancestor of either; (4) a stepfather or stepmother of the taxpayer; a son or daughter of a brother or sister of the taxpayer; (5) a brother or sister of the father or mother of the taxpayer; (6) a son-in-law, daughter-in-law, father-in-law, mother-in-law, brother-in-law, or sister-in-law of the taxpayer; and (7) an individual (other than a spouse of the taxpayer) who has as a principal place of abode the home of the taxpayer and is member of the taxpayer's household. The term dependent does not include any individual who is not a citizen or national of the United States unless such individual is a resident of the United States or a country contiguous to the United States. An individual is not a member of the taxpayer's household and thus cannot be a dependent under the tax code if at any time during the year the relationship between such individual and the taxpayer is in violation of local law.

For VEBA purposes, dependent is defined as a member's spouse, any child of the member or the member's spouse who is a minor or a student (within the meaning of I.R.C. § 151(e)(4)); any other minor child residing with the member and any other individual who an association in good faith believes to be a dependent as described in I.R.C. § 152(a).

Statutory and Regulatory Reference: I.R.C. §§ 152(a), (b)(3), and (b)(5); Treas. Reg. §§ 1.152-1 and -2; 1.501(c)(9)-2(b)(3).

Treatise Reference: Tax Mgmt. (BNA), No. 394, *Employee Fringe Benefits*.

dependent care assistance program A separate written plan of an employer for the exclusive benefit of its employees to provide them with dependent care assistance, i.e., the payment of, or provision of, services which, if paid for by the employee, would be considered expenses for household and dependent care services necessary for gainful employment within the meaning of I.R.C. § 21(b)(2).

The Code generally provides a limited exclusion from the employee's gross income for amounts paid or incurred by the employer pursuant to a dependent care assistance plan for dependent care expenses incurred with respect to qualifying dependents, *i.e.*, dependents who are either under age 13 or physically or mentally incapable of caring for themselves. For taxable years beginning after 1986, the exclusion is limited to $5,000 per year ($2,500 in the case of a married individual filing separately). The exclusion is further limited in that an employee cannot exclude amounts paid to another dependent of the employee under age 19 at the close of the taxable year of the payment. The amount of excludable dependent care assistance is also subject to an earned income limitation and nondiscrimination requirements. An employee who excludes amounts from income under a dependent care assistance program cannot claim a credit under I.R.C. § 21 for expenses for household and dependent care services. For taxable years beginning in 1988, the employer must include on the employee's W-2 the total amount incurred for dependent care assistance.

Statutory and Regulatory Reference: I.R.C. § 12. *See also* I.R.C. §§ 21, 6051(a)(9); Treas. Reg. § 1.44A-1, 1.125-2 (Q&A 4).

Case and Other Interpretive Reference: IRS Notice 89-111, 1989 I.R.B. 19 (where dependent care assistance is provided to employee in-kind (e.g., through an on-site day care facility), the limits apply to the fair market value of the assistance without regard to the actual cost to the employer). Notice also provided guidance on how to comply with the reporting requirements of §§ 129(d)(6) and 6051(a)(9) *see also* PLR 8303037 (cost of kindergarten qualified as deductible expense for the care of a child, even though food and education were also provided); *and Zoltan v. Commissioner*, 79 T.C. 490 (1983), *acq.* 1984-2 C.B. 2 (cost of sending child to summer camp to provide for child's protection and well being was an expense incurred for the care of the child, if camp provided no significant educational services). *But see* Prop. Treas. Reg. § 1.125-2, Q&A-4(a)(2)(iv) (after January 1988, cost of overnight camp cannot qualify as a dependent care expense).

Treatise Reference: Tax Mgmt. (BNA), No. 394, *Employee Fringe Benefits*; *Employee Benefits Law* 968 (1991).

determination date   For a qualified retirement plan, the date prescribed by law for testing the plan's benefits or contributions to determine if it will be subject to the top-heavy rules for the next PLAN YEAR. Specifically, the "determination date" for any plan year is (1) the last day of the previous plan year, or (2) for a plan's first plan year, the last day of that year.

The determination date is essentially a snapshot of the accumulated benefits under a plan taken at a designated point in time.

Example: If a plan uses the calendar year as its plan year, the determination date for 1991 would be December 31, 1990, unless 1991 was the plan's first year in existence, in which case it would be December 31, 1991 (which, in this case would also serve as the determination date for the plan's second year of existence, 1992). If the plan was top-heavy on that date, the top-heavy rules would apply for the entire ensuing plan year, regardless of whether, during that year, the level of benefits of key employees fell to 60 percent or less of total plan benefits (the top-heavy criterion). Similarly, if, on December 31, 1991, the plan was not top-heavy, the top-heavy rules would not apply to the plan until, at the earliest, the 1993 plan year (for which the determination date would be December 31, 1992), even if the benefits of key employees rose above 60 percent during 1992.

See TOP-HEAVY.

Statutory and Regulatory Reference: I.R.C. § 416(g)(3)(C).

Treatise Reference: Tax Mgmt. (BNA), No. 353, *Owner Dominated Plans — Top-Heavy and H.R. 10 Plans*.

determination letter   A letter issued by an IRS district office to the sponsor of a qualified retirement plan stating that, as of the date of the letter, the plan, on paper, complies with the Internal Revenue Code's qualification requirements. The plan must be operated in accordance with those requirements to maintain its qualified status.

Although a plan that does not obtain a determination letter may still be treated as qualified if it meets all of the Code's tests, in light of the complexity of the law, it is almost always advisable to obtain a determination letter when the plan is adopted as well as after it is amended or after the applicable law has changed.

A favorable determination letter effectively assures the PLAN SPONSOR that the IRS will treat the plan as qualified so long as the law does not change, the plan is operated in accordance with its terms, and the plan, in its operation, does not discriminate in favor of highly compensated employees.

Often, the IRS, upon receipt of a determination letter application, will require certain plan amendments or clarifications before it will issue a favorable letter. This process acts as a failsafe device to help make certain that the plan, as drafted, complies with all pertinent qualification requirements.

In addition, when a plan terminates, it is generally advisable to apply for and obtain a favorable "termination determination" letter, i.e., an IRS ruling stating that no aspect of the proposed termination will adversely affect the plan's prior qualified status. This assures the plan sponsor, as well as each participant and beneficiary, that the plan will be treated as qualified up to its termination date and that its assets, and benefits distributed from it, will continue to receive the favorable tax treatment applicable to qualified retirement plans.

Applications for determination letters must be filed using IRS Form 5300. Applications for termination determination letters or for approval of a plan MERGER, asset transfer, or consolidation, are filed on IRS Form 5310.

Statutory and Regulatory Reference: ERISA §§ 3001-02; I.R.C. § 7476.

Case and Other Interpretive Reference: See Rev. Proc. 90-1, 1990-1 I.R.B. 8 (procedures for rulings and determination letters, Associate Chief Counsel, Technical), Rev. Proc. 89-9 1989-1 C.B. 780 (master and prototype plans); Rev. Proc. 89-13, 1989-1 C.B. 801 (regional prototype plans); and *IRS Alert Guideline Package — Worksheets for Plan Qualification*. The alert guideline package contains the IRS' internal standards for determining the qualification of retirement plans under I.R.C. § 401(a).

Treatise Reference: Tax Mgmt. (BNA), No. 360, *(ERISA) — Qualified Plans — IRS Determination Letter Procedures*, generally for a discussion of the IRS' determination letter process; *Employee Benefits Law* 461-65 (1991).

DI benefits   *See* SOCIAL SECURITY DISABILITY INCOME BENEFITS.

disability retirement benefits   Payments made in lieu of wages to an employee who has retired by reason of total and permanent disability. Under I.R.C. § 22, a "qualified individual" may take a federal income tax credit equal to 15 percent of such payments for the year. Qualified individuals are individuals who (1) have attained age 65 before the close of the taxable year, or (2) have retired on disability before the close of the taxable year and, when retired, were permanently and totally disabled. An individual's § 22 amount is the initial amount as appropriately reduced.

disabled

See PERMANENT AND TOTAL DISABILITY, SECTION 22 AMOUNT

Statutory and Regulatory Reference: Former I.R.C. § 105(d); I.R.C. § 22, 106.

Treatise Reference: Tax Mgmt. (BNA), No. 389, *Disability and Medical Reimbursement Benefit Plans*.

disabled   An individual is disabled if he or she is unable to engage in any substantial gainful activity by reason of any medically determinable physical or mental impairment which can be expected to result in death or to be of long-continued and indefinite duration. An individual is not considered disabled unless he or she furnishes proof of the existence of the disability. The "substantial gainful activity" is the activity in which the individual was customarily engaged before the disability. A determination as to whether impairment causes disability is determined on a case-by-case basis.

Example: The following types impairments would ordinarily be considered as preventing substantial gainful activity: loss of use of two limbs, diabetes, multiple sclerosis, inoperable and progressive cancer, damage to the brain resulting in loss of judgment, intellect, or memory, psychosis or severe psychoneurosis, permanent and total loss of speech.

See PERMANENT AND TOTAL DISABILITY, SOCIAL SECURITY DISABILITY INCOME BENEFITS.

Statutory and Regulatory Reference: I.R.C. § 72(m)(7); Treas. Reg. §§ 1.72-17(f) and 1.72-17A(f).

discount factor   The interest rate factor that is used in calculating the PRESENT VALUE of a future payment, e.g., a plan benefit. Discount factors are used in the qualified retirement plan context in, among other things, determining the amount of an employee's benefit that is to be "cashed-out" under the voluntary or involuntary CASH-OUT rules, determining actuarial equivalence among multiple benefits forms, applying the I.R.C. § 412 MINIMUM FUNDING STANDARD, and determining an employee's benefit upon plan TERMINATION.

See ACTUARIAL ASSUMPTIONS.

Treatise Reference: Tax Mgmt. (BNA), No. 371, *Employee Plans—Deductions, Contributions, and Funding*.

discrimination   The favoring of an employer's highly compensated employees by the terms or operation of a plan. Qualified retirement plans may not discriminate either in their terms or in operation in favor of such employees. The Internal Revenue Code contains detailed rules designed to ensure that a qualified retirement plan will not discriminate. In addition to these specific rules, qualified plans must satisfy the "general nondiscrimination rule" in I.R.C. § 401(a)(4). This rule provides that a qualified plan cannot discriminate as to benefits or contributions in favor of highly compensated employees (within the meaning of I.R.C. § 414(q)). If a plan passes all of the other Code nondiscrimination tests but fails to satisfy this general rule in some aspect of its draftsmanship or operation, a plan will not qualify, even if it has previously received a favorable IRS DETERMINATION LETTER. A defined contribution plan is usually tested under § 401(a)(4) for nondiscrimination as to contributions and a defined benefit plan for discrimination as to benefits; however, a plan need only show that it does not discriminate as to benefits *or* contributions to meet § 401(a)(4). Therefore, if a defined contribution plan can show that it does not discriminate as to benefits, or a defined benefit plan can show that it does not discriminate as to contributions, the plan will satisfy § 401(a)(4).

The following example shows how a plan might pass the Code's specific nondiscrimination test for minimum VESTING, yet still violate § 401(a)(4) because its vesting schedule discriminates in operation.

Example: A defined contribution retirement plan that seeks to qualify under I.R.C. § 401(a)(4) contains a vesting schedule that applies equally to all participants and satisfies the requirements of I.R.C. §§ 401(a)(7) and 411. The vesting schedule calls for an employee to be 100 percent vested after four years of service. Over time, a disproportionately large number of nonhighly compensated employees relative to highly compensated employees leave the employer before becoming vested. As a result, there is a pattern of forfeitures from the accounts of nonhighly compensated employees to those employees who remain in the plan, who largely tend to be highly compensated. Highly compensated employees' account balances thus disproportionately benefit from reallocated forfeitures. Where this effect is pronounced, it can constitute discrimination under § 401(a)(4).

See GENERAL NONDISCRIMINATION RULE.

Statutory and Regulatory Reference: I.R.C. § 401(a)(4); Prop. Treas. Reg. § 1.401(a)(4)-1-13 *et seq.*

Treatise Reference: *See* Tax Mgmt. (BNA), No. 351, *Pension Plans—Qualification*, and No. 352 *Profit-Sharing Plans—Qualification*; *see also Employee Benefits Law* 90-104 (1991).

disqualified person *See* PARTY IN INTEREST.

distress termination Under SEPPAA (the Single-Employer Pension Plan Amendments Act of 1986), a voluntary termination of a single-employer defined benefit plan required when an employer desires to terminate a plan but has insufficient assets to meet benefit liabilities. In a distress termination, the sponsoring employer is liable to the PBGC for all unfunded benefit liabilities as of the plan termination date, along with reasonable interest from the termination date. A distress termination must be triggered by one of four events: (1) liquidation in bankruptcy; (2) reorganization in bankruptcy; (3) a demonstration that, absent plan termination, the employer will be unable to continue in business; and (4) a demonstration that, solely as a result of the employment of covered employees, the costs of providing coverage have become unreasonably burdensome. A single-employer plan may terminate under a distress termination only if the plan administrator provides 60 days' advance notice of intent to terminate to affected parties and the PBGC (on Form 600) and sends to the PBGC a distress termination notice (Form 601) containing, among other things, the current value of plan assets. The PBGC must determine that one of the four necessary distress termination criteria has been met by each contributing sponsor or member of its controlled group (members do not have to meet the same test).

See PBGC, SEPPAA, STANDARD TERMINATION.

Statutory and Regulatory Reference: ERISA § 4041, 4048(a)(2); *see also* the regulations cited under standard terminations.

Treatise Reference: Tax Mgmt. (BNA), No. 357, *Plan Terminations and Mergers*; *Employee Benefits Law* 404-08 (1991).

distribution *See* LUMP-SUM DISTRIBUTION, MINIMUM REQUIRED DISTRIBUTION, PREMATURE DISTRIBUTION.

domestic relations order *See* QUALIFIED DOMESTIC RELATIONS ORDER.

E

EAP *See* EMPLOYEE ASSISTANCE PROGRAM.

early retirement age/earliest retirement age The youngest age under a qualified retirement plan, prior to an employee's reaching the plan's NORMAL RETIREMENT AGE, at which the employee may elect to receive benefits. Some plans require that employees' benefits be actuarially reduced if they retire early; in other plans, the effect of this reduction is mitigated by an employer's subsidizing early retirement.

Statutory and Regulatory Reference: *See* I.R.C. § 417(f)(3). *See also* ERISA § 3(24) (definition of normal retirment age); I.R.C. § 411(a)(8) (definition of normal retirement age for qualified plan purposes).

Treatise Reference: D. McGill & D. Grubbs, Jr., *Fundamentals of Private Pensions* 131 (6th ed. 1989).

earned income An individual's net earnings (gross earnings less deductions) from self-employment determined, in general: (1) only as to a business in which his or her personal services are a material income-producing factor; (2) without considering items that do not constitute gross income under the Internal Revenue Code and any deductions that relate to such items; (3) without regard to any deductions for contributions to qualified retirement plans allowed to the individual; and (4) by taking into account any deductions for the employer portion of Self-Employment Contributions Act (SECA) taxes allowed to the taxpayer. Certain other special rules apply in determining earned income. For instance, gains (other than capital gains) and net earnings from the sale, disposition, transfer, or licensing of the use of property by an individual whose personal efforts created such property are counted and certain types of income described in I.R.C. § 1402(c)(4) and (5) are disregarded.

See COMPENSATION.

Statutory and Regulatory Reference: I.R.C. §§ 401(c)(2) and 1402(a).

educational assistance plan A benefit plan set up by an employer to pay expenses incurred by, or on behalf of, an employee for the education of the employee. Expenses covered by such a plan include, but are not limited to, tuition, fees and similar payments, books, supplies, and equipment. Also covered are expenses relating to the provision, by the employer, of courses of instruction for its employees, including such expenses as books, supplies, and equipment. Educational assistance does not include payments for tools or supplies that may be retained by the employee after completing the course of instruction, and it does not include the value of meals, lodging, or transportation. A tax-favored educational assistance plan cannot provide for payment of courses involving sports, games, or hobbies. An educational assistance plan must benefit a classification of employees that does not discriminate in favor of employees who are officers, owners, or highly compensated, or their dependents. An employee's federal gross income generally does not include amounts paid or incurred by the employer for educational assistance pursuant to an educational assistance plan.

Statutory and Regulatory Reference: I.R.C. §§ 127 and 401(c)(1); Treas. Reg. §§ 1.127-1 and -2.

Treatise Reference: Tax Mgmt. (BNA), No. 394, *Employee Fringe Benefits*; *Employee Benefits Law* 963-66 (1991).

elapsed time method   An alternative method of calculating service that qualified retirement plans may use in determining an employee's length of credited service for participation, BENEFIT ACCRUAL, and VESTING purposes. This method credits an employee with service for the time that has passed between commencement of employment for the employer and SEPARATION FROM SERVICE regardless of the hours worked. Like the equivalencies sanctioned by Labor Department and/or Treasury regulations, using this convention saves a plan from the burden and expense of keeping detailed records of the hours worked by employees to determine their eligibility for benefits under a qualified plan.

Under the elapsed time method, an employee generally is charged with a one-year BREAK IN SERVICE (called a "period of severance") when he or she leaves the employer and does not return within a 12-consecutive-month period. Certain tem-

porary absences not constituting a separation from service, such as vacation time, must be counted as service for participation and vesting purposes.

See EQUIVALENCY.

Statutory and Regulatory Reference: *See* Treas. Reg. § 1.410(a)-7(a)(3). The original elapsed time method regulations were issued under IRS authority pursuant to Reorganization Plan No. 4 of 1978, which transferred jurisdiction from the Labor Department to the Treasury. The final regulations were issued by the IRS. *See* former Temp. 29 C.F.R. 2530.200b-9(a)(3)(ii).

Treatise Reference: See Tax Mgmt. (BNA), No. 351, *Pension Plans — Qualification* and No. 352, *Profit-Sharing Plans — Qualification*; *see also Employee Benefits Law* 87-88 (1991).

elective deferral   With respect to an employee for a given TAXABLE YEAR, it is the sum of employer contributions, to the extent not includable in the individual's gross income for the year, to: (1) an I.R.C. § 401(k) plan; (2) a simplified employee pension (SEP); and (3) an I.R.C. § 403(b) plan under a salary reduction agreement on the employee's behalf.

The aggregate amount deferred by an employee under those provisions for a given year cannot exceed a dollar cap specified in the Code. The cap for contributions to an I.R.C. § 401(k) plan and a § 401(k) plan or SEP was $8,575 for 1991, and is adjusted for inflation each year. The cap for contributions to a tax-deferred annuity is $9,500 (up to $12,500 for certain long-service employees of qualifying organizations).

The cap for tax-deferred annuities applies to increase the overall cap on elective deferrals, but does not increase the cap for I.R.C. § 401(k) plans. Thus, an employee without elective deferrals to a tax-deferred annuity would have a total cap of $8,575 for 1991.

See EXCESS DEFERRAL.

Statutory and Regulatory Reference: I.R.C. §§ 401(m)(4)(B) and 402(g); Treas. Reg. §§ 1.401(m)-1 and 1.402(g)-1; IRS Notice 90-17, 1990-8 I.R.B. 19.

Treatise Reference: Tax Mgmt. (BNA), No. 358, *Cash or Deferred Arrangements*.

eligibility   *See* PARTICIPATION.

eligibility computation period   A 12-consecutive-month period used in determining whether an employee has worked for an employer for a sufficient length of time to become eligible to participate in the employer's qualified retirement plan.

When an employee first comes to work for an employer, the initial eligibility computation period that the plan must use is the 12-month period beginning with the date the employee begins work ("employment commencement date") and ending with the first anniversary thereof. After the first such period, the plan may choose to calculate future years of service for eligibility purposes based on its PLAN YEAR. Where a qualified plan changes its eligibility computation period in this manner, however, it must credit an employee who has performed at least 1,000 hours of service in each of the two overlapping computation periods with two years of service for eligibility purposes even though this may result in the double counting of certain hours.

Example: A qualified retirement plan uses a calendar year as its plan year and converts its eligibility computation period to the plan year after the initial year. Employee X begins work for the employer on July 1, 1991, and completes 1,000 hours of service by the first anniversary of his or her employment commencement date, July 1, 1992. Of these 1,000 hours, 500 are attributable to the period beginning January 1, 1992, and ending July 1, 1992. The plan then converts X's eligibility computation period to the plan year. Between July 2, 1992, and December 31, 1992, X completes another 500 hours of service, giving him or her 1,000 hours for the 1992 plan year. X must be credited with two years of service (by virtue of having performed at least 1,000 hours of service in each of the two eligibility computation periods), even though 500 of the hours were counted in each of the two overlapping periods.

In general, qualified plans may only require that an employee perform one YEAR OF SERVICE before becoming eligible to participate.

Statutory and Regulatory Reference: I.R.C. § 410(a)(1)(A)(ii); 29 C.F.R. §§ 2530.202b-2(a) and (b).

Treatise Reference: Tax Mgmt. (BNA), No. 351, *Pension Plans—Qualification*.

eligible deferred compensation plan   A DEFERRED COMPENSATION arrangement meeting the requirements of I.R.C. § 457. Such a plan may only be established by an employer that is a state, a subdivisions of a state, an instrumentality or political subdivision of a state, or an entity other than a governmental unit that is exempt from federal income tax. If a plan meets the various qualification requirements of § 457, including the ELIGIBLE EMPLOYER requirement described above, amounts deferred and any income thereon will only be taxed to employees when such amounts are paid or otherwise made available. In general, an employee may not defer more than the lesser of $7,500 or one-third of his or her salary under a § 457 plan for any year.

See COVERAGE, PARTICIPATION.

Statutory and Regulatory Reference: I.R.C. §§ 457(a), (b) and (e); Treas. Reg. § 1.457-1 *et seq.* (*Note:* These regulations do not reflect amendments made to § 457 by the Tax Reform Act of 1986, Pub. L. No. 99-514, or subsequent legislation).

Treatise Reference: See Tax Mgmt. (BNA), No. 385, *Deferred Compensation Arrange-*

ments; *see also Employee Benefits Law* 235 (1991).

eligible employee   Any employee who has met the requirements for benefiting from a plan. For a plan to be a qualified retirement plan, a broad cross-section of employees must be eligible to benefit from it.

See ELIGIBLE EMPLOYER.

Statutory and Regulatory Reference: *See* I.R.C. §§ 410(a) and (b).

Treatise Reference: Tax Mgmt. (BNA), No. 351, *Pension Plans – Qualification*.

eligible employer   An employer permitted to establish a deferred compensation plan under I.R.C. § 457. Employers in this class are (1) a state; (2) a political subdivision of a state; (3) any agency or instrumentality of a state or political subdivision of a state; and (4) any organization other than a governmental unit that is exempt from federal income tax.

Statutory and Regulatory Reference: *See* I.R.C. § 457(e)(1).

Treatise Reference: *See* Tax Mgmt. (BNA), No. 385, *Deferred Compensation Arrangements*.

employee   Common law employees are individuals who perform services for a person who has the legal relationship of employer to the worker under the usual common law rules. For purposes of ERISA and the Code (e.g., the income tax withholding rules), the word "employee" means common law employee. The common law employer/employee relationship exists when an individual for whom services are performed has the right to control and direct the individual performing the services. The employer's control must cover not only what the employee does, but also how it is done for the employer/employee relationship to exist.

Some factors to consider in determining whether this control exists include, integration (i.e., the integration of a worker's services into the business operations shows he or she is subject to direction and control), right of discharge (i.e., the threat of discharge which causes a worker to obey an employer's instructions indicates an employer/employee relationship), right to delegate (if services must be rendered personally, the employer has an interest not only in the results but also how the work is done, and this indicates an employer/employee relationship), hiring, firing, and paying (these factors show control characteristic of an employer/employee relationship), and tools and place of work (where the employer supplies the instrumentalities, tools, and place of work an employer/employee relationship is indicated).

See EMPLOYER.

Statutory and Regulatory Reference: ERISA § 3(6) – any individual employed by an employer; I.R.C. § 132(f) – retired and disabled employees and surviving spouses of employees treated as employees. I.R.C. § 72(t) (tax on early distributions) – employee includes any participant or, in the case of an IRA, the individual for whose benefit the IRA was established. I.R.C. §§ 3121(d), 3306(i), 3401; Employment Tax Regs. § 31.3121(d)-1; Internal Revenue Manual, Chapter 4600, Employment Tax Procedures, Ex. 4640-1, p. 4600-21 (referring to factors to be analyzed as elements of control in determining whether an employer/employee relationship exists).

Case and Other Interpretative Reference: *United States v. Silk*, 331 U.S. 704 (1947), and *Bartels v. Birmingham*, 332 U.S. 126 (1947)(employee includes workers who are such as a matter of economic reality).

Note that some glosses are added to the term employee for various purposes and under various particular statutes: For example, *Allied Chemical & Alkali Workers v.*

Pittsburgh Plate Glass Co., 404 U.S. 157 (1971)(retired employees are not employees within the definition of the NLRA and not provided the protection of that Act; ordinary construction of employee means someone who currently works for another for hire, thus excluding retired workers).

employee assistance program (EAP)

A program set up by an employer to assist employees in dealing with problems affecting employee health that require confidentiality, such as substance abuse, marital discord, and employment problems. An EAP typically includes a confidential hot line for employees arranged through a counseling agency. The initial counselor contacted evaluates the employee's needs, provides some initial counseling, and refers the employee to the appropriate provider for additional assistance.

Treatise Reference: Tax Mgmt. (BNA), *Financial Planning*, Para. 425, *Insurance Planning* (1991).

employee benefits

Employer-furnished benefits provided under an employee pension benefit plan or an employee welfare benefit plan.

See EMPLOYEE WELFARE BENEFIT PLAN, EMPLOYEE PENSION BENEFIT PLAN.

Statutory and Regulatory Reference: ERISA § 3(4).

employee benefit plan

An employee welfare or pension benefit plan or a plan that is both an employee welfare benefit plan and an employee pension benefit plan.

See EMPLOYEE WELFARE BENEFIT PLAN.

Statutory and Regulatory Reference: ERISA § 3(3).

Case and Other Interpretive Reference: Pane v. RCA Corp., 868 F.2d 63, 10 EB Cases 2079 (3d Cir. 1989) (employer severance plan held ERISA-covered benefit plan – plan

authorized by employer's board of directors; management identified potential class of participants; and it required administrative scheme). *See also Sayble v. Blue Cross*, 208 Cal. App. 3d 1108, 256 Cal. Rptr. 820, 10 EB Cases 2178 (Cal. Ct. App. Mar. 20, 1989) (employer's purchase of employee health insurance through multiple employer trust not ERISA-covered employee benefit plan – employer did not administer plan; role limited to paying policy premiums and there was no opportunity for employer abuses).

employee contributions

Voluntary or mandatory contributions by an employee to a qualified retirement plan. Such contributions (as distinguished from elective employee pretax deferrals to a § 401(k) or similar arrangement) are not deductible by the employee, but the employee is not taxed on the growth of contributed funds until they are withdrawn. A qualified plan is not required to provide for voluntary contributions; however, because voluntary contributions are counted in determining the TOP-HEAVY status of a plan, it may be desirable to restrict or prohibit them in plans that are in danger of becoming top-heavy. In addition, employee contributions must be taken into account in applying the nondiscrimination tests of I.R.C. § 401(m). Although there these contributions are not subject per se to a dollar limit, they are counted as ANNUAL ADDITIONS and, hence, are subject to the I.R.C. § 415 limits. In addition, contributions by highly compensated employees that exceed those permitted under I.R.C. § 401(m) must be distributed or otherwise corrected in a timely manner for a § 401(a) plan to remain qualified.

After-tax employee contributions increase an employee's basis in the plan benefit. Therefore, distributions, to the extent attributable to such contributions, are treated as a tax-free return of basis to the employee.

See QUALIFIED RETIREMENT PLAN; *See also* ELECTIVE DEFERRAL.

Statutory and Regulatory Reference: *See* I.R.C. §§ 401(m) and 416; Treas. Reg. § 1.401(m)-1(f)(6) (definition—note that I.R.C. § 401(m) contains nondiscrimination rules applicable to employee and matching contributions to qualified plans). *See also* ERISA § 203(a)(1) and I.R.C. § 411(a)(1) (VESTING in employee contributions); ERISA § 203(a)(3)(D) and I.R.C. § 411(a)(3)(D) (withdrawal of mandatory contributions); ERISA § 204(c) and I.R.C. § 411(d)(5) (voluntary employee contributions under defined benefit plans); ERISA § 204(c)(2) and I.R.C. § 411(c)(2) (determining benefit derived from employee contributions); ERISA § 204(c)(2)(C) and I.R.C. § 411(c)(2)(C) (definition of mandatory employee contribution); ERISA § 4044(a)(2) (allocation of plan assets to employee contributions); I.R.C. § 72(d) (surplus assets attributable to employee contributions); I.R.C. § 72(e)(8) (recovery of employee contributions); I.R.C. § 72(f) (computing employee contributions for purposes of the rules governing the taxation of annuities); I.R.C. § 72(o) (deductibility of employee contributions); I.R.C. § 414(h) (designation of contributions as employee contributions; I.R.C. § 414(h)(2) ("pick-ups" of employee contributions under certain governmental plans).

Case and Other Interpretive Reference: *See* Rev. Rul. 76-47, 1976-1 C.B. 109 (conversion factors for allocating accrued benefits under a defined benefit plan where NORMAL RETIREMENT AGE is not age 65 between employee contributions and employer contributions for minimum vesting purposes. *See also* Rev. Rul. 78-57, 1978-1 C.B. 128 (mandatory employee contributions to a defined benefit plan will be considered a separate plan for purposes of the I.R.C. § 415 limits on benefits that may be earned under qualified plans); and Rev. Rul. 78-202, 1978-1 C.B. 125 (providing rules for calculating accrued benefits derived from employee contributions payable in a lump sum and before normal retirement age).

Treatise Reference: *See* Tax Mgmt. (BNA), No. 358, *Cash or Deferred Arrangements*; *see also Employee Benefits Law* 121 (1991).

employee-pay-all VEBA   A voluntary employees' beneficiary association (VEBA) providing for the payment of life, sick, accident, or other benefits to its members or their dependents to which all contributions are made by employees and thus no employer funding is required. The I.R.C. § 419 account limits for welfare benefit funds do not apply to employee-pay-all VEBAs that cover at least 50 employees and that have certain experience-rating refund restrictions.

See VEBA, WELFARE BENEFIT FUND.

Statutory and Regulatory Reference: I.R.C. §§ 419, 419A, 501(c)(9).

Treatise Reference: Tax Mgmt. (BNA), No. 395, *Section 501(c)(9) and Self-Funded Employee Benefits*.

employee pension benefit plan   Any plan, fund, or program established or maintained by an employer or by an employee organization that either provides retirement income to employees or results in deferral of income by employees extending to the termination of employment or beyond. A plan meeting that definition is an employee pension benefit plan regardless of the how contributions made to the plan are calculated, benefits under the plan are calculated, or benefits under the plan are distributed. Thus, a defined benefit plan or a defined contribution plan is an employee pension benefit plan for purposes of ERISA.

See EMPLOYEE ORGANIZATION.

Statutory and Regulatory Reference: ERISA § 3(3).

employee organization   Any labor union or any other organization or group in which employees participate and which exists for the purpose, in whole or in part, of dealing with employers concerning an employee benefit plan or other employment matters. It also includes any employees' beneficiary association organized for the purpose, in whole or in part, of establishing such a plan.

See EMPLOYEE BENEFIT PLAN.

Statutory and Regulatory Reference: ERISA § 3(4).

employee stock ownership plan   *See* ESOP.

employee stock purchase plan   A plan that gives employees a systematic method of buying stock of the employer by providing an option price, to employees only, of 85 percent of the FAIR MARKET VALUE of the stock at the time the option is granted or at the time it is exercised, whichever is less. Employees who would own more than 5 percent of the stock of the employer, its parent, or its subsidiary, after the option is granted cannot be granted an option under the plan. Employees who do receive options under the plan and meet holding period requirements are not taxed on the bargain element of the option; the employer likewise gets no DEDUCTION for its contribution for federal income tax purposes.

See BARGAIN ELEMENT.

Statutory and Regulatory Reference: *See* I.R.C. § 423.

Treatise Reference: Tax Mgmt. (BNA), No. 7, *Stock Options (Statutory) — Qualification*.

employee welfare benefit plan   Any plan, fund, or program that was established or maintained by an employer or an employee organization, or by both, to the extent that such plan, fund, or program was established or is maintained for the purpose of providing for its participants or their beneficiaries through the purchase of insurance or otherwise (1) medical, surgical, or hospital care or benefits in the event of sickness, accident, disability, death or unemployment, or vacation benefits, apprenticeship or other training programs, or day care centers, scholarship funds, or prepaid legal services, or (2) any benefit described in § 302(c) of the Labor Management Relations Act, 1947 (other than pensions on retirement or death, and insurance to provide such pensions). Also known as a welfare plan.

See WELFARE BENEFIT PLAN.

Statutory and Regulatory Reference: ERISA § 3(1).

Case and Other Interpretive Reference: *Massachusetts v. Morash*, 402 Mass. 287, 522 N.E.2d 409, 10 EB Cases 1245 (1988), *rev'd in part*, 490 U.S. 107, 10 EB Cases 2233 (1989) (employer's policy of paying employees for unused vacation time from general assets held not ERISA-covered welfare benefit plan since employees' rights to benefits were contingent on future occurrence and benefits not payable on a regular basis from fund that accumulates over time); *Purser v. Enron Corp.*, 10 EB Cases 1561 (W.D. Pa. 1988) (change of control contract providing for severance benefits is ERISA-covered welfare benefit plan rather than individual employment contract; contract stated employer intended to provide benefits to a class of beneficiaries).

employer   Under ERISA, any person acting directly as an employer, or indirectly in the interest of an employer, in relation to an employee benefit plan. It includes a group or association of employers acting for an employer in such capacity. To further defining the terms employer and employee used within the ERISA definition, the common law definition of these words must be examined. Consult the definition of employee for this common law definition.

See EMPLOYEE.

Statutory and Regulatory Reference: ERISA § 3(5).

employer-pay-all split-dollar insurance

A variation of split-dollar life insurance for which the employee does not make a contribution to payment for the life insurance policy. The employer pays the entire premium. The policy is treated as a split-dollar policy even though the premium is not split since the proceeds are split appropriately. The tax consequences of this type of arrangement are the same as for the standard split-dollar policy (i.e., employee includes in gross income the value of the benefit received and the employer cannot deduct the premium payments as an ordinary and necessary business expense).

See SPLIT-DOLLAR LIFE INSURANCE.

Statutory and Regulatory Reference: I.R.C. § 264.

Case and Other Interpretive Reference: See Rev. Rul. 64-328, 1964-22 C.B. 11 (defining split-dollar life insurance). *See also* Rev. Rul. 79-50, 1979-1 C.B. 138 (treatment of shareholder split-dollar); Rev. Rul. 78-420, 1978-2 C.B. 67 (treatment of third-party split-dollar) and *Genshaft v. Commissioner*, 64 T.C. 282 (1975) (employer pay-all split dollar treated as split dollar).

Treatise Reference: Richey, *Evaluating and Designing Split-Dollar Life Insurance*, Sixth Annual Notre Dame Estate Planning Institute (1981); Tax Mgmt. (BNA), No. 386, *Insurance Related Compensation*.

employer real property

Real property and related personal property that is leased by a plan to the sponsoring employer (or to an affiliate of the employer). For purposes of the ERISA prohibited transaction rules, a plan cannot acquire or hold any employer real property that is not a qualifying employer real property. Furthermore, there is a 10 percent limitation with respect to the acquisition and holding of qualifying employer real property by plans that are not individual account plans.

See QUALIFYING EMPLOYER REAL PROPERTY, PROHIBITED TRANSACTION.

Statutory and Regulatory Reference: ERISA § 407(d)(3).

employer security

For purposes of the ERISA prohibited transaction rules, a security issued by a plan-sponsoring employer (or by an affiliate of the employer). Contracts for life insurance, health insurance or annuities with one or more insurers generally are not treated as securities for these purposes. A plan cannot acquire or hold any employer security that is not a qualifying employer security and ERISA generally imposes a 10 percent limitation with respect to acquisitions and holding of qualifying employer securities by plans that are not individual account plans. Violations of this requirement generally are treated as violations of the prohibited transaction restriction.

See PROHIBITED TRANSACTION, EMPLOYER PROPERTY, QUALIFYING EMPLOYER SECURITY, QUALIFYING EMPLOYER PROPERTY.

Statutory and Regulatory Reference: See ERISA §§ 406-07.

endowment policy

A life insurance policy with a maturity date, whereby if the insured lives until the maturity date, the insured is paid the face amount of the policy. If the insured dies before the maturity date, the face amount is paid to the insured's beneficiary. An endowment policy's terminal reserve (i.e., total amount of premiums received plus interest accumulated less the total cost of risk distribution (this should represent the insurer's set-aside to be applied to its obligation at maturity of the policy)) is designed to equal the face amount at maturity, so that after the maturity date there is no longer an insurance element to the policy (the insurer bears no risk since it is required to pay out the same amount regardless of the insured's death). Premiums generally are greater for endowment policies than for WHOLE LIFE since the cash reserve accumulates more rapidly and equals the face amount of the contract at the end of the endowment period.

Statutory and Regulatory Reference: *See* I.R.C. §§ 72, 2039, 2042, 6052; Treas. Reg. § 1.72-1; 1.73-2; 20.2042-1(a)(2).

Treatise Reference: *See* Tax Mgmt. (BNA), *Financial Planning*, Para. 425, *Insurance Planning* (1991).

enrolled actuary   A person who is enrolled by the Joint Board for the Enrollment of Actuaries established under Title III, Subtitle C of ERISA.

Statutory and Regulatory Reference: *See* ERISA § 103(a)(4)(C); I.R.C. § 7701(a)(35); (definition of actuary); *see also* ERISA § 3041-43 (enrollment of actuaries).

entry date   The date on which an employee must be permitted to participate in a qualified retirement plan. This date must be the earlier of the first day of the first PLAN YEAR after the employee satisfies the plan's ELIGIBILITY (participation) requirements, or six months after the date the employee first satisfies those requirements.

Qualified retirement plans often meet this test by calling for two entry dates per year: one on the first day of the plan year and the other six months thereafter. A plan that complies with the Internal Revenue Code's age and service requirements may still be disqualified because it fails to satisfy the rules regarding entry dates.

Example 1: A retirement plan uses an age 21 and one YEAR OF SERVICE requirement as permitted under I.R.C. § 410(a). It has one annual entry date: the first day of the plan year. The plan will not qualify since it is possible that its entry date rules could delay an employee's admission longer than the AGE AND SERVICE RULES allow. For instance, if an employee turns age 21 and completes the service requirement on January 2 and the plan year is the calendar year, the individual would not be admitted until January 1 of the next year. This would be later than the earlier of the first day of the next plan year or six months after the employee has satisfied the maximum allowable age and service requirements. Providing for two annual entry dates, the first on the first day of the plan year and the other six months thereafter would cure this problem as to all potential participants.

As the above Example indicates, a plan must satisfy the age and service requirements for all possible cases. The fact that no employee currently eligible to participate would be admitted later than ERISA requires will not enable a plan to satisfy this requirement unless this is also true for all conceivable factual situations. A plan, however, may use a single annual entry date and still qualify if it adjusts its age and service requirements downward accordingly.

Example 2: A retirement plan uses the calendar year as its plan year. To participate, it requires that an employee reach age 20 and complete one year of service. It has one annual entry date, falling on the first day of the plan year. This plan will satisfy the Code's requirements as to eligibility because all employees will be admitted by the earlier of the first day of the plan year beginning after they have reached age 21 and completed one year of service or six months after they meet these requirements.

Statutory and Regulatory Reference: ERISA § 202(a)(4); I.R.C. §§ 410(a)(4)(A)-(B); Treas. Reg. § 1.410(a)-4(b) (1).

Treatise Reference: See Tax Mgmt. (BNA), No. 351, *Pension Plans — Qualification*, and No. 352, *Profit-Sharing Plans — Qualification*; *Employee Benefits Law* 102-03 (1991).

equity split-dollar life insurance   For a standard split-dollar life insurance plan, the employer's interest in the policy is the greater of the policy's cash value or the aggregate amount of the premiums contributed by the employer, so that the employer receives any increase in the cash surrender value that exceeds the amount the employer paid in premium contributions. In an equity split-dollar plan, the employee has an interest in this excess amount. The employer's interest is limited to the employer's premium contributions, so that the employer owns the lesser of the policy's cash value or its premium contributions rather than the total cash value.

See SPLIT-DOLLAR LIFE INSURANCE.

Statutory and Regulatory Reference: *See* I.R.C. § 264.

Case and Other Interpretive Reference: *See* Rev. Rul. 64-328, 1964-22 C.B. 11 (defining split-dollar life); *see also* Rev. Rul. 79-50, 1979-1 C.B. 138 (treatment of shareholder split-dollar); Rev. Rul. 78-420, 1978-2 C.B. 67 (treatment of third-party split-dollar); and *Genshaft v. Commissioner*, 64 T.C. 282 (1975) (employer pay-all split dollar treated as split dollar).

Treatise Reference: *See* Tax Mgmt. (BNA) No. 386, *Insurance-Related Compensation*. *See also* Richey, *Evaluating and Designing Split-Dollar Life Insurance*, Sixth Annual Notre Dame Estate Planning Institute (1981).

equivalency   Under a qualified retirement plan, a formula for crediting employees with hours of service based on certain estimates or assumptions. Equivalencies, in general, are designed to allow the employer to use an estimating method of computing the service of its employees rather than having to maintain detailed records of hours worked. Labor Department regulations specifically approve equivalencies based on (1) hours worked, (2) regular time hours, (3) days of employment, (4) weeks of employment, (5) semi-monthly periods of employment, (6) months of employment, (7) shifts of employment, (8) earnings, and (9) the elapsed time method.

Example: Under an hours worked equivalency, only hours for which services are performed are counted. Thus, the employer may ignore such hours as vacation or sick leave. Since this will result in employees being credited with fewer hours of service than they would have if the plan did not use this equivalency, a plan using an hours worked equivalency must count 870 hours worked as 1,000 hours of service and 435 hours worked as 500. An employer does not have to apply this rule ratably to each hour worked. Thus, an employee who worked 420 hours in a computation period would only be considered to have 420 hours of service under this equivalency. Once the employee completes 435 hours worked in a computation period, however, the plan must credit the employee with 500 hours of service (and 870 or more must be credited as 1,000).

See ELAPSED TIME METHOD, HOUR OF SERVICE.

Statutory and Regulatory Reference: *See* 29 C.F.R. § 2530.200b-3 *et seq*.

Case and Other Interpretive Reference: *See Standard Oil of California v. Commissioner*, 78 T.C. 541 (1982) (plans may also use their own equivalencies so long as they credit service at least as liberally as one of the approved methods).

Treatise Reference: See Tax Mgmt. (BNA), No. 351, *Pension Plans — Qualification*, and No. 352, *Profit-Sharing Plans — Qualification*; *see also Employee Benefits Law* 84-89 (1991).

ERISA   The Employee Retirement Income Security Act of 1974, as amended (Pub. L. No. 93-406); the statute that established the basic requirements for qualified plans. ERISA is divided into four titles: a labor title (Title I); a tax title (Title II), a title coordinating jurisdiction among the federal agencies responsible for its enforcement (Title III), and a title governing plan termination insurance (Title IV).

This wide-ranging piece of legislation regulates the organization and operation of private sector employee retirement and welfare plans. In the years following its enactment, Congress has modified the statute in several significant aspects. Among the most notable modifications were those enacted by the Multiemployer Pension Plan Amendments Act of 1980, the Economic Recovery Tax Act of 1981, the Tax Equity and Fiscal Responsibility Act of 1982, the Deficit Reduction Act of 1984 (also known as the Tax Reform Act of 1984), the Retirement Equity Act of 1984, the Single-Employer Pension Plan Amendments Act, the Tax Reform Act of 1986, the Omnibus Budget Reconciliation Act of 1987, and the Revenue Reconciliation Act of 1990.

The authority for administering and enforcing ERISA is divided among three federal agencies: the Internal Revenue Service (IRS), the Department of Labor (DOL), and the Pension Benefit Guaranty Corporation (PBGC).

The IRS, generally, is responsible for administering the tax-qualification requirements imposed by the Internal Revenue Code. Favorable federal income tax results flow from a determination that a retirement-type plan "qualifies" under the Code.

The IRS also administers the Code provisions governing the taxation of non-qualified deferred compensation arrangements, welfare benefits, and other types of employee benefit plans such as employee stock option and stock ownership plans, which receive favorable federal income tax treatment.

The Labor Department is generally responsible for administering ERISA's non-tax provisions. The DOL supervises compliance with ERISA's reporting and disclosure and prohibited transaction rules. The Labor Department also promulgates regulations in many areas, such as the crediting of service to plan participants, the standards for fiduciary conduct, and the rules governing reporting and disclosure. DOL also enforces ERISA's civil and criminal sanctions and has an advisory role (to the IRS) concerning the tax qualification of retirement plans.

Note that ERISA enacted identical provisions in many areas in both the labor provisions and the Internal Revenue Code. For instance, the Code's provisions governing age and service requirements, vesting, and benefit accrual have their analogues in the labor statute. Similarly, I.R.C. § 4975, imposing a penalty tax on certain prohibited transactions, has its parallel provisions in the labor statute (ERISA § 406). Thus, most employee pension and welfare benefit plans come under the concurrent jurisdiction of the IRS and DOL.

The Pension Benefit Guaranty Corporation (PBGC) is a quasi-governmental corporation established by ERISA under the Labor Department's jurisdiction. Its function is to ensure that, should certain qualified defined benefit pension plans which are funded on an actuarially estimated basis terminate with insufficient assets to pay participants and their beneficiaries certain statutorily guaranteed benefits, such amounts will be paid. The PBGC thus acts as insurer of the private pension system, collecting premiums to be used to pay benefits when the employer's plan lacks sufficient funds. The PBGC also promulgates regulations, primarily in the area of funding.

Treatise Reference: See Tax Mgmt. (BNA), No. 351, *Pension Plans — Qualification*, and No. 361, *Reporting and Disclosure Under ERISA; see also Employee Benefits Law*, 36-50 (1991).

ERISA plan   A qualified or nonqualified deferred compensation plan or arrangement, or a welfare plan that is subject to ERISA.

Treatise Reference: See generally Tax Mgmt. (BNA), No. 351, *Pension Plans – Qualification*, and No. 361, *Reporting and Disclosure Under ERISA*; *Employee Benefits Law* 19-35 (1991).

ESOP (employee stock ownership plan)
An ESOP is a qualified stock bonus, or combination stock bonus/money purchase pension plan designed to invest its assets primarily in the common stock of the sponsoring employer or that of its parent or subsidiary corporation.

ESOPs fall into two broad categories: tax-credit ESOPs (TCESOPs), and "leveraged" ESOPs. The tax credit for which TCESOPs were eligible was based on the level of the employer's payroll. This credit has been repealed. Leveraged ESOPs generally use a loan from a third-party lender to help them acquire employer securities for allocation to participants. Typically the employer will guarantee the loan to the ESOP. Such loans are specially exempted from ERISA's prohibited transactions rules.

See MONEY PURCHASE PLAN, PROHIBITED TRANSACTION, AND STOCK BONUS PLAN.

Statutory and Regulatory Reference: *See* ERISA § 407(c)(6) (definition); I.R.C. §§ 409(a) and 4975(e)(7) (voting rights); Treas. Reg. § 54.4975-7. *See also* ERISA § 205(b)(2) and I.R.C. § 401(a)(11)(C) (spouse's survivor benefits); ERISA § 408(b)(3) and I.R.C. § 4975(d)(3) (definition of leveraged ESOP); ERISA § 408(e) and I.R.C. § 4975(d)(13) (exemptions from the prohibited transaction rules for loans to acquire ESOP stock); I.R.C. § 72(e)(5)(D) (taxation of distributions of dividends on ESOP stock); I.R.C. § 133 (lender's partial exclusion from gross income of interest on ESOP securities acquisition loans); I.R.C. §§ 401(a)(22) and 409(e)(voting rights);

I.R.C. §§ 401(a)(23) and 409(h)(2) (cash distribution option); I.R.C. § 401(a)(28) (diversification requirements applicable to ESOP stock); I.R.C. §§ 404(a)(9) and (k) (deduction limits for contributions to ESOPs); I.R.C. § 409(c) (vesting); I.R.C. § 409(d) (84-month holding period rule for employer securities); I.R.C. § 409(h) (employee put option requirement for ESOP stock); I.R.C. § 411(a)(11)(C) (mandatory distribution of dividends paid on ESOP stock); I.R.C. § 415(c)(6) (maximum annual allocations to participants' accounts); I.R.C. § 1042 (non-recognition rule for certain transfers of stock to an ESOP or eligible worker-owned cooperative followed by acquisition of qualified replacement securities); I.R.C. §§ 4978 and 4978A (excise taxes on certain dispositions by an ESOP of employer securities); I.R.C. § 4980(c)(3) (REVERSION of certain qualified plan assets transferred to an ESOP); I.R.C. § 6047(e) (reporting requirements).

Treatise Reference: See Tax Mgmt. (BNA), No. 354, *ESOPs; see also Employee Benefits Law* 194-208; 287-92 (1991); D. McGill & D. Grubbs, Jr., *Fundamentals of Private Pensions* 675 (6th ed. 1989).

excess aggregate contributions   Under a qualified retirement plan, the excess for any PLAN YEAR of the total amount of employee contributions, employer matching contributions, and any employer contributions that, under Treasury regulations, may be counted as employee or matching contributions, over the maximum amount of such contributions permitted for the year under the nondiscrimination tests of I.R.C. § 401(m)(2).

See EMPLOYEE CONTRIBUTIONS, MATCHING CONTRIBUTIONS.

Statutory and Regulatory Reference: *See* Treas. Reg. § 1.401(m)-1.

Treatise Reference: Tax Mgmt. (BNA), No. 358, *Cash or Deferred Arrangements*; *Employee Benefits Law* 212-14 (1991).

excess benefit percentage

Under a qualified defined benefit plan that is integrated with Social Security, the percentage of compensation at which employees earn employer-derived benefits on their compensation above the plan's INTEGRATION LEVEL.

Example: A defined benefit plan provides that employees will earn an annual benefit equal to 1 percent of their FINAL AVERAGE COMPENSATION per YEAR OF SERVICE on all compensation up to $30,000. For compensation in excess of $30,000, the rate at which benefits are earned increases to 2 percent. This plan's excess benefits percentage is 2 percent.

See BASE BENEFIT PERCENTAGE, DEFINED BENEFIT EXCESS PLAN, EXCESS PLAN, INTEGRATION.

Statutory and Regulatory Reference: *See* I.R.C. § 401(l)(3)(A)(ii). Treas. Reg. § 1.401(l)-1(c)(14). Note that in the above Example, that part of compensation on which an employee earns benefits at the 1 percent rate is known as the "base benefit percentage." *See* I.R.C. § 401(l)(3)(A)(ii); Treas. Reg. § 1.401(l)-1(c)(3).

Treatise Reference: Tax Mgmt. (BNA), No. 356, *Qualified Plans—Integration*.

excess benefit plan

A plan maintained by an employer solely for the purpose of providing benefits for certain of its employees over and above the limits on annual additions or benefits under qualified retirement plans imposed by I.R.C. § 415.

See NONQUALIFIED DEFERRED COMPENSATION PLANS.

Statutory and Regulatory Reference: ERISA §§ 3(36), 4(b)(5), 201(a)(7), and 301(a)(9).

Treatise Reference: Tax Mgmt. (BNA), No. 385, *Deferred Compensation Arrangements; Employee Benefits Law* 235-36 (1991).

excess contribution

Contributions to an I.R.C. § 401(k) CASH OR DEFERRED ARRANGEMENT on behalf of highly compensated employees that are greater than the amount allowed under the actual deferral percentage (ADP) test. Excess contributions will disqualify the I.R.C. § 401(k) arrangement unless they are either distributed to the highly compensated employees by the end of the following PLAN YEAR or recharacterized as elective contributions. A distribution of excess contributions to the highly compensated employees must be made on the basis of the respective portions of the excess contributions attributable to each of them. The individuals receiving a distribution of excess contributions must take the amounts received into income for the same year as they would have taken them into income had they initially elected to take the contributions in cash.

See RECHARACTERIZATION, ACTUAL DEFERRAL PERCENTAGE (ADP).

Statutory and Regulatory Reference: *See* I.R.C. § 401(k)(8); Treas. Reg. § 1.401(k)-1(f); Prop. Treas. Reg. § 1.401(k)-1. *See also* I.R.C. §§ 402(g)(2) (refund of elective deferrals), 4979 (tax on excess deferrals).

Treatise Reference: Tax Mgmt. (BNA), No. 358, *Cash or Deferred Arrangements*.

excess contribution percentage

For a PLAN YEAR, for a qualified defined contribution excess plan that is integrated with Social Security, the percentage of compensation at which employer contributions (and forfeitures) are allocated to participants' accounts with respect to their compensation above the plan's INTEGRATION LEVEL.

See BASE CONTRIBUTION PERCENTAGE, DEFINED CONTRIBUTION EXCESS PLAN, EX-

CESS PLAN, INTEGRATION (SOCIAL SECURITY).

Statutory and Regulatory Reference: I.R.C. §§ 401(a)(5) and 401(l)(2)(B); Treas. Reg. § 1.401(l)-1(c)(15).

Treatise Reference: Tax Mgmt. (BNA), No. 356, *Qualified Plans — Integration*.

excess deferral   The amount of elective deferral in excess of the I.R.C. § 402(g) dollar cap for the year. This amount is included in the employee's income for the year in which the employer contributions were made. By April 15 of the following year, the excess deferral can be distributed to the employee without further tax. If such a distribution is not made, the employer is subject to an excise tax under I.R.C. § 4979.

See ELECTIVE DEFERRAL.

Statutory and Regulatory Reference: I.R.C. § 402(g); I.R.C. § 401(m)(4)(B) (definition of elective deferral for purposes of the excess deferral limits); I.R.C. § 401(a)(30) (refund of excess deferrals).

Treatise Reference: Tax Mgmt. (BNA), No. 358, *Cash or Deferred Arrangements*.

excess distribution   A distribution from one or more qualified retirement plans that exceeds the percentage and dollar limits of I.R.C. § 4980A. For distributions that occur during a participant's lifetime, that Code section imposes a 15 percent penalty tax on distributions in excess of the applicable limits received during a single calendar year. Code § 4980A also imposes a similar penalty tax on excess retirement plan "accumulations" (benefits) held on a participant's behalf at the time of the participant's death. The tax applies to the total of all distributions (or, in the case of the penalty estate tax, plan accumulations) held on the participant's behalf under any qualified plan, tax-sheltered annuity, or individual retirement arrangement. There are exemptions for distributions rolled over into other qualified plans or IRAs or amounts previously taxed under I.R.C. § 72(f), as well as other exclusions set forth in Treasury regulations.

Statutory and Regulatory Reference: I.R.C. § 4980A; Temp. Treas. Reg. § 54.4981A-1T.

Treatise Reference: Tax Mgmt. (BNA), No. 370, *Qualified Plans — Taxation of Distributions*; *Employee Benefits Law* 191-92 (1991).

excess plan   A qualified defined benefit plan or defined contribution plan that integrates with Social Security using the "excess" method. Under the excess method, a plan provides one level of benefits on a participant's compensation up to the plan's integration level and another, higher level on compensation above the integration level.

Example: A defined contribution plan provides employees with an annual employer contribution equal to 5 percent of their annual salary on salary up to the plan's integration level of $30,000. For compensation over $30,000, the plan calls for the employer to contribute 7 percent.

The 5 percent benefit in the above example is called the "base contribution percentage" (in a defined benefit plan it would be the "base benefit percentage") and the 7 percent benefit the "excess contribution percentage" (or, if the example was a defined benefit plan, the "excess benefit percentage").

Defined benefit plans may integrate with Social Security using either the excess method or the "offset" method. *See* OFFSET PLAN. Defined contribution plans may only integrate with Social Security by using the excess method.

See BASE BENEFIT PERCENTAGE, BASE CONTRIBUTION PERCENTAGE, EXCESS BENEFIT PERCENTAGE, EXCESS CONTRIBUTION PERCENTAGE, INTEGRATION LEVEL, INTEGRATION (SOCIAL SECURITY).

Statutory and Regulatory Reference: I.R.C. §§ 401(a)(5) and 401(l); Prop. Treas. Reg. § 1.401(l)-1(c)(16).

Treatise Reference: Tax Mgmt. (BNA), No. 356, *Qualified Plans — Integration*; *Employee Benefits Law* 129 (1991).

Excess retirement accumulation   *See* EXCESS DISTRIBUTION.

exclusion allowance (§ 403(b) tax-deferred annuities)   The amount of contributions to a tax-deferred annuity that the employee may exclude from gross income under a statutory formula.

In general, an employee's exclusion allowance for a TAXABLE YEAR is computed by multiplying 20 percent of "includible compensation" (generally compensation includable in gross income) by years of service and then subtracting the total amount the employee has excluded under this method for any previous year.

See CATCH-UP ELECTION, SECTION 403(b) PLAN, TAX-DEFERRED ANNUITY.

Statutory and Regulatory Reference: *See* I.R.C. § 403(b)(2); Treas. Reg. § 1.403(b)-1(d). *See also* I.R.C. §§ 402(g) (deferral limits for § 403(b) plans) and § 415 (contribution limits unaffected by exclusion allowance).

Treatise Reference: Tax Mgmt. (BNA), No. 388, *Tax-Deferred Annuities — Section* 403(b); *Employee Benefits Law* 216-21 (1991).

exclusion ratio (annuities)   *See* ANNUITY EXCLUSION RATIO RULE.

exclusive benefit rule   A rule requiring that it must be impossible under a qualified retirement plan, at any time before all of its liabilities to employees and their beneficiaries are satisfied, for any of the plan's assets to be used for purposes other than providing benefits to covered employees or their beneficiaries and paying the plan's administrative costs.

Statutory and Regulatory Reference: ERISA § 404(a)(1)(A); I.R.C. § 401(a)(2); Treas. Reg. § 1.401-2.

Treatise Reference: *See* Tax Mgmt. (BNA), No. 351, *Pension Plans — Qualification*; *see also Employee Benefits Law* 43; 272-74 (1991).

executive bonus pension plan   An arrangement established by an employer under which a cash bonus or insurance premium amount is paid by the employer for an employee (usually an executive). The employer makes the payment and takes an ordinary and necessary business expense deduction for the bonus (or premium) to the employee, and, in the case of a bonus, the employee can use the after-tax balance to fund his or her own pension or life insurance payments. These are also known as "Section 162" plans since they are basically payments of COMPENSATION deductible by the employer as a business expense under I.R.C. § 162.

See BONUS LIFE INSURANCE.

Statutory and Regulatory Reference: ERISA § 3(4); I.R.C. §§ 61, 101, and 162; Treas. Reg. §§ 1.61-1(a); 1.162-9.

Case and Other Interpretive Reference: Rev. Rul. 58-90, 1958-2 C.B. 88 (for a company to take a business deduction for premiums paid for policy owned by an executive, (1) the premium payments must constitute compensation to the executive, (2) the total amount of compensation paid to the executive must not be unreasonable, and (3) the company must not be a beneficiary of the policy, directly or indirectly).

Treatise Reference: Tax Mgmt. (BNA), No. 386, *Insurance- Related Compensation*.

experience gains/losses   The difference, using the FUNDING METHOD used to determine costs under a plan, between the plan's actual liabilities during a given period and its liabilities that were projected at the beginning of the period. Experience gains and losses include changes in benefits under the Social Security Act or in other retirement benefits under federal or state law, and any change in the definition of the term "wages" in I.R.C. § 3121 or in the amount of wages taken into account under I.R.C. § 401(a)(5).

The amount of any experience gains or losses must be determined at least once every three years. It must be amortized by charging or crediting the plan's funding standard account in equal installments over a five year period. The amortization period was 15 years before the Revenue Act of 1987, and remains at 15 years for multiemployer plans.

See FUNDING STANDARD ACCOUNT.

Statutory and Regulatory Reference: ERISA §§ 302(b)(2)(B)(iv) and (b)(3)(B)(ii); I.R.C. §§ 412(b)(2)(iv) and (b)(3)(B)(ii); Prop. Treas. Reg. § 1.412(b)-1(f).

Treatise Reference: Tax Mgmt. (BNA), No. 371, *Employee Plans—Deductions, Contributions, and Funding.*

extended due date (of tax return) The new date on which a taxpayer must file a tax return with the IRS after it has been extended either by the taxpayer's agreement with the IRS or by unilateral legislative or regulatory/administrative action.

extension of amortization periods A rule under which a qualified retirement plan subject to the Internal Revenue Code's minimum funding standard may request more time from the Secretary of Labor to pay off the items charged to its funding standard account than is normally provided by statute. I.R.C. § 412 allows the Secretary to extend the amortization period for any liability by up to 10 years. To grant an extension, the Secretary must find that it would help carry out ERISA's purposes and would provide adequate protection to participants and beneficiaries. The Secretary must also find that failure to grant an extension would (1) result in a substantial risk that the plan would not be continued or that its benefits would be curtailed; or (2) be adverse to the interests of participants in the aggregate.

See FUNDING STANDARD ACCOUNT, MINIMUM FUNDING STANDARD.

Statutory and Regulatory Reference: ERISA § 304; I.R.C. § 412(e); Rev. Proc. 79-408, 1979-2 C.B. 191 (guidelines for plan administrators seeking an extension of amortization periods).

Treatise Reference: Tax Mgmt. (BNA), No. 371, *Employee Plans—Deductions, Contributions, and Funding.*

F

fair market value   The price that a willing buyer would pay a willing seller in an open market for property or services if each party were under no compulsion to buy or sell, respectively and both parties were fully informed as to all material circumstances surrounding the transaction. ERISA § 3(26) uses the term current value for fair market value.

See CURRENT VALUE.

Federal Insurance Contributions Act (FICA) Tax   *See* SOCIAL SECURITY TAX.

Federal Unemployment Tax Act (FUTA) *See* UNEMPLOYMENT TAX.

fiduciary/fiduciary duty   In general, a person who occupies a relationship of particular trust with respect to an employee benefit plan covered by ERISA, and the standard of conduct imposed upon such a person, respectively.

ERISA provides standards governing the conduct of fiduciaries. The fiduciary duty rules also regulate transactions between a plan and a "party in interest" (the term used in ERISA's labor title) or a "disqualified person" (the term used to describe the same classes of individuals in I.R.C. § 4975).

Who is a Fiduciary? ERISA § 3(21) provides a "transactional" definition of fiduciary. Under it, a person (juridical or natural) becomes a fiduciary by virtue of that person's actual responsibilities with respect to the plan, rather than by virtue of any job title. Specifically, a person is considered a fiduciary to the extent that the person:

(1) Exercises any discretionary authority or discretionary control respecting management of the plan or exercises any authority or control respecting management or disposition of its assets;

(2) Renders investment advice for a fee or other compensation, direct or indirect, with respect to any moneys or other property of the plan, or has any authority or responsibility to do so; or

(3) Has any discretionary authority or discretionary responsibility in the administration of the plan.

A person is also a fiduciary to the extent that he or she has been delegated by the plan's "named fiduciary" under ERISA § 405(c)(1)(B) to perform any of the above-referenced duties.

The statute provides that one is a fiduciary with respect to a plan "to the extent that" he or she engages in one or more of the enumerated functions. This means that one can be a fiduciary with respect to certain aspects of the plan and not others. For instance, someone who has discretionary control with respect to the investment of 25 percent of a plan's assets would be considered a fiduciary with respect to those assets only, unless the person was also subject to liability under ERISA for breaches by a cofiduciary.

ERISA and the Code exempt certain classes of persons from classification as fiduciaries despite the fact that they are literally persons who perform the statutorily enumerated functions with respect to a plan. Specifically, ERISA § 405(c)(1)(B) provides that an investment company will not be considered a fiduciary solely because a plan's money or other property is invested in securities that the company has issued if the company is registered under the Investment Company Act of 1940. That section also provides that such an investment company's investment adviser or principal underwriter will not be deemed a fiduciary by virtue of such transactions and such companies will not, by engaging in such transactions, be considered parties in interest with respect to the plan.

An attorney, accountant, or actuary is not considered a fiduciary with respect to a plan solely because he or she renders professional services in connection with the plan.

Fiduciary Responsibilities. Part 4 of Title I of ERISA sets forth the fiduciary responsibility rules. These rules apply to any employee pension or welfare benefit plan maintained by an employer, a labor organization, or both, except for:

(1) Governmental plans;

(2) Church plans;

(3) Plans established to comply with applicable workmen's compensation, unemployment, or disability insurance laws;

(4) Plans maintained outside the United States for nonresident aliens;

(5) Excess plans (plans designed to provide employees with benefits in excess of the Code § 415 limits);

(6) Unfunded "top hat" plans, i.e., plans for key executives; and

(7) Certain plans described in I.R.C. § 736 that provide for payments to retired or deceased partners of a partnership

Named Fiduciary Requirement. ERISA § 402(a)(1) requires that an employee benefit plan subject to its provisions be maintained pursuant to a written instrument and that the instrument must name a person who will serve as the plan's "named fiduciary." The named fiduciary is liable for the plan's operation and administration. A plan may designate more than one person as the named fiduciary. If it does so, the persons so designated will be jointly and severally liable for the plan's operation and administration. ERISA § 405, however, provides that the named fiduciary may designate one or more persons to carry out specific responsibilities with respect to the plan. This includes the authority to appoint a person to act as investment manager for the plan's assets.

Duties of the Fiduciary. (1) General. ERISA § 404(a)(1) requires that a fiduciary must discharge his or her duties with respect to the plan solely in the interest of its participants and beneficiaries. Those duties must be discharged for the exclusive purpose of: (1) providing benefits to participants and their beneficiaries; and (2) defraying reasonable expenses of administering the plan.

(2) *Prudence.* A fiduciary must also satisfy the "prudent man rule." This rule, contained in ERISA § 404(a)(1)(B), requires that a fiduciary discharge his duties "with the care, skill, prudence, and diligence under the circumstances then prevailing that a prudent man, acting in a like capacity and familiar with such matters would use in the conduct of an enterprise of a like character and with like aims."

(3) *Diversification.* ERISA § 404(a)(1)(C) requires that a fiduciary diversify the investment of plan assets "so as to minimize the risk of large losses, unless, under the circumstances, it is clearly prudent not to do so." This requirement does not apply to plans that, by their nature, must invest in certain assets, such as an Employee Stock Ownership Plan (ESOP) that invests in the securities of the sponsoring employer. ERISA provides that, an "eligible individual account plan" (generally a defined contribution plan), will not violate the diversification requirement by the plan's investing in employer securities and/or employer real property.

(4) *Indicia of Ownership.* ERISA § 404(b) provides that a fiduciary may not, except insofar as Labor Department regulations permit, maintain the indicia of ownership in any plan assets outside the jurisdiction of the U.S. district courts.

Special Rule Where Self Direction Is Allowed. Under a special exception provided by ERISA § 404(c), where a plan having individual accounts allows participants or beneficiaries to direct the investment of their accounts, a participant or beneficiary is not, by virtue of this right, considered a fiduciary, but the plan's fiduciaries will be relieved of their duties with respect to the assets over which the right of self direction is exercised.

Liability for Breach by a Cofiduciary. In addition to any other liability that a fiduciary may incur under Title IV of ERISA, ERISA § 405 provides that a fiduciary will be liable for any breach by another fiduciary under the following circumstances:

(1) If he participates knowingly in, or knowingly undertakes to conceal, an act or omission of such other fiduciary, knowing such act or omission constitutes a breach;

(2) If, by his failure to comply with ERISA § 404(a)(1) in the administration of his specific responsibilities which gave rise to his status as a fiduciary, he has enabled such other fiduciary to commit a breach; or

(3) If he has knowledge of a breach by such other fiduciary, unless he makes reasonable efforts under the circumstances to remedy the breach.

See DISQUALIFIED PERSON, PROHIBITED TRANSACTION.

Statutory and Regulatory Reference: ERISA §§ 3(21)(A) and 404-06.

Treatise Reference: Tax Mgmt. (BNA), No. 351, *Pension Plans—Qualification*; *Employee Benefits Law* 265-300 (1991).

final average compensation   Generally, the average of the participant's average annual compensation from the employer for the highest (general definition) or final (integration definition) five years of a participant's participation in a qualified defined benefit plan before retirement.

See AVERAGE ANNUAL COMPENSATION, INTEGRATION (SOCIAL SECURITY).

Statutory and Regulatory Reference: I.R.C. § 401(a)(5)(D)(ii); Treas. Reg. § 1.401-4(c)(2)(vi)(c).

Treatise Reference: Tax Mgmt. (BNA), No. 356, *Qualified Plans—Integration*.

fiscal year   The 12-consecutive-month period used by an entity (e.g., the sponsoring employer) to maintain its records of income and expenses for financial accounting purposes, if it is other than the calendar year.

Statutory and Regulatory Reference: *See* I.R.C. § 7701(a)(24).

5 percent owner   For a corporation, any person who owns (or is considered as owning within the meaning of I.R.C. § 318) more than 5 percent of the outstanding stock of the corporation or stock possessing more than 5 percent of the total combined voting power of all stock of the corporation. For noncorporate taxpayers a 5 percent owner is any person who owns more than 5 percent of the capital or profits interest in the employer.

See TOP-HEAVY.

Statutory and Regulatory Reference: I.R.C. §§ 414(q)(1) and (3); 416(i)(1); Treas. Reg. § 1.414(q)-1T, Q&A 8.

Treatise Reference: *See* Tax Mgmt. (BNA), No. 351, *Pension Plans — Qualification* (for definition of highly compensated employee), and No. 353, *Owner-Dominated Plans — Top-Heavy and H.R. 10 Plans* (for discussion of the top-heavy rules).

flat benefit/flat benefit plan A defined benefit plan that provides employees with a retirement benefit expressed as either a specific dollar amount or a specific percentage of compensation, regardless of the individual's length of service with the sponsoring employer. Defined benefit plans are generally either "flat" benefit plans or "unit" benefit plans.

Example: A plan provides all employees who retire at NORMAL RETIREMENT AGE with a benefit of 30 percent of career average compensation, or one that provides such employees with a benefit of $30,000 per year.

See UNIT BENEFIT PLAN.

Treatise Reference: Tax Mgmt. (BNA), No. 351, *Pension Plans — Qualification*.

flexible benefit plan A cafeteria plan under which employees may redirect their salary into a tax-favored account and use that amount to purchase benefits from a menu of various benefits, such as dependent care or certain medical payments, or cash. Since a cafeteria plan allows employees to choose the benefits they desire, these plans are often referred to as "flexible" benefit or spending plans.

See CAFETERIA PLAN.

Statutory and Regulatory Reference: I.R.C. § 125.

Treatise Reference: Tax Mgmt. (BNA), No. 397, *Cafeteria Plans. Employee Benefits Law* 976-78 (1991).

flexible premium adjustable life insurance A life insurance contract that provides for the payment of premiums not fixed by the insurer as to timing and amount. The concept includes any contract that, under state law, provides annuity benefits, other than as a settlement option. The policies were designed in the late 1970s as an investment vehicle to compete with bank accounts and high yield bonds. Flexible premium contracts issued before January 1, 1985, are subject to rules limiting their cash values. These policies are more commonly known as universal life insurance policies.

See UNIVERSAL LIFE INSURANCE.

Statutory and Regulatory Reference: I.R.C. § 101(f).

Treatise Reference: Dorsett, *Universal Life Emerges From "Product Revolution,"* TRUST AND ESTATES 22 (July 1983).

flexible spending arrangement (FSA) A type of cafeteria plan under which participants can defer pretax dollars, using them to pay for medical or dependent care expenses. Only incurred expenses may be reimbursed (subject to reimbursement maximums); the maximum amount of reimbursement that is reasonably available to a participant for a period of coverage may not substantially exceed the total premium (including both employer-paid and employee-paid portions of the premium) for that participant's coverage. The maximum amount of reimbursement is not substantially in excess of the total premium if the amount is less than 500 percent of the premium. Under the applicable regulations, an employer that establishes a health FSA or a dependent care FSA, will be subject to special regulations governing FSAs in addition to the standard cafeteria plan regulations. For example, under a health FSA, the maximum reimbursement amount must be available at all times during the period of coverage. Generally, the period of coverage must be 12 months.

Example: An employee elects coverage under a health FSA for a calendar year in the amount of $300, and agrees to forego $25 per month in salary during that calendar year. The employee must be eligible to receive the entire $300 reimbursement at all times during the year, reduced by any prior reimbursement amounts. Thus, if the employee has $300 of medical expenses in February, the entire $300 claim must be reimbursed even though only $50 has been taken from the employee's salary.

See CAFETERIA PLAN, FLEXIBLE BENEFIT PLAN.

Statutory and Regulatory Reference: I.R.C. § 125; Treas. Reg. §§ 1.125-1 and -2.

Treatise Reference: Tax Mgmt. (BNA), No. 397, *Cafeteria Plans; Employee Benefits Law* 976-78 (1991).

forfeitability   The possibility that an employee will lose rights to an accrued benefit under a retirement or welfare benefit plan before becoming fully and irrevocably vested in that benefit.

See SUBSTANTIAL RISK OF FORFEITURE, VESTING.

forfeiture   The loss of benefits (generally as specified in a qualified or nonqualified deferred compensation plan) resulting from an employee's having committed a specified act (e.g., going to work for a competitor of the employer) or having failed to satisfy a specified condition or group of conditions (e.g., leaving employment before all accrued benefits have vested). The conditions under which employer-derived accrued benefits may be subject to forfeiture in a qualified

retirement plan are limited by the vesting rules of I.R.C. §§ 411 (the "regular" vesting rules) and 416 (the more rapid vesting requirements that apply for any PLAN YEAR in which the plan is top-heavy).

In a nonqualified deferred compensation arrangement, the employee recognizes income and the employer becomes eligible to take an offsetting compensation DEDUCTION when the employee's benefits become transferable or not subject to a substantial risk of forfeiture.

See SUBSTANTIAL RISK OF FORFEITURE, TOP-HEAVY, VESTING.

Statutory and Regulatory Reference: *See* I.R.C. § 411(a) and Treas. Reg. § 1.411(a)-3T (regular post-Tax Reform Act of 1986 vesting rules for qualified plans); and Treas. Reg. § 1.411(a)(3) (pre-TRA 1986 qualified plan regular vesting rules) *see also* I.R.C. § 416(b) and Treas. Reg. § 1.416-1, V-1 to V-7 (top-heavy vesting rules).

I.R.C. § 83(a); Treas. Reg. § 1.83-1(a)(1) (rules for nonqualified plans) and I.R.C. § 402(b)(1) (rules for trusts of nonqualified plans, which invoke I.R.C. § 83 principles).

Treatise Reference: *See* Tax Mgmt. (BNA), No. 384, *Restricted Property—Section 83.*

forfeiture restrictions   *See* SUBSTANTIAL RISK OF FORFEITURE.

forward averaging   A method of computing the federal income tax due on a lump-sum distribution from a qualified retirement plan in which the tax is determined in effect as if the distribution were received over a period of five years. Once the five theoretical installments are calculated, they are added together and paid in the year of the distribution. This method generally reduces the tax that would otherwise be payable by preventing "bunching" of income and by taxing the distribution separately from the taxpayer's other income for the year. Both of these features generally will reduce the effective tax rate on the distribution. Both participants and beneficiaries are eligible to use forward averaging on qualifying distributions (see LUMP SUM DISTRIBUTION), but this treatment may only be elected once per lifetime and, in general, only after age 59½.

Before the Tax Reform Act of 1986 (TRA 1986), Pub. L. No. 99-514, participants were eligible to use 10-year forward averaging on qualifying distributions (generally the same as 5-year averaging, except that it is over 10 theoretical years). Certain individuals who reached age 50 by January 1, 1986, may still elect to use 10-year averaging, provided they agree to have their distribution taxed under pre-1987 tax rates.

Statutory and Regulatory Reference: I.R.C. § 402(e)(4); Treas. Reg. §§ 1.402(e)(4)(A)-(B).

Treatise Reference: *See* Tax Mgmt. (BNA), No. 370, *Qualified Plans – Taxation of Distributions*; *see also Employee Benefits Law* 181-84 (1991).

4/40 vesting   A special accelerated vesting schedule that the IRS required certain qualified retirement plans to provide before the enactment of the top-heavy plan rules of I.R.C. § 416. Before the Tax Equity and Fiscal Responsibility Act of 1982 (TEFRA), Pub. L. No. 97-248, many IRS district offices took the position, based on ERISA's legislative history, that, where the facts indicated that the plan's proposed 10-year CLIFF VESTING schedule (the longest statutory vesting schedule allowed at that time) would, in operation, discriminate in favor of highly compensated employees, they would not issue a favorable DETERMINATION LETTER unless the plan was amended to provide for 4/40 vesting. This schedule vests employees 40 percent after 4 years of service, increasing in 5 percent annual increments in years 5 and 6, and then increasing in 10 percent annual in-

crements in years 7 through 11, to the point where, after 11 years of service, the employee is fully vested.

See TOP-HEAVY, VESTING.

Treatise Reference: *See generally* Tax Mgmt. (BNA), No. 351, *Pension Plans – Qualification*.

401(h) account   *See* SECTION 401(k) ACCOUNT.

401(k) plan   *See* SECTION 401(k) PLAN.

403(b) annuity plan/403(b) annuity
See SECTION 403(b) PLAN.

fractional rule   One of three statutory BENEFIT ACCRUAL rules designed to prevent excessive "BACKLOADING" of benefits that a qualified defined benefit plan may satisfy (the other two are the 3 percent rule and the 133⅓ percent rule). Under the fractional rule, the annual benefit to which a participant is entitled upon separating from the employer's service before reaching the plan's NORMAL RETIREMENT AGE must be at least a ratable share of the benefit he or she would have received had the employee worked until normal retirement age.

Example: Under a qualified defined benefit plan having a normal retirement age of 60, employees accrue benefits at the following rates: 1.25 percent of compensation in years of service 1 to 15, 1.5 percent in years 16-30, and 1.75 percent for all years thereafter. This plan would fail the fractional test. Consider employee A who separated from service after 10 years and who began work for the employer at age 20. For the plan to pass the test, A should be entitled to 10/40ths, or 25 percent of his or her NORMAL RETIREMENT BENEFIT at SEPARATION FROM SERVICE. Instead, A will only have earned 21.3

percent of this amount. This conclusion is based on the following calculation:

Step 1: Determine the Plan's Normal Retirement Benefit

(1.25 percent × 15 years =) 18.75 percent +

(1.50 percent × 15 years =) 22.50 percent +

(1.75 percent × 10 years =) 17.50 percent =

58.75 percent

Step 2: Determine the Employee's Benefit at Separation From Service as a Percentage of the Normal Retirement Benefit

12.50 percent (benefit after 10 years) +

58.75 percent (benefit after 40 years) =

21.3 percent

Step 3: Determine the Ratable Amount of the Normal Retirement Benefit to Which the Employee Would Be Entitled Based on Years of Service at Separation

58.75 percent × .25 = 14.69 percent

A's actual benefit after 10 years here (12.5 percent) is less than the benefit needed to satisfy the fractional rule (14.69 percent).

See 3 PERCENT RULE, 133¹/3 PERCENT RULE.

Statutory and Regulatory Reference: ERISA § 204(b)(1)(C); I.R.C. § 411(b)(1)(C); Treas. Reg. § 1.411(b)-1(b)(3).

Case and Other Interpretive Reference: Rev. Rul. 81-11, 1981-1 C.B. 227 (rules for applying the fractional rule following a BREAK IN SERVICE).

Treatise Reference: See Tax Mgmt. (BNA), No. 351, *Pension Plans—Qualification; see also Employee Benefits Law* 124 (1991).

frozen plan   A qualified retirement plan in which ACCRUAL of benefits has stopped, but which remains in existence pending its formal termination or until it may complete the distribution of its assets to participants and beneficiaries.

See TERMINATION.

Treatise Reference: See generally Tax Mgmt. (BNA), No. 357, *Plan Terminations and Mergers.*

FSA   *See* FLEXIBLE SPENDING ACCOUNT.

full funding limitation   A federal tax law limit that caps the amount an employer maintaining a qualified pension plan subject to the I.R.C. § 412 MINIMUM FUNDING STANDARD is required or allowed to contribute on a deductible basis for a year. The full funding limitation is the lesser of: (1) the accrued liability of the plan for the plan year, less the value of plan assets; or (2) 150 percent of the current liability over the value of the plan's assets. This limit generally will affect the level of required contributions when a plan's assets are large relative to its benefit liabilities.

See FUNDING STANDARD ACCOUNT.

Statutory and Regulatory Reference: See ERISA § 302(c)(6), I.R.C. § 412(c)(6) (effect on FUNDING); ERISA § 302(c)(7), I.R.C. § 412(f)(7) (definition); and *see* ERISA § 302(b)(7)(E) and I.R.C. § 412(b)(7)(E) (multiemployer plans).

Case and Other Interpretive Reference: Rev. Rul. 81-12, 1981-1 C.B. 229 (illustrating how accrued liability to determine the full funding limitation (under pre-OBRA 1987 law) can be calculated)[the Omnibus Budget Reconciliation Act of 1987, Pub. L. No. 100-203].

Treatise Reference: See Tax Mgmt. (BNA), No. 371, *Employee Plans—Deductions, Contributions, and Funding; Employee Benefits Law* 137 (1991).

fully insured plan   A qualified retirement plan that meets the following requirements: (1) the plan is funded entirely by the purchase of individual insurance contracts; (2) the contracts provide for level annual premium payments to be paid extending no later than the RETIREMENT AGE of each participant in the plan, and commencing with the date the individual became a participant (or the benefits were increased); (3) benefits provided by the plan are equal to the benefits provided under each contract at normal retirement age and are guaranteed by an insurance carrier to the extent premiums have been paid; (4) premiums payable for the PLAN YEAR and all prior plan years under the contracts have been paid before lapse or there is reinstatement of the policy; (5) no rights under the contracts have been subject to a security interest at any time during the plan year; and (6) no policy loans are outstanding at any time during the plan year.

A plan meeting these requirements is not required to meet the MINIMUM FUNDING STANDARD.

See FUNDED PLAN.

Statutory and Regulatory Reference: ERISA § 301(b); I.R.C. §§ 412(h)(2) and (i).

Treatise Reference: Tax Mgmt. (BNA), No. 371, *Employee Plans — Deductions, Contributions, and Funding.*

funded current liability percentage The percentage determined by dividing the value of the plan's assets by the plan's CURRENT LIABILITY. For this purpose, a plan's current liability means all liabilities to employees and their beneficiaries under the plan.

This percentage is used in determining whether and the extent to which a plan that is not a multiemployer plan must make any additional charge to its funding standard account.

See FUNDING STANDARD ACCOUNT.

Statutory and Regulatory Reference: ERISA § 302(d)(8)(B); I.R.C. § 412(l)(8)(B).

Treatise Reference: Tax Mgmt. (BNA), No. 371, *Employee Plans — Deductions, Contributions, and Funding.*

funded plan A plan that has assets or annuity contracts from which the plan's expenses and liabilities are to be paid. Any plan with a trust qualified under I.R.C. § 401(a) or a tax-deferred annuity under I.R.C. § 403(b) is required to be funded, except the following plans: (1) a profit-sharing or stock bonus plan; (2) a fully insured plan; (3) a governmental plan; (4) a church plan that has not elected to have the participation, VESTING, FUNDING, and certain other provisions of the I.R.C. § 401(a) apply; (5) a plan that has not, at any time after September 2, 1974, provided for employer contributions; and (6) a plan of an I.R.C. § 501(c)(8) or § 501(c)(9) organization, if no part of the contributions to or under the plan are made by employers of plan participants.

A NONQUALIFIED PLAN can be considered to be funded for purposes of ERISA. If so, it is subject to the participation, vesting, accrual, funding, and fiduciary standards of ERISA Title I.

See FULLY INSURED PLAN, FUNDING STANDARD ACCOUNT, FUNDING WAIVER, FULL FUNDING LIMITATION.

Statutory and Regulatory Reference: *See* ERISA §§ 201(2), 301(a)(3), and 401(a)(1); I.R.C. § 412(a), (h), and (i).

Treatise Reference: *See* Tax Mgmt. (BNA), No. 371, *Employee Plans — Deductions, Contributions, and Funding.*

funding Contribution of assets to a trust or purchase of annuities to cover a plan's expenses and liabilities.

See FUNDED PLAN.

funding method The method used by a plan for determining the required amount of funding. This method must be the same as the method used by the plan in determining normal costs, accrued liability, past service liabilities, and experience gains and losses.

ERISA's minimum funding standards do not limit the employer to the use of a particular funding method. Rather, under ERISA § 302(c) and I.R.C. § 412(c), the employer may choose from any actuarial cost method deemed reasonable. Once the method is chosen, however, the minimum funding standard comes into play, ensuring that sufficient contributions are made to meet the costs generated by the chosen method.

In general, accepted actuarial methods for funding defined benefit plans fall into two broad categories:

(1) Accrued benefit cost methods; and

(2) Projected benefit methods.

Accrued benefit cost methods consider the entire amount necessary to fund a plan's past service liability to be due in the first plan year in which that liability arises. Thus, for a plan with significant past service liabilities, these methods accelerate the rate at which the employer must fund this type of liability. This can be desirable where the employer needs a large current deduction because employer deductions under § 404 for defined benefit plans are geared to the amount necessary to satisfy the minimum funding standard.

In contrast, projected benefit methods generally treat past service liability as accruing over an employee's entire career. Projected benefit methods thus even out the employer's annual liability more than accrued benefit cost methods, avoiding large jumps in liability in the year a past service liability arises.

The ACTUARIAL ASSUMPTIONS used for the funding method must be reasonable, and the method itself must be reasonable. To be reasonable, the method must take into account normal cost, all liabilities of the plan (whether accrued or not), and all of the plan participants, retirees, and employees eligible to participate. A reasonable funding method cannot take into account anticipated benefit changes or anticipated future participants.

See NORMAL COST, FUNDING.

Statutory and Regulatory Reference: See ERISA § 302(b)(1); I.R.C. § 412(c); Treas. Reg. § 1.412(c)(3)-1.

Treatise Reference: Tax Mgmt. (BNA), No. 371, *Employee Plans — Deductions, Contributions, and Funding; Employee Benefits Law* 140-43; 729-31 (1991).

funding standard account   An account required to be maintained by qualified pension plans that are subject to ERISA and the Internal Revenue Code's MINIMUM FUNDING STANDARD. The account is a recordkeeping system under which certain items, such as payments, are credited and certain expenses, relating to the funding of plan benefits, are reflected as charges. If, at the end of a PLAN YEAR, there is a negative balance in the account, I.R.C. § 4971 imposes an initial penalty excise tax on the employer equal to 10 percent of the "ACCUMULATED FUNDING DEFICIENCY." An additional 100 percent penalty excise tax is imposed if the deficiency is not corrected within a statutory "correction period."

The following items are charged to the funding standard account:

(1) Normal costs for the plan year;

(2) The amount needed to amortize, in equal annual installments over 30 years, any unfunded past service liability arising in connection with services rendered before the plan was adopted;

(3) The amount needed to amortize in equal annual installments over 30 years, separately for each plan year, any net increase in the plan's unfunded past service liability arising from plan amendments adopted in that year;

(4) The amount needed to amortize in equal annual installments over five years (15 years for years beginning before 1988 and for multiemployer plans), separately for each plan year, any "net experience loss" under the plan; and

(5) The amount needed to amortize, in equal annual installments over 10 years (30 for years beginning before 1988 and for multiemployer plans) separately for each plan year, any net loss resulting from changes in the plan's actuarial assumptions.

(6) When the employer switches from the alternative minimum funding standard to the regular funding standard, the excess of the debit balance in the regular funding

account over any debit balance in the alternative minimum funding standard account must be made up by amortizing the excess over five years.

In addition, there are separate amortization rules for waived funding deficiencies. In the case of business hardship, the IRS can waive the contribution which would otherwise be required to satisfy the minimum funding standard. When that occurs, there is technically a funding deficiency, but it is temporarily waived. This "waived funding deficiency" is amortized and charged to the funding standard account over a period of five years (15 years for years beginning before 1988 and for multiemployer plans).

The credit side of the funding standard account is basically the mirror image of the charge side.

Each plan year, the minimum funding standard account is credited with the amount actually contributed to the plan in that year. In addition, the following amounts are credited to the funding standard account:

(1) The amount needed to amortize in equal annual installments over 30 years, separately for each plan year, any net decrease in the plan's unfunded past service liability attributable to plan amendments adopted during the year;

(2) The amount needed to amortize in equal annual installments over five years (15 for years beginning before 1988 and multiemployer plans), separately for each plan year, any "net experience gain" for the plan year;

(3) The amount needed to amortize in equal annual installments over 10 years (30 for years beginning before 1988 and multiemployer plans), separately for each plan year, any net gain attributable to changes in actuarial assumptions;

(4) The amount of any waived funding deficiency for the plan year; and

(5) When the plan has been using the alternative minimum funding standard, the amount needed to amortize, over five years, the excess, if any, of the deficit balance in the funding standard account over the deficit balance in the alternative minimum funding standard account.

Statutory and Regulatory Reference: See ERISA § 302(b), I.R.C. § 412(b), and Treas. Reg. § 1.412(c) *et seq.* (items of charges and credits); ERISA § 302(e) and I.R.C. § 412(m) (required installment payments of funding standard account liabilities); and I.R.C. § 4971 (excise tax on failure to satisfy minimum funding standard).

Case and Other Interpretive Reference: Rev. Rul. 77-2, 1977-1 C.B. 120 (a change in a qualified pension plan's benefit structure that becomes effective in a plan year after the plan year for which charges and credits to the funding standard account are being calculated will not be considered in that year's computation); Rev. Rul. 81-137, 1981-1 C.B. 232 (defined benefit plans maintained by employers under common control must maintain separate funding standard accounts); Rev. Rul. 86-47, 1986-1 C.B. 215 (adjustments to the funding standard account for spinoff of a plan).

Treatise Reference: Tax Mgmt. (BNA), No. 371, *Employee Plans — Deductions, Contributions, and Funding. See also* D. McGill & D. Grubbs, Jr., *Fundamentals of Private Pensions* 301 (6th ed. 1989).

funding waiver   A rule that allows the IRS to waive the application of the I.R.C. § 412 MINIMUM FUNDING STANDARD to a qualified pension plan for a year in which the employer incurs certain substantial business hardships. An employer is eligible for this waiver if it, or in the case of a multiemployer plan 10 percent of contributing employers, is unable to satisfy the minimum funding standard for the year without substantial business hardship and "if application of the (minimum funding) standard would be adverse to the interests of plan participants in the aggregate." The waiver may be granted as to all or part of the minimum funding standard liability for the year.

"Substantial business hardship," for this purpose, includes situations where (1) the employer is operating at an economic loss; (2) there is substantial unemployment or underemployment in the employer's trade or business or in the relevant industry; (3) sales and profits of the industry concerned are depressed or declining; and (4) it is reasonable to expect that the plan will be continued only if the waiver is granted.

Statutory and Regulatory Reference: ERISA § 303, I.R.C. § 412(d) (general rule); ERISA § 303(d)(1), I.R.C. § 412(d)(4) (application for, due date of); ERISA § 303(e), I.R.C. § 412(f)(4) (notice requirements to affected parties) and ERISA § 304(b), I.R.C. § 412(f) (prohibition on plan benefit increases during a period when a waiver of the minimum funding standard is in effect).

Treatise Reference: *See* Tax Mgmt. (BNA), No. 371, *Employee Plans—Deductions, Contributions, and Funding; see also Employee Benefits Law* 465-68 (1991).

G

general counsel memorandum (GCM)
A type of legal memoranda prepared by the Chief Counsel's office of the IRS. They are written in response to requests from IRS employees for advice in preparing revenue rulings, technical advice memoranda, and private letter rulings. GCMs are substantial authority for taking a position on a tax return, and can therefore be used to escape the penalty for substantial understatement of income tax.

general nondiscrimination rule   As set forth in I.R.C. § 401(a)(4), the rule provides that a qualified retirement plan must not discriminate as to benefits or contributions in favor of highly compensated employees within the meaning of I.R.C. § 414(q). A plan must satisfy the general rule both on paper (that is, the PLAN DOCUMENT, by its terms, must not discriminate) and in operation.

See DISCRIMINATION.

Statutory and Regulatory Reference: I.R.C. § 401(a); Treas. Reg. § 1.401(a)(4)-1 *et seq.*

GLSP   *See* GROUP LEGAL SERVICE PLAN.

golden handcuffs   A contract between an employer and an employee (generally an executive) requiring bonus retirement payments of cash, stock, real estate, or other property (on which the employee has already been taxed) to be returned in whole or part if the employee leaves the company. The contract is often applicable where the employee would leave the employer to be employed with a competitor. The contract can require the employee to collateralize the repayment obligation with, for instance, a life insurance policy. Some contracts require the payment to be held in trust, for example in a secular trust.

See SECULAR TRUST, LIFE INSURANCE CONTRACT.

Treatise Reference: Tax Mgmt. (BNA), No. 394, *Employee Fringe Benefits*.

golden parachute payment   Amounts paid to executives or disqualified individuals that are in the nature of compensation and that are contingent upon a change in corporate control. The payment may be cash or property and may be made not only to, but also for the benefit of, a disqualified individual. To be treated as a golden parachute payment, the aggregate present value of the payment must be at least three times the employee's average salary for the preceding five years. The payer of a parachute payment may be a target company, acquiring company, or a shareholder of either company. The recipient of the parachute payment must be a disqualified individual, defined as any employee or independent contractor who performs services for the target corporation and who is a highly compensated individual, an officer, or a shareholder. A highly compensated individual in this instance must be a member of the group of the highest paid one percent of employees, and no individual with annual compensation less than $75,000 will be treated as highly compensated. The number of individuals treated as officers is limited to 50 employees, or, if less, the greater of three employees or 10 percent of the employees of the corporation. Only an individual who owns stock with a value exceeding the lesser of $1 million or one percent of the total value of all of the target company's stock is treated as a disqualified individual.

See DISQUALIFIED INDIVIDUAL, HIGHLY COMPENSATED EMPLOYEE.

Statutory and Regulatory Reference: I.R.C. § 280G; Prop. Treas. Reg. § 1.280G-1.

Treatise Reference: Tax Mgmt. (BNA), No. 394, *Employee Fringe Benefits*.

governmental plan   A qualified retirement plan established and maintained by the U.S. government, a state or political subdivision thereof, or an agency or instrumentality of such government.

Statutory and Regulatory Reference: ERISA § 3(32); I.R.C. § 414(d).

Treatise Reference: Tax Mgmt. (BNA), No. 372, *Defined Benefit Plans of Churches and State and Local Governments*; *Employee Benefits Law* 34-35 (1991).

graded vesting   A vesting schedule in which an increasing percentage of an employee's employer-derived accrued benefits become vested each year, until 100 percent vesting has been reached. For purposes of the qualified plan regular (non-top heavy) vesting rules, plans using graded vest-

ing must vest employees in their employer-derived contributions at least as rapidly as is called for under a statutory seven-year graded vesting schedule. Under that schedule, a plan must provide at least 20 percent vesting after three years, 40 percent after four, 60 percent after five, 80 percent after six, and 100 percent after seven years.

Top-heavy plans may satisfy a more rapid six-year graded vesting schedule which vests an employee 20 percent per YEAR OF SERVICE until he or she is 100 percent vested.

See CLIFF VESTING, 4/40 VESTING, VESTING.

Statutory and Regulatory Reference: ERISA § 203(a)(2)(B); I.R.C. §§ 411(a)(2)(B), 416(b)(1)(B); Treas. Reg. §§ 1.411(a)-3T(c), 1.416-1, Q&A V-1.

Treatise Reference: Tax Mgmt. (BNA), No. 351, *Pension Plans—Qualification*, and Tax Mgmt. (BNA), No. 353, *Owner-Dominated Plans—Top-Heavy and H.R. 10 Plans*.

gross income   All income from whatever source derived, including but not limited to: (1) compensation for services, including fees, commissions, fringe benefits, and similar items; (2) income derived from business; (3) gains from dealings in property; (4) interest; (5) rents; (6) royalties; (7) dividends; (8) alimony and separate maintenance payments; (9) annuities; (10) income from life insurance and endowment contracts; (11) pensions; (12) discharge-of-indebtedness income; (13) a partner's distributive share of the gross income of a partnership; (14) "income in respect of a decedent" within the meaning of I.R.C. § 691; and (15) income from an interest in an estate or trust.

Statutory and Regulatory Reference: I.R.C. § 61(a).

group annuity contract/plan   A FUNDING mechanism for a pension plan in which the employer purchases a group annuity contract to fund the plan's benefits. Although a trust can be used to hold the annuity contract, this is not necessary because the insurance company from which the contract is purchased is treated as a qualified trust for purposes of the Internal Revenue Code.

See ANNUITY.

Statutory and Regulatory Reference: I.R.C. § 401(f).

group health plan   Under ERISA, an employee welfare benefit plan providing medical care to participants and beneficiaries directly or through insurance, reimbursement, or otherwise. (*See* the definition under medical care for what can be covered by these plans.) Note that the term medical care in this situation includes dental and vision coverage. Since a group health plan includes any plan maintained by an employer to provide medical care to employees, or former employees, or their families, it encompasses individual as well as group health insurance policies and employee-pay-all plans.

Under the Internal Revenue Code, the term refers to any plan of, or contributed to, by an employer (including a self-insured plan) to provide medical care (directly or through insurance, reimbursement, or otherwise) to employees, former employees, or their families whether or not provided through an on-site facility or through a cafeteria plan or other flexible benefit arrangement. A "large group health plan" is defined as a group health plan as defined above that covers employees of at least one employer that normally employees at least 100 employees on a typical business day during the previous calendar year.

See MEDICAL CARE.

Statutory and Regulatory Reference: *See* ERISA § 607(1), I.R.C. §§ 213(d) (defining medical care), §§ 4980B(g)(2), 5000(b). *See also* Treas. Reg. § 1.196-1, 1.162-26, Q&A 7.

Treatise Reference: Tax Mgmt. (BNA), No. 389, *Disability and Medical Reimbursement Benefits*; *Employee Benefits Law* 949 (1991).

group legal service plan   A separate written plan of an employer for the exclusive benefit of its employees or their spouses or dependents to provide the employees, spouses, and dependents with specified benefits consisting of personal legal services through prepayment of, or provision in advance for, legal fees in whole or in part by the employer. The plan must meet discrimination, eligibility, and contribution limitation requirements. Gross income of the employee, spouse or dependents does not include the amounts contributed by the employer or the value of the legal services provided. The exclusion from income is only allowed to the extent the value of the insurance against legal costs incurred by the individual for the year does not exceed $70. The plan can only reimburse for the cost of "personal legal services," i.e., legal services provided to a participating employee, spouse, or dependent that were not connected with, or directly pertaining to, a trade or business of the employee, spouse or dependent; the management, conservation, or preservation of property held by the employee, spouse or dependent for the production of income; or the production or collection of income by the employee, spouse, or dependent.

Statutory and Regulatory Reference: *See* I.R.C. § 120; Treas. Reg. § 1.120-3. *See also* Prop. Treas. Reg. §§ 1.120-2, § 1.125-2.

Case and Other Interpretive Reference: GCM 39485 (March 6, 1986) (since group legal service plan must involve prepayment for legal services, a plan may not provide for the direct payment or reimbursement by the employer of legal fees for personal legal services already incurred).

Treatise Reference: Tax Mgmt. (BNA), No. 394, *Employee Fringe Benefits*; *Employee Benefits Law* 960-63 (1991).

group paid-up life insurance An employer-offered insurance plan to provide postretirement insurance for which employees purchase permanent life insurance protection by making contributions to the plan during their working lives, so that the policy is fully paid-up when the employee retires. The employer does not contribute funds toward the purchase of this permanent insurance, but instead provides temporary insurance protection through term insurance. The amount of term insurance will decrease as the amount of paid-up life insurance increases. As group-term life insurance coverage, the insurance is subject to favorable federal income tax treatment.

See GROUP-TERM LIFE INSURANCE, TERM INSURANCE.

Statutory and Regulatory Reference: I.R.C. §§ 79 and 264; Treas. Reg. § 1.79-1(d) (allocation of premium between term and permanent features).

Treatise Reference: Tax Mgmt. (BNA), No. 386, *Insurance-Related Compensation*.

group-term life insurance The Internal Revenue Code does not define group-term life insurance, but the Treasury regulations provide that in order to qualify as group-term life insurance under I.R.C. § 79, a life insurance plan must: (1) include a general death benefit excludable from the recipient's gross income under I.R.C. § 101, i.e., it must be paid pursuant to a life insurance contract; (2) be furnished to a group of employees with membership determined solely on the basis of age, marital status, or other factors related to employment; (3) accomplish 1 and 2, above, under a policy or policies (a master group policy or a group of individual policies) carried directly or indirectly by the employer; and (4) pay benefits in amounts computed under a formula that precludes individual selection. Group-term life benefits may be offered in different amounts or percentages of pay for different categories of employees, and may be provided to employees under one or more group or individual life insurance contracts, through employer contributions, employee contributions, or both. Up to $50,000 of group term life insurance generally may be provided through employer contributions without having the cost of that coverage included in the employee's federal gross income.

Statutory and Regulatory Reference: I.R.C. §§ 79, 101 and 162; Treas. Reg. §§ 1.79-1, -2, and 1.79-3(d) (Table I costs showing excludable premium amounts); 1.101-1(a)(1); 1.61-2(d)(2)(ii)(b) and 1.132-6(e)(2) (coverage on life of dependent or spouse not subject to I.R.C. § 79 but rather included in employee's gross income); *but see* IRS Notice 89-110, 1989-49 I.R.B. 17 (until further notice from IRS, cost of coverage for spouse or dependent up to $2,000 qualifies as a de mimimis fringe under § 132); *see also* Prop. Treas. Reg. 1.125-2 Q&A-1(a).

Case and Other Interpretive Reference: Rev. Rul. 75-91, 1975-1 C.B. 39 (group insurance policy providing life insurance protection in level premium five-year term with no cash-surrender value, paid-up value, or other equivalent benefits, covering employees only while included in the plan, and paid for by the employer's contributions can be considered group term life insurance). *See also* PLR 8116010 (life insurance violated § 79 since supplemental policies were individually selected rather than according to a formula based on age, years of service, compensation or position); *Towne v. Commissioner*, 78 T.C. 791 (1982) (add-on policy to corporation's group-term life plan for an additional plan on the life of the president; plan could not qualify as an addition to the plan since it involved individual selection).

Treatise Reference: Tax Mgmt. (BNA), No. 386, *Insurance-Related Compensation*.

group universal life policy (GULP) A life insurance policy that combines the characteristics of a group-term life insurance plan with the characteristics of a universal life policy (which is basically term insurance with an interest-bearing cash value or savings account). The arrangement thus provides employees with group-term life insurance at group rates while allowing them to accumulate a cash value account earning interest on a tax-free basis.

See GROUP-TERM LIFE INSURANCE, UNIVERSAL LIFE INSURANCE.

Statutory and Regulatory Reference: I.R.C. § 79; Treas. Reg. § 1.79-1.

Treatise Reference: Tax Mgmt. (BNA) No. 386, *Insurance-Related Compensation*.

GULP *See* GROUP UNIVERSAL LIFE POLICY.

H

H.R. 10 plan *See* KEOGH PLAN.

hardship withdrawal The withdrawal by an employee of funds from a § 401(k) plan before reaching age 59½. The reason for the withdrawal must be to meet an immediate and heavy financial need that the employee cannot meet through other resources. Financial needs that justify a hardship withdrawal include the following: (1) medical expenses; (2) purchase of a principal residence; (3) payment of tuition for post-secondary education for the employee or his or her spouse or children; and (4) payment of amounts necessary to prevent eviction of the employee or foreclosure on his or her mortgage. There are requirements regarding amounts that may be withdrawn to satisfy the financial hardship, e.g., the amount withdrawn may not exceed the financial need.

Statutory and Regulatory Reference: I.R.C. § 401(k)(2)(B)(IV); Treas. Reg. § 1.401(k)-1(d) (2).

Treatise Reference: Tax Mgmt. (BNA), No. 358, *Cash or Deferred Arrangements*; *Employee Benefits Law* 209-10 (1991).

health and accident benefit plan An arrangement for the payment by an employer of benefits to employees in the event of personal injuries or sickness. If the benefits are provided for personal injuries or sickness through accident or health insurance, the amounts received are not included in gross income. Amounts received by employees under an accident or health plan are treated as if received "through accident or health insurance" and hence are not taxed to the employee, whether insured or uninsured. Benefits received for personal injuries or sickness that are attributable to employer contributions are not taxable to the employee; benefits paid directly by the employer to the employee are considered taxable income to the recipient. If the benefits are received, however, as amounts to reimburse the employee for medical expenses incurred by the employee, or the employee's spouse or dependents, and are not related to previously deducted medical expenses, the amounts received are not taxable, and the employer generally may deduct them as reasonable and necessary business expenses under I.R.C. § 162.

See DISABLED, MEDICAL CARE, MEDICAL REIMBURSEMENT PLAN.

Statutory and Regulatory Reference: I.R.C. §§ 104, 105, 106, 162; Treas. Reg. 1.162-10.

Treatise Reference: Tax Mgmt. (BNA), No. 389, *Disability and Medical Reimbursement Benefits*; *Employee Benefits Law* 946-49 (1991).

health benefits account *See* SECTION 401(H) ACCOUNT.

Health Maintenance Act of 1973 Federal law originally enacted to encourage the development of HMOs. It requires employers subject to minimum wage standards who employ 25 or more employees, as well as states and their political subdivisions, to include in a health benefit plan offered to employees the option of membership in a "qualified health maintenance organization" (HMO) if an HMO has made a proper request (meeting specific form, content, and timing requirements) for such inclusion. A qualified HMO is an one that provides basic and supplemental health services pursuant to the regulations of the Secretary of Health and Human Services (42 C.F.R. §§ 110.601 to .605), and has a fiscally sound operation and adequate provision against the risk of insolvency. Many state HMO laws mirror the federal act, although some state laws tend to be more restrictive.

See HEALTH MAINTENANCE ORGANIZATION.

Statutory and Regulatory Reference: Health Maintenance Amendments Act of 1988, P.L. 100-517 (1988); 42 U.S.C. § 300e-9 (1982); 42 C.F.R. §§ 110.801 to .810 (regulations issued before 1988 Amendments Act).

Treatise Reference: *HMOs: An Employer Guide to Complying with the Federal HMO Act*, Hewitt Associates, 100 Half Day Road, Lincolnshire, Illinois 60015.

health maintenance organization (HMO) An alternative health care delivery system to the traditional fee-for-services/indemnity arrangement whereby the health care provider receives a fixed premium each month on behalf of each participating employee, and the provider is then obligated to provide a comprehensive range of health care services. Health care services are provided to HMO members through primary care physicians who treat the members within the scope of their expertise and refer members to specialists within the HMO when necessary. There are three basic types of HMOs allowed by federal regulation: (1) staff model HMOs (physicians who provide basic health care services are employees of the HMO); (2) group practice HMOs (HMO contracts with physicians practicing together in a group that primarily provides services to members of the HMO); and (3) individual practice associations (IPAs) (HMO contracts with various individual physicians to provide basic health care services to members). The use of an HMO represents a trade-off whereby health care recipients agree to restrict nonemergency covered services to physicians and services provided by the HMO, but thereby obtain a broader set of benefits than under a basic hospital/major medical plan with lower out-of-pocket costs. Many HMOs are qualified under the federal Health Maintenance Organization Act, as well as under the various state laws, but the absence of federal qualification is not currently any indication of the quality of the HMO; most HMOs that are not federally qualified are such because they do not seek federal funding and generally are regulated by state law.

See HEALTH MAINTENANCE ACT OF 1973.

Statutory and Regulatory Reference: Health Maintenance Organization Act of 1973, 42 U.S.C. § 300e-9(a).

Treatise Reference: *Employee Benefits Law* 1030 (1991); Mamorsky, *Employee Benefits Handbook*, Ch. 31 (1987); Tax Mgmt. (BNA), *Financial Planning*, Para. 425, *Insurance Planning* (1991).

highly compensated employee For purposes of qualified retirement plans, VEBAs, group legal services plans, § 401(k) plans, and employee benefits (as defined in I.R.C. § 132), any employee who, during the year or the preceding year, (1) was at any time a five percent owner, (2) received COMPENSATION from the employer in excess of $75,000 (as adjusted), (3) received compensation from the employer in excess of $50,000 (as adjusted) and was in the top-paid group employees for such year, or (4) was at any time an officer and received compensation greater than 50 percent of the amount in effect under § 415(b)(1)(A) for such year (the defined benefit limitation).

Statutory and Regulatory Reference: I.R.C. § 132(h)(7), 401(k)(5), 414(q), 505(b)(5); Treas. Reg. § 1.414(q)-1T, Q&A 2-4.

highly compensated individual For purposes of cafeteria plans, this term has the same meaning as highly compensated employee.

For purposes of health benefits (self-insured), an individual who is (1) one of the five highest paid officers, (2) a shareholder who owns (within the application of I.R.C. § 318) more than 10 percent in value of the stock of the employer, or (3) among the highest paid 25 percent of all employees (other than employees described in I.R.C. § 105(h)(3)(B) who are not participants (i.e., employees who have not completed three years of service; employees who have not attained age 25; part-time or seasonal employees; employees not included in a unit of employees covered by a collective bargaining agreement; employees who are nonresident aliens and who receive no earned income from the employer that constitutes income from sources within the United States)).

See HIGHLY COMPENSATED EMPLOYEE.

Statutory and Regulatory Reference: I.R.C. § 105(h)(5) (health plans); I.R.C. § 125(e)(2) (cafeteria plans).

highly compensated participant For cafeteria plans, a participant in such a plan who is (1) an officer, (2) a shareholder owning more than 5 percent of the voting power or value of all classes of stock of the employer, (3) highly compensated, or (4) a spouse or dependent within the meaning of I.R.C. § 152 of an individual described above.

Statutory and Regulatory Reference: I.R.C. § 125(e)(1); Treas. Reg. § 1.105-11(d).

HMO *See* HEALTH MAINTENANCE ORGANIZATION.

hour of service An hour for which an employee is paid or entitled to pay for performing duties for an employer during a computation period or for excused absences such as vacation, holiday, illness, incapacity, layoff, jury duty, military duty, or leave of absence, or an hour for which an employee is awarded back pay. Hours of service are used in determining whether an employee is eligible to participate in a plan, and, if so, his or her entitlement to accrued benefits and his or her level of VESTING in such benefits.

See EQUIVALENCY, YEAR OF SERVICE.

Statutory and Regulatory Reference: *See* ERISA § 202(a)(3)(C); *see also* I.R.C. § 410(a)(3)(C); 29 C.F.R. § 2530.200b-2(a)(2).

Treatise Reference: *See* Tax Mgmt. (BNA), No. 351, *Pension Plans – Qualification*; *see also Employee Benefits Law* 85-87 (1991).

HSOP A medical benefits account described in I.R.C. § 401(h) (one to pay retiree medical benefits) established as part of a combined money purchase pension plan-Employee Stock Ownership Plan (ESOP). HSOPs allow the sponsoring employer to provide for retiree medical benefits for its current employees without having to accrue such future liabilities currently for financial accounting purposes in accordance with Financial Accounting Standards Board (FASB) Standard 106, as would be required if such benefits were provided outside the qualified plan context.

See SECTION 401(H) ACCOUNT.

Statutory and Regulatory Reference: I.R.C. § 401(h).

hybrid plan   A qualified retirement-type plan that has characteristics typical of both defined benefit and defined contribution plans. A money purchase pension plan is the most common type of hybrid plan, as it provides for individual employee accounts, like a defined contribution plan, but in other respects, such as the applicability of the I.R.C. § 412 minimum funding standard, is treated as a defined benefit pension plan. Other types of hybrid plans include target benefit plans and cash balance plans.

See CASH BALANCE PLAN, MONEY PURCHASE PLAN, TARGET BENEFIT PLAN.

Treatise Reference: *See generally* Tax Mgmt. (BNA), No. 351, *Pension Plans — Qualification.*

I

immediate annuity   An annuity contract in which payments are begun shortly after the contract is purchased.

See ANNUITY.

Statutory and Regulatory Reference: I.R.C. § 72(u)(4).

incentive stock option (ISO)   A compensatory option granting an employee (generally a key executive) the right to purchase employer securities or those of its corporate parent or subsidiary at a predetermined price under a plan that satisfies certain requirements entitling the employee to favorable federal income tax treatment.

For an option to qualify as an ISO, the period during which the employee has the right to exercise the option may not exceed 10 years. The initial option exercise price must equal or exceed the FAIR MARKET VALUE of employer stock as of the date the option was granted. Certain other qualification requirements also apply.

The chief tax benefit of ISOs for employees is that they are not taxed at the time of the option grant or exercise and that the employee generally will be eligible for capital gains treatment when he or she ultimately sells or disposes of the stock in a taxable transaction. The chief detriment of ISOs (from the employer's perspective) derives from the fact that the employer may not take a compensation DEDUCTION with respect to ISO stock.

See   QUALIFIED STOCK OPTION, RESTRICTED STOCK OPTION.

Statutory and Regulatory Reference: I.R.C. § 421-25; Prop. Treas. Reg. §§ 1.421-7 to -8 and 1.422A-1 *et seq*. and Temp. Treas. Reg. § 14a.422A-2.

Treatise Reference: Tax Mgmt. (BNA), No. 7, *Stock Options (Statutory) – Qualification*.

incidental benefit rule   A rule derived from the requirement that the principal purpose of a retirement plan must be to provide pensions to employees at retirement, in the case of a defined benefit plan, or to enable employees to share in the profits of their employer, in the case of a profit-sharing plan. Although this must be the principal purpose, a plan may carry a limited amount of life, health, and accident insurance on behalf of covered employees if the provision of such coverage is incidental to the principal purpose of the plan.

Example: Life insurance benefits generally are incidental where the plan provides a preretirement death benefit no greater than 100 times the monthly annuity benefit provided under the plan. A postretirement death benefit generally is incidental if the benefit does not exceed 50 percent of the participant's base salary in effect in the year preceding the year of retirement.

Statutory and Regulatory Reference: I.R.C. § 401(a)(9)(G); Treas. Reg. § 1.401-1(b)(1)(ii).

Case and Other Interpretive Reference: See Rev. Rul. 54-51, 1954-1 C.B. 147 (investment by a profit-sharing plan in whole life insurance for participants is considered "incidental" where the trust funds used have not been accumulated for at least two years if (1) the total life insurance premium for each participant is less than one-half of the total of contributions allocated to him or her at any particular time; and (2) the plan requires the trustee to convert the contract's entire value at or before retirement to provide periodic income so that no portion of such insurance's value may be used to continue life insurance protection after retirement). Such protection, however, may be extended to an employee who continues to work past the plan's NORMAL RETIREMENT AGE. *See* Rev. Rul. 57-213, 1957-1 C.B. 157; Rev. Rul. 66-143, 1966-1 C.B. 79. Rev. Rul. 54-51, *supra*, was extended to money purchase pension plans in Rev. Rul. 66-143, 1966-1 C.B. 79.

In Rev. Rul. 61-164, 1961-2 C.B. 99, the IRS ruled that the distribution by a qualified profit-sharing plan's trust of life, health, or accident insurance for participants will be considered "incidental" to the plan's main purpose of deferring compensation if it does not exceed 25 percent of the contributions allocated to a participant's account). *See also Raymond J. Moore v. Commissioner*, 45 B.T.A. 1073, *acq.* C.B. 1943, 17.

Rev. Rul. 76-353, 1976-2 C.B. 112, provides that the cost of a decreasing amount whole life insurance policy with level premiums will be considered incidental and subordinate to the primary purpose of a defined contribution plan in accordance with Rev. Rul. 61-164 if the total premium for each participant never exceed 25 percent of the funds allocated to the participant's account.

In a pension plan or annuity plan funded with insurance contracts, the life insurance benefit is deemed to be incidental where the life insurance benefit is no greater than 100 times the monthly annuity to which the participant is entitled. *See* Rev. Rul. 60-83, 1960-1 C.B. 157.

See also Rev. Rul. 85-15, 1985-1 C.B. 132, for guidance on how plans may satisfy the incidental benefit rule after being amended solely to provide for the preretirement survivor annuity provisions enacted by the Retirement Equity Act of 1984 (REA), Pub. L. No. 98-397, and Rev. Rul. 74-307, 1974-2 C.B. 126; Rev. Rul. 60-84, 1960-1 C.B. 159; Rev. Rul. 61-164, 1961-2 C.B. 99.

Treatise Reference: See Tax Mgmt. (BNA), No. 351, *Pension Plans—Qualification*, and No. 352, *Profit-Sharing Plans—Qualification*; *see also Employee Benefits Law* 143-44 (1991).

income averaging In addition to forward averaging (a tax reduction technique applicable to lump-sum distributions from qualified retirement plans), under prior law, in the nonpension context, certain taxpayers could "income average" on their personal income tax returns. This concept is different from the concept of "income" or "forward" averaging for employee benefit plan purposes, and was designed to avoid penalizing taxpayers whose income increased dramatically from the level of prior years.

See FORWARD AVERAGING.

Statutory and Regulatory Reference: See former I.R.C. §§ 1301-05.

individual account plan A qualified plan that holds each employee's benefits in a separate account.

See DEFINED CONTRIBUTION PLAN.

Statutory and Regulatory Reference: ERISA § 3(34).

individual level premium actuarial cost method An actuarial method that spreads out an employer's obligation to make FUND-

ING contributions to a qualified defined benefit plan over a period of several years in equal annual increments.

See FUNDING STANDARD ACCOUNT, MINIMUM FUNDING STANDARD.

Treatise Reference: *See generally* Tax Mgmt. (BNA), No. 371, *Employee Plans—Deductions, Contributions, and Funding.*

individual retirement account/arrangement *See* IRA, INDIVIDUAL RETIREMENT PLAN.

individual retirement plan An individual retirement account (IRA) described in I.R.C. § 408(a) or an individual retirement annuity (IRAN) described in I.R.C. § 408(b).

Statutory and Regulatory Reference: I.R.C. § 7701(a)(37).

Treatise Reference: *Employee Benefits Law* 29-31; 216-25 (1991).

individual retirement annuity (IRAN) *See* IRA.

information return A report that must be filed with the IRS by specified parties or with respect to specified transactions or situations and that relates primarily to the tax liability of a party other than the one filing the report.

Example: Pension plans to which the VESTING standards apply must file an annual registration statement with the Secretary of the Treasury; all qualified plans must report annually on their qualification, financial condition, and operations to the extent required by the Secretary; and defined benefit plans to which the MINIMUM FUNDING STANDARD applies must file a periodic actuarial report. Failure to file required information returns can subject the plan to penalties.

Statutory and Regulatory Reference: I.R.C. §§ 6057 (vesting registration), 6058 (annual qualification), 6059 (actuarial report), and 6652 (failure to file penalties).

in-service distributions A distribution from a qualified retirement plan made while the participant is still actively employed by the employer maintaining the plan. Pension plans, since their principal purpose is to provide benefits for retirement, generally may not provide for in-service distributions. A profit-sharing or stock bonus plan, however, may permit in-service distributions under certain circumstances. In general, in-service distributions are subject to federal income tax under the same basis recovery rules that apply to qualified plan distributions generally (i.e., ratable basis recovery under I.R.C. § 72). They may also be subject to the premature distribution tax of I.R.C. § 72(t) unless one of the exceptions listed in that section applies. Plan loans are not considered in-service withdrawals.

See ANNUITY, ANNUITY EXCLUSION RATIO RULE, PARTICIPANT LOAN, PREMATURE DISTRIBUTION.

Statutory and Regulatory Reference: Treas. Reg. § 1.401-1(b).

Treatise Reference: Tax Mgmt. (BNA), No. 370, *Qualified Plans—Taxation of Distributions; Employee Benefits Law* 180–81 (1991).

insolvency For purposes of multiemployer pension plans, an employer whose liabilities, including withdrawal liability to the plan, exceed the employer's assets (determined at the commencement of the liquidation or dissolution) where the employer's liquidation or dissolution value is determined without regard to its withdrawal liability. ERISA limits the withdrawal liability of such an employer to the sum of: (1) 50 percent of the plan's unfunded vested benefits allocable to the employer; and (2) that portion of the 50 percent of unfunded vested benefits allocable to that employer that do not exceed its liquidation or dissolution value: (a) as of the commencement of the liquidation or dissolution; and (b) after reducing the employer's liquidation or dissolution value to 50 percent of allocable unfunded vested benefits as provided in (1), above.

See MULTIEMPLOYER PLAN, WITHDRAWAL LIABILITY.

Statutory and Regulatory Reference: ERISA §§ 4225(b), (d).

Treatise Reference: Tax Mgmt. (BNA), No. 359, *Multiemployer Plans – Special Rules*.

insurable interest   A legal doctrine that limits the categories of those who may purchase an insurance policy on a particular person's life, by requiring that the purchaser have an insurable interest in the life of the insured so that ostensibly the purchaser has an interest in the insured person's longevity. It is generally an interest arising from the relations of the purchaser and the insured, either as a creditor or surety of the insured, or from the ties of blood or marriage to the insured, which justify a reasonable expectation of benefit from the continuance of the insured's life. The expectation of benefit does not have to be a pecuniary interest; a parent has an insurable interest in the life of his or her child and the natural affection in this case protects the life of the insured. A policy issued with a purchaser who does not have an insurable interest is void as against public policy.

Example: Employee X has no present ownership interest in Company A but wants to buy an insurance policy to fund her buy-out of a nonfamily member who is sole proprietor of Company A. X lacks an insurable interest.

Statutory and Regulatory Reference: I.R.C. §§ 101(a), 7702.

Case and Other Interpretive Reference: *Atlantic Oil Co. v. Patterson*, 331 F.2d 576 (5th Cir. 1964); *Thomson Sans v. United States*, 454 F.2d 954 (7th Cir. 1978).

Treatise Reference: *Couch on Insurance* § 24.148 (2d ed. 1984).

insurance contract plan   A qualified retirement plan that is funded entirely by individual or group insurance or annuity contracts purchased from a licensed insurance company. The insurance contract generally must provide for level premium payments payable no less frequently than annually.

Statutory and Regulatory Reference: ERISA § 301(b); I.R.C. § 412(i); Treas. Reg. § 1.412(i)-1.

Treatise Reference: *Employee Benefits Law* 29 (1991).

integration level   Under an integrated qualified retirement plan, the amount of a participant's compensation above a certain level where the rate of employer contributions or benefit accruals attributable to such contributions is higher than the rate applied to compensation below that level.

Example: A defined contribution plan provides for an annual allocation of employer contributions to participants' accounts of 5 percent of their compensation for their first $30,000 of annual salary and of 7 percent on compensation over $30,000. The plan's integration level is $30,000.

See DEFINED BENEFIT EXCESS PLAN, DEFINED CONTRIBUTION EXCESS PLAN, INTEGRATION (SOCIAL SECURITY), OFFSET PLAN.

Statutory and Regulatory Reference: I.R.C. § 401(l)(5)(A); Prop. Treas. Reg. § 1.401(l)-1(c)(20).

Treatise Reference: Tax Mgmt. (BNA), No. 356, *Qualified Plans – Integration*.

integration (Social Security)   The reduction of benefits or contributions under a qualified retirement plan to take into account Social Security benefits or contributions to which the participant is entitled under the Internal Revenue Code's "permitted disparity" rules. Although the integration rules historically were based on Social Security benefits or contributions, the Tax Reform Act of 1986 (TRA 1986), Pub. L. No. 99-514, codified them and created a set of mathematical formulas that are only loosely related to Social Security. If not for the Social Security integration rules, a plan benefit structure that reduced benefits or contributions to take account of Social Security benefits or contributions would tend to benefit highly compensated employees disproportionately, and therefore fail to qualify under I.R.C. § 401(a)(4) because the Social Security tax (which is being offset against the participant's plan benefit) is regressive in nature.

See BASE BENEFIT PERCENTAGE, BASE CONTRIBUTION PERCENTAGE, DEFINED BENEFIT EXCESS PLAN, DEFINED CONTRIBUTION EXCESS PLAN, OFFSET PLAN.

Statutory and Regulatory Reference: I.R.C. §§ 401(a)(5) and (l) and Treas. Reg. § 1.401(l)-1-6.

Case and Other Interpretive Reference: For the IRS' pre-TRA 1986 integration rules, *see* Rev. Rul. 71-446, 1971-2 C.B. 187; Rev. Rul. 75-480, 1975-2 C.B. 131; and Rev. Rul. 78-252, 1978-1 C.B. 123. In Rev. Rul. 78-178, 1978-1 C.B. 117, the IRS ruled that benefits provided under a qualified pension plan may not be integrated with unemployment compensation benefits.

See also Rev. Rul. 79-236, 1979-2 C.B. 160 (pre-TRA 1986 integration rules for plans of related employers); Rev. Rul. 80-307, 1980-2 C.B. 136 (plan funded solely with mandatory EMPLOYEE CONTRIBUTIONS that has the effect of denying participation to nonhighly compensated employees or causing them to receive a lower level of benefits expressed as a percentage of compensation discriminates within the meaning of I.R.C. § 401(a)(4), despite literal compliance with the integration rules); Rev. Rul. 83-53, 1983-1 C.B. 88

(pre-TRA 1986 adjustment factors for certain preretirement death benefits). Other pre-1986 integration rulings include Rev. Rul. 83-97, 1983-1 C.B. 72 (adjustment factors); Rev. Rul. 83-110, 1983-2 C.B. 70 (target benefit plans); Rev. Rul. 84-45, 1984-1 C.B. 115 (use of estimated Primary Insurance Amount in offset plan); Rev. Rul. 86-51, 1986-1 C.B. 205 (integrated pension plan maintained jointly by unaffiliated employers will not fail to qualify under I.R.C. § 401(a) solely because compensation on which benefits are based is compensation of employee received from all employers maintaining the plan); Rev. Rul. 86-74, 1986-1 C.B. 205 (changes in pre-TRA 1986 integration rules to take into account effect of the Social Security Act Amendments of 1983 (Pub. L. No. 98-21).

Treatise Reference: See Tax Mgmt. (BNA), No. 356, *Qualified Plans – Integration*; *see also Employee Benefits Law* 119; 129 (1991); D. McGill & D. Grubbs, Jr., *Fundamentals of Private Pensions* 191 (6th ed. 1991).

interest assumption   In a qualified defined benefit plan, for purposes of the Internal Revenue Code's minimum funding standard, the assumption used by the plan's actuary in estimating the rate of investment return on plan assets, or the interest rate that is used in determining the present value of a participant's or beneficiary's benefit or the actuarial equivalent of a plan benefit when expressed in another form. For single employer defined benefit plans, the interest assumption, like all actuarial assumptions, generally must be reasonable. For multiemployer plans, individual assumptions can be unreasonable, so long as the combined effect of all the plan's actuarial assumptions is "reasonable in the aggregate."

Liabilities and benefits upon plan termination are also calculated based on an interest assumption. In this case, it is generally the PBGC's immediate or deferred rates at the time a distribution of benefits occurs, although, when valuing benefits over $25,000, the maximum interest rate that can be used is capped at 120 percent of the PBGC immediate rate. Finally, unfunded vested benefits, for purposes of calculating an employer's withdrawal liability under a multiemployer plan, are calculated based on certain actuarial assumptions, including an interest assumption.

See ACTUARIAL ASSUMPTIONS, MINIMUM FUNDING STANDARD, FUNDING STANDARD ACCOUNT, MULTIEMPLOYER PLAN, WITHDRAWAL LIABILITY.

Statutory and Regulatory Reference: See generally ERISA §§ 302(b) (5), (c) (3); I.R.C. § 412(b)(5), (c)(3) (general rules). For the rules governing interest assumptions in the context of the valuation of plan assets, *see* PBGC Reg. 29 C.F.R. § 2619. For the interest assumption cap on benefits over $25,000, *see* ERISA § 205(g)(1), I.R.C. § 417(e), Treas. Reg. §§ 1.411(a)-11 and 1.417(e)-1. For rules governing permissible actuarial assumptions in calculating withdrawal liability under a multiemployer plan, *see* ERISA § 4213(b).

Case and Other Interpretive Reference: See Rev. Rul. 79-237, 1979-2 C.B. 190 (application of the minimum funding standard to terminating plans); Rev. Rul. 81-213, 1981-2 C.B. 101, (guidelines for calculating the amortization of experience gains and losses). For arbitration cases dealing with the reasonableness of actuarial assumptions in calculating withdrawal liability, *see Penn Textile Corp. v. Textile Workers Pension Fund*, 3 EB Cases 1609 (1982) (Pritzker, Arb.); *Great Atlantic & Pacific Tea Co. v. UFCW & Food Employers Pension Plan*, AAA Case No. 55-621-0006-85 MEEP (July 16, 1986) (Pillsbury, Arb.); *Eberhard Food, Inc. v. REEC Joint Pension Fund*, 6 EB Cases 1961 (1985) (Glover, Arb.); *Paperworkers Local 286 Pension Plan v. Kardom Indus.*, 6 EB Cases 2398 (1985) (Nagel, Arb.); *Foodtown Stores, Inc. v. Kansas City Area Retail Food Store Employees Pension Fund*, AAA Case No. 57-261-0001

(Sept. 26, 1985) (O'Laughlin, Arb.); *Palmer Coking Coal Co. v UMWA 1950 & 1974 Pension Plans*, 5 EB Cases 2369 (1984) (Gordon Arb.); *Calvert & Youngblood Coal Co. v. UMWA 1950 and 1974 Pension Plans*, 5 EB Cases 2361 (1981) (Polak Arb.); *Buy-Low, Inc. v. Board of Trustees, Food Workers Pension Fund*, 5 EB Cases 2641 (1984) (Bowles, Arb.); *Hertz Corp. v. Commission Drivers Local 187 Pension Fund*, 4 EB Cases 1367 (1983) (Mittleman, Arb.).

Treatise Reference: Tax Mgmt. (BNA), No. 371, *Employee Plans — Deductions, Contributions, and Funding*; *Employee Benefits Law* 421-22; 748-49; 752-58 (1991).

interested parties   All employees of an employer who are eligible to participate in a qualified plan of the employer or whose principal place of employment is the same as the principal place of employment of an employee who is eligible to participate in the plan. In the case of a collectively bargained plan, all employees covered by the collective bargaining agreement are considered interested parties. All interested parties must be given prior notice if the employer requests a DETERMINATION LETTER with respect to a plan.

Statutory and Regulatory Reference: ERISA § 3001; Treas. Reg. § 1.7476-1.

Internal Revenue Code   The Internal Revenue Code of 1986, as amended, 26 U.S.C. § 1 *et seq.*; the body of law governing the federal taxation of individuals and business entities, including, among other things, income, estate and gift, and excise taxes.

investment in the contract   The aggregate amount of premiums or other consideration paid for an annuity contract as of the annuity starting date, minus any amounts received before that date which are excludable from income. When compared to the expected return from the annuity, the investment in the contract controls the amount of payments under the contract that can be received tax free.

See ANNUITY EXCLUSION RATIO RULE.

Statutory and Regulatory Reference: I.R.C. §§ 72(c)(1) and 72(e)(8).

investment manager   A fiduciary, other than a trustee or named fiduciary (as defined in ERISA § 402(a)(2)), who has the power to manage, acquire, or dispose of any asset of a plan. The investment manager must either be registered as an investment adviser under the Investment Advisers Act of 1940 (15 U.S.C. § 80a-1 *et seq.*), a bank (as defined in that same Act), or an insurance company qualified to perform asset management, acquisition, and disposition services under the laws of more than one state. The investment manager also must acknowledge in writing that he or she is a fiduciary with respect to the plan. Note that the responsibility to manage and control trust assets resides with the trustee, but a trustee who is a named fiduciary under ERISA § 402 may delegate that responsibility to one or more investment managers pursuant to a written plan provision. Although the trustee thus relieves himself of the responsibility to manage trust assets, the trustee may have a continuing responsibility to monitor the performance of the investment manager.

See QPAM.

Statutory and Regulatory Reference: ERISA §§ 3(38), 403(a)(2).

Case and Other Interpretive Reference: DOL Adv. Op. 77-68A (Sept. 9, 1977), *Brock v. Berman,* 673 F. Supp. 634, 8 EB Cases 1689 (D. Mass. 1987) (trustee may have continuing obligation to monitor investment manager).

involuntary termination   Under SEP-PAA, a plan termination initiated by the PBGC rather than the plan administrator. In specific situations, the PBGC may seek a court-ordered involuntary termination of a pension plan where the action is necessary to protect the interests of participants or the PBGC insurance system. Specific situations where this is authorized include cases where the plan has failed to meet the Internal Revenue Code's minimum funding standard, will be unable to pay benefits when due, or has made a large distribution to a participant who is a substantial owner, leaving the plan with unfunded vested benefits, and situations where the PBGC's long-term loss may be reasonably expected to increase unreasonably if the plan is not terminated. The court decree will include provision for appointment of a trustee to terminate the plan and a trustee may be appointed to administer the plan while the proceedings are pending. The PBGC will request and will receive appointment as this trustee.

Note that a plan may be terminated involuntarily notwithstanding the plan sponsor's commitment to continue maintaining the plan pursuant to a collective bargaining agreement.

See SEPPAA, TERMINATION.

Statutory and Regulatory Reference: See ERISA §§ 4042, 4048; *see also* the regulations discussed under standard termination.

Case and Other Interpretive Reference: In re Chateaugay Corp., 9 EB Cases 2209, 89 B.R. 779 (S.D.N.Y. 1988), *aff'd sub nom. PBGC v. LTV Corp.,* 875 F.2d 1008 (2d Cir. 1989), *rev'd,* 110 S. Ct. 2668, 12 EB Cases 1593, 53 USLW 4831 (1990) (Supreme Court upheld PBGC restoration of plans involuntarily terminated based on LTV's failure to meet minimum funding standards and its apparent inability to make further contributions when LTV later agreed in collective bargaining to adopt several follow-on plans).

Treatise Reference: Tax Mgmt. (BNA), No. 357, *Plan Terminations and Mergers*; *Employee Benefits Law* 408-11 (1991).

IRA (individual retirement arrangement) A private pension arrangement permitted for individuals with earned income. Individuals with earned income (generally income from the performance of services) for the taxable year may make deductible contributions to such arrangements subject to certain limits. Such contributions (together with any rollover contributions held by the IRA) will grow tax-free until they are distributed to the IRA owner or his or her beneficiary. An individual retirement account (also commonly referred to as an IRA) is a trust organized or created in the United States for the exclusive benefit of an individual or his or her beneficiaries that must satisfy certain requirements. Except for rollover contributions, the IRA's plan document generally must provide that no contribution will be accepted for a taxable year in excess of $2,000 on behalf of any individual. Its trustee must be a bank or other person that demonstrates to the IRS' satisfaction that it is capable of administering IRAs in accordance with the federal tax law rules.

Individual retirement annuities (IRANs) are similar to IRAs except that their benefits are funded through commercial annuity or endowment contracts. The owner's annual contribution to such plans goes to pay the annual premium on this contract.

See ACTIVE PARTICIPANT, CONDUIT IRA, ROLLOVER.

Statutory and Regulatory Reference: For the definition and qualification requirements for individual retirement arrangements, *see* I.R.C. §§ 408(a); Treas. Reg. § 1.408-2 (IRAs); and I.R.C. § 408(b) and Treas. Reg. § 1.408-3 (IRANs). For the general limits on the deductibility of IRA contributions, *see* I.R.C. § 219 and Treas. Reg. § 1.219-1; for the definition of "active participant," for purposes of the deduction cutback rules, *see* I.R.C. § 219(g) and Treas. Reg. § 1.219-2. For the rules limiting the payment of death benefits under an IRA, *see* I.R.C. §§ 408(a)(6) and (b)(3). For the IRS reporting requirements applicable to IRAs, *see* I.R.C. §§ 408(i), 408(o)(4), and 6693 (penalty for failure to file); for the rules governing the tax treatment of an IRA owner upon borrowing or pledging his or her IRA, *see* I.R.C. § 408(e)(3). The 10 percent penalty tax on premature distributions from an IRA appears at I.R.C. § 72(t). I.R.C. § 4973 contains the excise tax on excess IRA contributions and I.R.C. § 4974 contains the penalty tax for failure to make certain IRA distributions.

Case and Other Interpretive Reference: See Rev. Rul. 84-146, 1984-2 C.B. 97 (administrative fees for an IRA, paid out of taxpayer's personal funds, are deductible under I.R.C. § 212, even if the deductible limits of I.R.C. § 219 are exceeded for the year; *but see* Rev. Rul. 87-10, 1987-1 C.B. 136, denying a deduction for brokerage fees paid separately by an IRA owner); Rev. Rul. 85-62, 1985-1 C.B. 153 (earnings credited to an IRA, which are attributable to a non-IRA companion account maintained at the same financial institution, are deemed to be interest earned by the IRA owner; when these amounts are credited to the IRA account, they are treated as being contributed by the IRA owner); Rev. Rul. 86-78, 1986-1 C.B. 208 (detailing the financial disclosure that the trustee or issuer of an IRA must provide to the IRA owner).

Treatise Reference: See Tax Mgmt. (BNA), No. 355, *IRAs and SEPs. See also* D. McGill & D. Grubbs, Jr., *Fundamentals of Private Pensions* 715 (6th ed. 1989).

J

joint and survivor annuity An annuity, provided under a qualified retirement plan or otherwise, that calls for payments for the life or life expectancy of one individual, and for some level of payments to continue to a second individual upon the death of the first ("primary") annuitant.

Example: A qualified retirement plan provides benefits to participants in annuity form. Under an optional benefit form elected by participant A, payments of $2,000 per month will be made jointly to A and his or her designated beneficiary for A's life, beginning when A retires. If A predeceases the beneficiary, the plan will continue to make annuity payments to the beneficiary of $1,000 per month.

See QUALIFIED JOINT AND SURVIVOR ANNUITY (QJSA).

Statutory and Regulatory Reference: See generally I.R.C. §§ 401(a)(11) and 417 and Treas. Reg. § 1.401(a)(11).

Treatise Reference: See Tax Mgmt. (BNA), No. 370, *Qualified Plans—Taxation of Distributions*; *Employee Benefits Law* 12; 161 (1991).

joint and survivor annuity, qualified

See QUALIFIED JOINT AND SURVIVOR ANNUITY (QJSA).

joint and survivor annuity with term certain A joint and survivor annuity provided under a qualified retirement plan or otherwise under which, even if all of the designated payees die, a minimum number of payments will nonetheless be made to someone, generally the annuitant's estate or designated beneficiary.

Example: A purchases a joint and survivor annuity for himself and B, with a guaranteed 10-year term certain. After two years, both A and B die. The issuer of the contract (generally an insurance company) will have to make eight more years of payments to the relevant estate or designated secondary beneficiary.

See JOINT AND SURVIVOR ANNUITY.

Statutory and Regulatory Reference: See generally I.R.C. §§ 72 and 402 and the regulations promulgated thereunder.

Treatise Reference: Tax Mgmt. (BNA), No. 370, *Qualified Plans—Taxation of Distributions*.

K

Keogh plan   A qualified retirement plan established by or on behalf of a self-employed person that is generally subject to the same requirements and limits as a qualified retirement plan, plus certain additional restrictions. The Tax Equity and Fiscal Responsibility Act of 1982 (TEFRA), Pub. L. No. 97-248, eliminated many of the tax law distinctions that once existed between Keogh plans and regular or "corporate" qualified plans in an effort to make qualified plans a tax-neutral consideration in determining in what form a company should do business. The terms "Keogh plan" (derived from the name of the Congressman who introduced the bill allowing these plans), and "H.R. 10 PLAN" (derived from the number of that bill) are synonymous.

For examples of these special restrictions, *see* I.R.C. §§ 404(a)(8) (imposing special limits on the deductibility of plan contributions); 401(c)(1) (setting forth a different definition of compensation than the one that generally applies for determining benefits under qualified plans); and 402(e)(4)(a)(iii) and (iv) (denying favorable tax status on lump-sum distributions to self-employed individuals upon SEPARATION FROM SERVICE, but granting it upon such an individual's becoming disabled.

Treatise Reference: Tax Mgmt. (BNA), No. 353, *Owner-Dominated Plans — Top-Heavy and H.R. 10 Plans*.

key employee   An employee who, at any time during the plan year or any of the four preceding plan years, is (1) an officer of the employer and has an annual COMPENSATION greater than 50 percent of the amount in effect under the I.R.C. § 415(b)(1)(A) contribution and benefit limitations for the plan year; or (2) 1 of the 10 employees having annual compensation from the employer of more than the limitation in effect under I.R.C. § 415(c)(1)(A) and owning the largest interest in the employer, (3) a 5 percent owner of the employer, or (4) a 1 percent owner of the employer having annual compensation from the employer of more than $150,000. Under the test in (1), above, no more than 50 employees, or, if less, the greater of 3 or 10 percent of the employees, are treated as officers. The key employee rules are part of the top-heavy rules.

See 5 PERCENT OWNER, OFFICER, TOP-HEAVY.

Statutory and Regulatory Reference: See I.R.C. § 416(i) and Treas. Reg. § 1.416-1, Q&A T-12 to T-21. For the dollar limit applicable to defined benefit plans, *see* I.R.C.

§ 415(b)(1)(A); for the dollar limit on defined contribution plans, *see* I.R.C. § 415(c)(1)(A).

Treatise Reference: Tax Mgmt. (BNA), No. 353, *Owner-Dominated Plans — Top-Heavy and H.R. 10 Plans*; *Employee Benefits Law* 115; 284; 956-57 (1991).

key-man insurance   An individual life insurance policy owned by a corporation on the life of a "key man," i.e., an individual who is a key executive or professional in a business on whom the success of the corporation is dependent, with proceeds of the policy payable to the corporation to protect against the loss of the leader. The employer cannot deduct any amounts paid as premiums on an individual life insurance policy, including a key-man policy, if the employer is directly or indirectly a beneficiary under the policy.

Statutory and Regulatory Reference: I.R.C. § 264; Treas. Reg. § 1.264-1 (premiums not deductible whether or not employer is beneficiary of policy).

Case and Other Interpretive Reference: *Emeloid v. Commissioner*, 189 F.2d 230 (3d Cir. 1951) (corporate purchase of life insurance on life of corporate officer is a valid business purpose); *Harrison v. Commissioner*, 59 T.C. 578 (1973), *acq.*, 1973-2 C.B. 2 (definition of key man expanded to include individuals not officers or employees, as long as close business relationship exists between insured and insuring company). *See also L.C. Thomsen & Sons v. United States*, 484 F.2d 954 (7th Cir. 1973); *Klinck v. Commissioner*, 11 T.C.M. 1224 (1952) (deduction of premium on life insurance policy on officer disallowed) and PLRs 6508270960A and 6303205600A (deductions for premiums disallowed where insurance payable to stockholders in proportion to stock holdings).

Treatise Reference: Tax Mgmt. (BNA), *Financial Planning*, Para. 425, *Insurance Planning* (1991).

L

Labor-Management Relations Act of 1947 (LMRA)   Also known as the Taft-Hartley Act, the LMRA contains requirements for payments to trust funds under collectively bargained arrangements. The trust funds are commonly known as Taft-Hartley plans or jointly administered plans. The substantive requirements for jointly administered plans are found in LMRA § 302(c)(5). The failure to comply with these requirements is subject to criminal penalties.

Statutory and Regulatory Reference: 29 U.S.C. § 186(c).

lapse restriction   A restriction having a fixed expiration date that applies to property other than money given an employee or independent contractor by the employer as COMPENSATION for services ("restricted property"). If such a restriction either makes the property subject to a substantial risk of forfeiture (e.g., the employee will forfeit the property if he or she goes to work for a competitor of the employer within five years) or renders the property nontransferable (e.g., if the employee intends to sell the property within five years of its receipt, he or she must first offer to sell it back to the employer at a predetermined price), the property will not be taxable to the employee, and the employer may not take its offsetting compensation DEDUCTION, until the restrictions lapse.

In contrast, a restriction which, by its terms, will never lapse (e.g., a requirement that if the employee ever sells the property he or she must first offer to sell it back to the employer at a predetermined price) does not affect the timing of the employee's recognition of income or of the employer's compensation deduction; rather such nonlapse restrictions will only be taken into account in determining the property's FAIR MARKET VALUE.

See RESTRICTED PROPERTY, SUBSTANTIAL RISK OF FORFEITURE, TRANSFERABILITY RESTRICTION.

Statutory and Regulatory Reference: I.R.C. §§ 83(a), (c), and (d); Treas. Reg. § 1.83-1 *et seq*.

Treatise Reference: Tax Mgmt. (BNA), No. 384, *Restricted Property—Section* 83.

late retirement/late retirement age   The retirement of an employee and resulting entitlement to benefits under a retirement-type plan, occurring after the employee has worked past the employer's normal retirement age as specified in the plan. A plan may withhold employer contributions/benefits during the period of employment after normal retirment age (subject to the minimum distribution rules). Benefits must then be actuarially increased upon later commencement, with certain exceptions.

See NORMAL RETIREMENT AGE.

Statutory and Regulatory Reference: Prop. Treas. Reg. § 1.411(b)-2(b)(4)(iii).

Treatise Reference: Tax Mgmt. (BNA), No. 351, *Pension Plans—Qualification*, and No. 352, *Profit-Sharing Plans—Qualification*; *Employee Benefits Law* 158-59 (1991).

leased employee A person other than an employee of the employer who provides, under an agreement with an employee leasing organization and on a substantially full-time basis for more than one year, services for an employer of the type that historically have been provided by common-law employees. For qualified retirement plan purposes, leased employees are treated as employees of the employer who leases their services, rather than as employees of the leasing organization. This employment attribution rule, however, will not apply if the leasing organization covers the employees under a money purchase plan that provides a 10 percent annual nonintegrated employer contribution with full and immediate participation and VESTING.

Statutory and Regulatory Reference: I.R.C. § 414(n); Prop. Treas. Reg. § 1.414(n)-1 *et seq.*

Treatise Reference: Tax Mgmt. (BNA), No. 351, *Pension Plans—Qualification*.

leveraged ESOP A form of employee stock ownership plan (ESOP) that may borrow funds that it uses to purchase qualifying employer securities. Typically, a leveraged ESOP will borrow money from a bank, which it will use to purchase shares of stock from its sponsoring employer, with the employer guaranteeing the loan. Alternatively, the employer may borrow the funds directly from the lender and reloan them to the plan. The employer then makes annual contributions to the plan, which the ESOP uses to make the payments on the loan. As the loan is repaid, the employer securities are released from a plan suspense account and allocated to the accounts of participants. Such loan arrangements are not considered prohibited transactions.

See ESOP, PROHIBITED TRANSACTION.

Statutory and Regulatory Reference: ERISA § 408(b)(3); I.R.C. §§ 409, 4975(d)(3), (e)(7); Treas. Reg. § 54.4975-7.

Treatise Reference: Tax Mgmt. (BNA), No. 354, *ESOPs*; *Employee Benefits Law* 151; 338 (1991).

life annuity An annuity, provided under a qualified retirement plan or otherwise, where payments are to be made over a period measured by the life or life expectancy of one or more individuals or a commercial annuity having such a contingency (known as a "life contingency").

Example: A joint and survivor annuity calling for payments to be made jointly to individuals A and B during A's lifetime and, should A predecease B, for payments continuing to B for B's life would be a form of life annuity, as would an annuity payable to A alone for either his or her life or life expectancy. Further, an annuity for A's life with a guaranteed "term-certain," such as one calling for payments to A for A's life but, should A die before 10 years of payments are received, for payments to continue to A's beneficiary or estate until the 10-year period has elapsed, would be a life annuity because one of its contingencies is a "life contingency" (A's life).

See JOINT AND SURVIVOR ANNUITY.

Statutory and Regulatory Reference: I.R.C. §§ 72, 401(a)(11) and 417; Treas. Reg. § 1.401(a)-12(b) (1).

Treatise Reference: Tax Mgmt. (BNA), No. 134, *Annuities*, and No. 370, *Qualified Plans—Taxation of Distributions*.

life expectancy The remaining years that an individual who has reached a specified age is projected to live under actuarial tables of common usage in the insurance industry.

Statutory and Regulatory Reference: I.R.C. § 72(c)(3)(A); Treas. Reg. § 1.72-9 (containing tables used by the IRS in determining life expectancy).

Treatise Reference: Tax Mgmt. (BNA), No. 134, *Annuities* and No. 370, *Qualified Plans — Taxation of Distributions*.

life insurance contract For purposes of the Internal Revenue Code, any contract that is a life insurance contract under state law, but only if the contract meets the "cash value accumulation test" and the "guideline premium requirements" and falls within the "cash value corridor." The term includes a life insurance policy, a workers' compensation contract, an endowment policy, and an accident insurance contract. This definition generally is applicable for policies issued after 1984. Note however that even if a policy meets this definition, it will not be treated as a life insurance contract if it is a "variable policy" based on a "segregation asset account" and the investments in the account are not "adequately diversified," as described in I.R.C. § 817. Despite the above statutory definition of life insurance introduced for contracts issued after 1984, the nonstatutory definition of life insurance is important because a policy must not only meet the I.R.C. § 7702 statutory definition, but must also be life insurance under "applicable law." No statutory definition generally applies for policies issued before 1985 (unless it is a flexible premium contract), and a life insurance contract that fails the § 7702 definition may still be treated as life insurance for taxation purposes if it meets the definition of life insurance under local law, which generally focuses on the risk-shifting and risk-distribution.

See ENDOWMENT POLICY, FLEXIBLE PREMIUM ADJUSTABLE LIFE INSURANCE, VARIABLE LIFE INSURANCE CONTRACT.

Statutory and Regulatory Reference: I.R.C. §§ 101, 7702, 1035(b)(3), 817 (defining life insurance in the context of a tax-free exchange); Treas. Reg. §§ 1.101-1(a)(1); 20.2042-1(a); 1.101-2; 1.72-1; 1.72-2.

Case and Other Interpretive Reference: *See Helvering v. Le Gierse*, 312 U.S. 531 (1941) (life insurance involves the element of risk shifting and risk distributing); *Commissioner v. Treganowan*, 183 F.2d 288 (2d Cir. 1950) (existence of life insurance contract issued by commercial insurance company is not required in the definition of "insurance"). *See also* Rev. Rul. 65-222, 1965-2 C.B. 74; *Davis v. United States*, 323 F. Supp. 858 (S.D. W. Va. 1971) (distinguishing life insurance benefit from survivor benefit, i.e., death benefit, under a retirement system); *Barnes v. United States*, 86-2 U.S.T.C. Para. 9692 (7th Cir. 1986); Rev. Rul. 83-44, 1983-1 C.B. 228 (distinguishing life insurance and liability insurance).

Treatise Reference: Tax Mgmt. (BNA), No. 386, *Insurance-Related Compensation*; Tax Mgmt. (BNA) *Financial Planning*, Para. 425, *Insurance Planning* (1991).

limitation on contributions/benefits (I.R.C. § 415) A limit on the maximum amount of annual additions that may be made to a participant's account in a qualified defined contribution plan in any year or on the maximum total retirement benefit that may be provided a participant under a qualified defined benefit plan.

In a defined contribution plan, no participant may receive an annual addition for a year that exceeds the lesser of 25 percent of compensation or $30,000 (the $30,000 limit is adjusted for inflation). Benefits under all defined contribution plans of a single employer in which an employee participates are aggregated in applying this limit.

In a defined benefit plan, the annual benefit a participant may earn, when expressed as a life annuity with payments starting at the participant's Social Security NORMAL RETIREMENT AGE, cannot exceed the lesser of his or her AVERAGE ANNUAL COMPENSATION for the three consecutive years that produce the highest average, or $90,000 (the $90,000 figure is adjusted for inflation after 1987). All defined benefit plans maintained by an employer in which an employee participates are aggregated in applying this limit.

Statutory and Regulatory Reference: I.R.C. § 415(b)(1) and Treas. Reg. § 1.415-3 to -5 (defined benefit plans); I.R.C. § 415(c)(1)(A) and Treas. Reg. § 1.415-6 (defined contribution plans). *See also* I.R.C. § 415(d) (providing for indexation of the $30,000 and $90,000 amounts in the formula for inflation); Treas. Reg. § 1.415-5 (inflation adjustment for defined benefit plans); and Treas. Reg. § 1.415-6(d) (inflation adjustment for defined contribution plans). I.R.C. § 401(a)(16) makes satisfaction of the applicable benefit/contribution limits of § 415 a qualification requirement for § 401(a) plans. Note that the above-cited regulations refer to the $25,000 and $75,000 limits rather than the $30,000 and $90,000 limits because they were promulgated in 1980, before the alteration of those limits by the Tax Equity and Fiscal Responsibility Act of 1982 (TEFRA), Pub. L. No. 97-248.

For the limits applicable to church plans, *see* I.R.C. § 415(c)(7); for the limits applicable to combinations of qualified retirement plans, *see* I.R.C. § 415(e). I.R.C. § 416(h) contains special rules modifying the normally applicable § 415(e) COMBINED PLAN LIMIT for certain TOP-HEAVY plans.

Case and Other Interpretive Reference: Rev. Rul. 75-481, 1975-2 C.B. 188 (rules for determining whether plan contributions and benefits satisfy the I.R.C. § 415 limits).

Treatise Reference: Tax Mgmt. (BNA), No. 370, *Qualified Plans — Taxation of Distributions*.

line of business   A portion of an employer's business identified by the property or services it provides to its customers. As a first step in identifying separate lines of business, employers must determine their lines of business by identifying all the property and services provided to customers during the testing year and then designating which portion of the property and services is provided by each business. Employers may use their discretion to determine their lines of business in a manner that conforms to their business operations and otherwise satisfies the proposed regulations under Internal Revenue Code § 414(r). Note that there generally is no requirement that a line of business provide only one type of property or services or only related types of property or services, so an employer may combine in a single line of business dissimilar types of property or services. Also, there generally is no requirement that all property or services of related types or of the same type be provided by a single line of business. The employer must keep in mind, however, that the line of business must go on to pass the separateness tests of the proposed I.R.C. § 414(r) regulations.

Example: Employer X is a conglomerate manufacturing and selling consumer food and beverage products and providing data processing services to private industry. Employer X determined that the consumer food products line and the consumer beverage products business will satisfy the separateness criteria of Prop. Treas. Reg. § 1.414(r)-3, so X apportions all the property and services it provides to customers between two lines of business, one providing all its consumer food and beverage products, and a second proving all its data processing services. Employer X has two lines of business for purposes of § 414(r).

See SEPARATE LINE OF BUSINESS (SLOB).

Statutory and Regulatory Reference: I.R.C. § 414(r); Prop. Treas. Reg. § 1.414(r).

Treatise Reference: Tax Mgmt. (BNA), No. 351, *Pension Plans — Qualification.*

lump-sum distribution   A distribution of a participant's entire interest in a qualified retirement plan within the same taxable year of the recipient where such distribution occurs because of the employee's death, DIS-ABILITY, separation from the employer's service, or after the employee reaches age 59½.

One lump-sum distribution in an individual's lifetime is eligible for favorable "forward averaging" tax treatment. To constitute a lump-sum distribution, the individual must receive a total distribution of all of his or her interests in all plans of the same type (profit-sharing and stock bonus plans or pension plans) within the year. The distribution need not be paid in a single installment, but in general all amounts payable to the recipient must be paid within the same TAXABLE YEAR of the recipient (generally the calendar year). Self-employed individuals may not qualify for forward averaging treatment for distributions upon SEPARATION FROM SERVICE but may do so if the triggering event is disability. For common-law employees, separation from service is a triggering event, but not disability. The recipient need not be the plan participant; it may be his or her beneficiary. Lump-sum distributions are also eligible for tax-free rollover treatment.

See FORWARD AVERAGING, ROLLOVER.

Statutory and Regulatory Reference: ERISA §§ 203(e) and 205(g) (mandatory lump-sum distribution); ERISA § 4041A(f) (rules applicable to certain terminated multiemployer plans); I.R.C. § 402(a)(5) (rollover rules);

I.R.C. § 402(e)(4) (forward averaging rules and definition of lump-sum distribution); I.R.C. §§ 411(a)(11) and 417(e) (mandatory lump-sum distributions).

Case and Other Interpretive Reference: Rev. Rul. 80-129, 1980-1 C.B. 86 (where the business of an employee's employer is terminated, but the employee continues at the same job for a successor employer, no separation from service has occurred; therefore the employee is not eligible to receive a lump-sum distribution); Rul. 81-141, 1981-1 C.B. 204 (similar rule where employee continues service for spun-off subsidiary of parent corporation); Rev. Rul. 81-26, 1981-1 C.B. 200 (promotion of employee from common-law employee to partner was not a separation from service for purposes of the lump-sum distribution rules); Rev. Rul. 83-57, 1983-1 C.B. 92 (distribution of employee's entire account balance in qualified plan was a lump-sum distribution even though an additional amount, which had been impounded by a court, was released in a later year); Rev. Rul. 85-89, 1985-1 C.B. 135 (where plan conditions the right to receive a lump-sum distribution as a benefit option upon the employee's satisfying certain financial conditions, it may discriminate within the meaning of I.R.C. § 401(a) (4). This rule was later incorporated into Treas. Reg. § 1.401(a)-4, prohibiting discretion from being vested in the trustee of a qualified plan to determine which of the plan's benefit options will be available to a participant).

The courts are divided on whether the disqualification of a plan for certain past years makes the recipient of an otherwise qualifying lump-sum distribution ineligible for the favorable tax treatment afforded by I.R.C. § 402(e). *See Benbow v. Commissioner*, 774 F.2d 740 (7th Cir. 1985); *Woodson v. Commissioner*, 651 F.2d 1094 (5th Cir. 1981), both of which uphold the favorable tax treatment. *But see Greenwald v. Commissioner*, 366 F.2d 538 (2d Cir. 1966), partially disqualifying a lump-sum distribution from favorable tax treatment where the distributing plan was retroactively disqualified for certain years during which the participant earned the benefit).

Treatise Reference: *See* Tax Mgmt. (BNA), No. 355, *IRAs and SEPs*, for a discussion of the rollover rules, and No. 370, *Qualified Plans — Taxation of Distributions*, for a discussion of the forward averaging and lump-sum distribution rules; *see also Employee Benefits Law* 181-85 (1991); D. McGill & D. Grubbs, Jr., *Fundamentals of Private Pensions* 738 (6th ed. 1989).

M

mandatory distribution *See* MINIMUM REQUIRED DISTRIBUTION.

mass withdrawal Under a multi-employer pension plan, a simultaneous withdrawal from participation in the plan of every one of the employers sponsoring it, or such a withdrawal accomplished by agreement or arrangement. When a mass withdrawal occurs, the plan sponsor must amend the plan to reduce its benefits and then match the plan's benefits to its assets. When the plan finds itself unable to pay the reduced benefits, it must notify the PBGC and go into insolvency. This, in turn, will trigger PBGC guaranteed benefits under ERISA's insolvency rules for multiemployer plans.

See INSOLVENCY, MPPAA, MULTI-EMPLOYER PLAN, WITHDRAWAL LIABILITY.

Statutory and Regulatory Reference: ERISA §§ 4041A, 4219(c)(1)(D); 29 C.F.R. Pts. 2670, 2675 (PBGC regulations).

Treatise Reference: Tax Mgmt. (BNA), No. 359, *Multiemployer Plans — Special Rules*; *Employee Benefits Law* 732-840 (1991).

master plan A qualified retirement plan operated by a financial institution or similar entity that an employer can adopt by executing a participation agreement. Generally, the sponsoring institution will obtain a favorable DETERMINATION LETTER from the IRS on the tax qualification of the overall plan. Adopting employers may then apply for individual IRS determination letters under a simplified procedure in which only the specifics of their individual adoption agreement are considered. Among the types of terms usually found in the adoption agreement are the level of plan benefits, its ELIGIBILITY requirements, its VESTING schedule, and its optional forms of benefit payment.

See DEFINED BENEFIT PLAN, DEFINED CONTRIBUTION PLAN, QUALIFIED RETIREMENT PLAN.

Statutory and Regulatory Reference: I.R.C. § 401(a) and the regulations promulgated thereunder.

Treatise Reference: See generally Tax Mgmt. (BNA), No. 360, *Qualified Plans — IRS Determination Letter Procedures*.

matching contribution (1) Any employer contribution made to a qualified retirement plan on behalf of an employee on account of a contribution by such employee, and (2) any employer contribution to the plan on behalf of an employee on account of an employee's elective pretax deferral of salary into the plan. Special nondiscrimination tests apply to matching contributions to qualified plans.

See ACTUAL CONTRIBUTION PERCENTAGE.

Statutory and Regulatory Reference: See I.R.C. §§ 401(a)(3)(C); 401(m)(4)(A); Treas. Reg. § 1.401(m)-1, *et seq.* (definition and non-discrimination tests); and ERISA § 203(a)(3)(F) and I.R.C. § 411(a)(3)(G) (rules governing forfeitures of matching contributions). *See also* IRS Notice 88-127, 1988-2 C.B. 538 (contributions that could be made at the plan sponsor's discretion if the employee contributed to the plan are considered matching contributions for tax purposes).

Case and Other Interpretive Reference: Rev. Rul. 90-105, 1990-52 I.R.B. 15 (contributions to a 401(k) plan or to another defined contribution plan as matching contributions within the meaning of I.R.C. § 401(m) are not deductible by the employer if the contributions are attributable to COMPENSATION earned by participants after the end of that taxable year).

Treatise Reference: Tax Mgmt. (BNA), No. 358, *Cash or Deferred Arrangements*; *Employee Benefits Law* 121 (1991).

maternity- or paternity-related leave of absence The absence from work of a participant in a qualified retirement plan for a period of time due to certain events relating to the birth, adoption, or caring for a child.

A qualified retirement plan may not treat certain maternity- or paternity- related absences as breaks in service for purposes of determining ELIGIBILITY for plan benefits and VESTING. Specifically, an absence cannot cause a one-year break if it occurred (1) because of the employee's pregnancy; (2) because of the birth of the employee's child; (3) because of the placement of a child with the employee in connection with the employee's adoption of the child; or (4) to care for the child for a period beginning immediately following such birth or placement.

Statutory and Regulatory Reference: ERISA §§ 202(b)(5) and 203(a)(3)(E); I.R.C. §§ 410(a)(5)(E) and (a)(6)(E); Treas. Reg. § 1.410(a)-9.

Treatise Reference: Tax Mgmt. (BNA), No. 370, *Qualified Plans — Taxation of Distributions*.

maximum age requirement A provision in a qualified defined benefit plan denying the right to participate to employees who begin work for the employer after reaching a specified age. Under ERISA as originally enacted, qualified defined benefit plans could prescribe maximum age limits for participation. Such plans could prohibit participation by employees who came to work for the employer within five years of the plan's NORMAL RETIREMENT AGE. Because FUNDING an employee's benefit under a defined benefit plan is based in part on the number of years between the date participation begins the NORMAL RETIREMENT DATE, this rule was designed to remove a disincentive to hiring older workers, i.e., the high cost of funding their benefits over a relatively short period. The Omnibus Budget Reconciliation Act of 1986 (OBRA 1986), Pub. L. No. 99-509, eliminated this rule, effective generally for plan years beginning after 1987 as to employees who have one or more hours of service in any such plan year. Under the revised rule, qualified plans may not bar an employee from participation or decrease an employee's rate of BENEFIT ACCRUAL on account of any increase in age or service.

Statutory and Regulatory Reference: ERISA § 202(a)(2); I.R.C. §§ 410(a)(2) and 411(b)(1)(G)-(H).

Treatise Reference: Tax Mgmt. (BNA), No. 351, *Pension Plans — Qualification*.

maximum benefits Under ERISA, there are limits on the total amount of annual benefits that a participant can accrue under a defined benefit plan, on the annual additions to a participant's account under a defined contribution plan, and on the total benefits a participant can accrue under all plans of the same employer. In addition to defined benefit and defined contribution plans, these limits apply to annuity plans under I.R.C. § 403(b), annuity contracts under I.R.C. § 403(a), and simplified employee pensions.

The annual limit for defined benefit plans is the lesser of a statutory dollar limit or the participant's average compensation for the three consecutive most highly compensated years of service with the employer. The statutory dollar limit is $90,000, but this figure is adjusted annually for inflation.

The annual limit for defined contribution plans is the lesser of a statutory dollar limit or 25 percent of the participant's compensation for the year. The dollar limit started at $30,000; it is not indexed for inflation until the defined benefit dollar limit has been indexed up to $120,000. At that time, the defined contribution dollar limit will be one-fourth of the defined benefit dollar limit.

If a participant is covered by both a defined contribution plan and a defined benefit plan of the same employer, a combined limit applies. A defined benefit fraction and a defined contribution fraction are added to yield the limit, known as the combined plan fraction.

The defined benefit fraction is the participant's projected annual benefit under the plan divided by the lesser of (1) 1.25 times the defined benefit plan dollar limit for the year, or (2) 1.4 times the percentage of compensation limit for the year.

The defined contribution fraction is the sum of annual additions to the participant's account divided by the lesser of (1) 1.25 times the defined contribution dollar limit in effect for the year and for each prior YEAR OF SERVICE with the employer, or (2) 1.4 times the

defined contribution plan percentage of compensation limit in effect for those years.

For a TOP-HEAVY PLAN, "1.0" is used in both fractions in place of "1.25." A top-heavy plan can regain the use of 1.25 in the fractions by paying additional minimum benefits to nonkey employees. This is not possible, however, if the plan is super top-heavy, i.e., one in which more than 90 percent of contributions or benefits inure to the benefit of key employees within the meaning of I.R.C. § 416(i).

Statutory and Regulatory Reference: I.R.C. §§ 404(j) (rule limiting employer's deduction for qualified plan contributions to amounts that may be accrued under the § 415 limits); 415(b) (defined benefit plan limits); 415(c) (defined contribution plan limits); 415(d) (cost-of-living adjustments in applicable dollar limits); 415(e) (limit applicable to certain combinations of plans); 415(c)(6) (ESOPs); 415(c)(7) (church plans); 415(l) (medical benefits provided under a qualified plan); and 416(h) (rule limiting the otherwise applicable COMBINED PLAN LIMIT in the case of certain top-heavy plans).

Treatise Reference: See Tax Mgmt. (BNA), No. 371, *Employee Plans—Deductions, Contributions, and Funding. See also* D. McGill & D. Grubbs, Jr. *Fundamentals of Private Pensions* 119 (6th ed. 1989).

maximum excess allowance   *See* BASE BENEFIT PERCENTAGE.

MCCA   *See* MEDICARE CATASTROPHIC COVERAGE ACT OF 1988.

MECM   See MODIFIED ENDOWMENT CONTRACT.

medical care For purposes of the medical expense deduction and COBRA CONTINUA-TION COVERAGE, amounts paid for the diagnosis, cure, mitigation, treatment, or prevention of disease, or for the purpose of affecting any structure or function of the body, as well as amounts paid for transportation primarily for and essential to medical care described above. It also includes amounts paid for insurance for medical care described above. In some circumstances, amounts (not in excess of $50 a night) paid for lodging while away from home primarily for and essential to medical care described above are treated as amounts paid for medical care if the medical care is provided by a physician in a licensed hospital (or its equivalent) and there is no significant element of personal pleasure, recreation, or vacation in the travel away from home. Medical care does not include anything that is merely beneficial to the general health of an individual, such as a vacation. Thus, if an employer maintains a fitness program, but the program does not relate to the relief of medical problems and generally is used by employees without regard to their physical condition, the program is not considered a program that provides medical care. However, if an employer maintains a drug treatment program intended to alleviate this specific health problem, the program is considered to provide medical care. Further, medical care does not include expenses paid for cosmetic surgery unless necessary to correct a congenital deformity, personal injury resulting from an accident or trauma, or disfiguring disease.

Statutory and Regulatory Reference: I.R.C. § 213(d); Treas. Reg. §§ 1.105-2 and -5, 1.213-1; Prop. Treas. Reg. § 1.162-26, Q&A-7(b)&(c).

Treatise Reference: Employee Benefits Law 946-54; 989-1003 (1991).

medical reimbursement plan Employer self-insured benefit plan through which amounts paid by an employer to the plan are used, directly or indirectly, to reimburse employees for expenses incurred for medical care for the employee, the spouse, or dependents. The reimbursements cannot be provided under an individual or group accident or health insurance policy or under an HMO or similar arrangement where such policy or plan involves the shifting of risk to an unrelated third party. Medical care in this context is defined in I.R.C. § 213(e). Amounts so reimbursed are excludable from the employee's gross income unless a § 213 medical expense deduction was taken on the employee's personal return for those amounts, and the employer takes a business deduction under I.R.C. §§ 162 or 212.

Example: A medical expense reimbursement plan will be treated as self-insured to the extent it involves a cost-plus, administrative services only, or other arrangement under which the employer or employees bear the risk instead of the insurance company or prepaid health plan.

Statutory and Regulatory Reference: I.R.C. §§ 105(b) and (h), 106, 162, 212, 213; Treas. Reg. §§ 1.105-2, 1.105-5 and -11, 1.106-1, 1.162-10, 1.213-1; Prop. Treas. Reg. §§ 1.125-1 and -2.

Treatise Reference: Tax Mgmt. (BNA), No. 389, *Disability and Medical Reimbursement Benefits; Employee Benefits Law* 946-54; 1050-51 (1991).

Medicare The federal government program to provide health benefits for senior citizens. Medicare Part A, automatic coverage, applies to all persons entitled to benefits; Medicare Part B, optional coverage, is paid for by those who desire the additional coverage. Part A focuses on the services rendered by institutional health providers (including hospitals and nursing homes). Those individuals eligible for Part A coverage are disability retirees (individuals deemed to be totally and permanently disabled for purposes of receiving Social Security regardless of age) and people over age 65 (individuals who have attained Social Security retirement age regardless of whether they are still employed). Part A coverage generally pays for inpatient hospital services such as room and board, drugs and biologicals administered in the hospital, appliances and equipment, supplies, diagnostic and therapeutic items, and nursing and doctor services. Part B coverage focuses on providing certain services (instead of focusing on the institution as with Part A), including physician services, out-patient hospital services, physical and occupational therapy services, diagnostic tests, ambulance services and rural health services. Part B coverage is voluntary and requires a monthly fee. Part B of the federal Medicare program is treated as an accident or health plan under I.R.C. § 106. Thus, payment of Part B premiums are not taxable to employees who are over age 65 and eligible for Medicare. However, amounts withheld from employees' compensation as payment of Part A may not be excluded from gross income as employer contributions to an accident or health plan.

See MEDICARE CATASTROPHIC COVERAGE ACT OF 1988 (MCCA).

Statutory and Regulatory Reference: Social Security Act, Title XVIII, 41 U.S.C. §§ 1395 *et seq.*; Medicare Catastrophic Coverage Act of 1988 (MCCA), P.L. No. 100-360; Technical Corrections to MCCA and Family Support Act of 1988, P.L. No. 100-485; I.R.C. §§ 106 and 3101(b).

Case and Other Interpretive Reference: Rev. Rul. 67-360, 1967-2 C.B. 71 (payment of Part B premiums not taxable to employees over age 65 and eligible for Medicare); Rev. Rul. 66-216, 1966 C.B. 100 (Part A payments not excludable from employee gross income).

Treatise Reference: Review of Medicare Supplement Insurance After Repeal of The Medicare Catastrophic Coverage Act, National Association of Insurance Commissioners (NAIC) (1990); *see also, All About Medicare*, National Underwriter (Cincinnati: The National Underwriter Co., 1990).

Medicare carve-out plan   A method of integrating private health coverage with Medicare whereby the private Medicare carve-out plan or policy applies its deductible and co-payments to the total bill to determine what amount it will reimburse. The Medicare carve-out plan then offsets or credits its payment responsibility by the amount of the Medicare payment.

Example: An individual incurs a $1,000 hospital bill. The Medicare carve-out plan has a $100 deductible, leaving a balance of $900. With a policy co-payment factor of 80 percent, the Medicare carve-out policy must reimburse $720 to the hospital. However, assuming a $500 Medicare payment, the carve-out policy is responsible for $220. Thus, the $1,000 hospital bill is paid $500 by Medicare, $220 by the Medicare carve-out policy, and $280 by the individual.

Treatise Reference: Guide To Health Insurance For People With Medicare (Buyer's Guide), National Association of Insurance Commissioners (NAIC) (1990); *Review of Medicare Supplement Insurance After Repeal of The Medicare Catastrophic Coverage Act*, NAIC (1990); Medicare Supplement Insurance Minimum Standards Model Act Model Regulations (NAIC) (1989).

Medicare Catastrophic Coverage Act of 1988 (MCCA)   The Act extending Medicare coverage to, among other things, out-patient prescription drugs and long-term nursing care. The increased tax burden imposed by MCCA to pay for the increased benefits was controversial because the costs were funded by a tax on the elderly. Thus, the Act was repealed in December 1989. Employers also opposed the maintenance of effort rule contained in the MCCA that would have required them to refund the cost of duplicative coverage created by the extension of Medicare to benefits already covered by the employer's plan or to extend additional benefits to employees.

Statutory and Regulatory Reference: Pub. L. No. 100-360 (enacting MCCA); Medicare Catastrophic Coverage Repeal Act of 1989, Pub. L. No. 101-234 (repealing MCCA).

Case and Other Interpretive Reference: Notice of the Health Care Financing Administration, 53 Fed. Reg. 49,233 (Dec. 6, 1989) (explaining the maintenance of effort rule).

Treatise Reference: See J.J. Hercenberg & W.L. Krasner, *The New Medicare Law: An Employer's Guide to Compliance and Health Plan Redesign*, A BNA Special Report (Washington: The Bureau of National Affairs, Inc., 1989); *see also Review of Medicare Supplement Insurance After Repeal of The Medicare Catastrophic Coverage Act*, National Association of Insurance Commissioners (NAIC) (1990).

Medicare supplement plan   A method of coordinating private health coverage with Medicare whereby the coverage of the private plan, called a Medicare Supplement plan or policy, in relation to Medicare coverage, is computed by reducing the health care provider's total bill by the Medicare payment and then applying the deductible and co-payment requirements (if they exist) of the Medicare Supplement policy to the unpaid balance.

Example: B has a hospital bill of $1,000. The Medicare payment to the hospital is $500. The $500 balance, which the participant is responsible for, is reduced by a $100 deductible leaving a balance of $400. If the plan has a co-payment factor of 80 percent, the plan must make a payment of $320. Thus, of the $1,000 bill, Medicare pays $500, Medicare Supplement plan pays $320, and the individual pays out of pocket $180.

See MEDICARE.

Treatise Reference: Guide To Health Insurance For People With Medicare (Buyer's Guide), National Association of Insurance Commissioners (NAIC) (1990); *Review of Medicare Supplement Insurance After Repeal of The Medicare Catastrophic Coverage Act*, NAIC (1990); Medicare Supplement Insurance Minimum Standards Model Act and Model Regulations (NAIC)(1989).

Medigap plan   A health insurance plan or policy that integrates with Medicare so that the Medigap policy pays only the Medicare deductible and co-payment amounts. Thus, the Medigap policy pays the dollar gaps in Medicare.

Treatise Reference: Guide To Health Insurance For People With Medicare (Buyer's Guide), National Association of Insurance Commissioners (NAIC) (1990); *Review of Medicare Supplement Insurance After Repeal of The Medicare Catastrophic Coverage Act*, NAIC (1990); Medicare Supplement Insurance Minimum Standards Model Act and Model Regulations (NAIC)(1989).

merged plan/merger   A consolidation of two or more plans into a single plan, ordinarily by amendment of the plan documents and transfer of the assets of the plans into a single trust. In this event, each participant in the plan must receive a benefit after the merger that is equal to or greater than the benefit he or she would have been entitled to receive immediately before the merger if the plan had been terminated.

Note that the benefit preservation rule of I.R.C. §§ 401(a)(12) and 414(l) described in the preceding paragraph also applies to asset transfers between qualified plans (transactions in which assets and liabilities are transferred between existing plans) and spin-offs (where an existing plan is divided into two or more plans).

See TERMINATION.

Statutory and Regulatory Reference: See I.R.C. §§ 401(a)(12) and 414(l); Treas. Reg. § 1.414(l)-1.

Treatise Reference: Tax Mgmt. (BNA), No. 357, *Plan Terminations and Mergers*; *Employee Benefits Law* 175-78 (1991).

MEWA *See* MULTIPLE EMPLOYER WELFARE ARRANGEMENT.

minimum accrual (1) A minimum percentage of normal retirement benefits that must be credited each year to a participant in a qualified defined benefit plan; or (2) a statutory level of benefits or contributions that must be credited to each nonkey employee in a top-heavy defined benefit or defined contribution plan.

See ACCRUAL, BACKLOADING, FRACTIONAL RULE, 133¹/₃ PERCENT RULE, 3 PERCENT RULE, TOP-HEAVY.

Statutory and Regulatory Reference: See ERISA § 204, I.R.C. § 411(b); Treas. Reg. § 1.411(b) (regular accrual rules applicable to defined benefit plans). *See also* I.R.C. § 416(c) and Treas. Reg. § 1.416-1, Q&A M-1 *et seq.* (top-heavy, minimum benefit, and contribution rules).

Treatise Reference: Tax Mgmt. (BNA), No. 351, *Pension Plans—Qualification.*

minimum benefit requirement A requirement that a TOP-HEAVY defined benefit plan provide a specified minimum benefit for all nonkey employees who are credited with at least 1,000 hours of service for the PLAN YEAR. The minimum benefit for the year is the participant's average compensation during the highest five consecutive plan years for which the plan was top-heavy, times the lesser of (1) 2 percent times the participant's number of years of service with the employer; or (2) 20 percent. The top-heavy minimum benefit is expressed as a LIFE ANNUITY, with no ancillary benefits, commencing at NOR-

MAL RETIREMENT AGE. If the participant's benefit is in a different form, it must be the ACTUARIAL EQUIVALENT of the normal form of minimum benefit.

Statutory and Regulatory Reference: I.R.C. § 416(c)(1); Treas. Reg. § 1.416-1, M-1, *et seq.*

Treatise Reference: Tax Mgmt. (BNA), No. 353, *Owner-Dominated Plans—Top-Heavy and H.R. 10 Plans.*

minimum contribution requirement (1) A requirement that a TOP-HEAVY defined contribution plan provide at least a specified ANNUAL ADDITION to the accounts of nonkey employees regardless of whether they are credited with 1,000 hours of service for the year. The minimum contribution for the year is 3 percent of compensation. If, however, the highest paid KEY EMPLOYEE receives a contribution of less than 3 percent, the minimum contribution for nonkey employees is that same percentage.

(2) A new funding standard imposed on an underfunded multiemployer plan that has entered reorganization. The minimum contribution requirement is the amount necessary to amortize the unfunded benefits of retirees over 10 years and all other unfunded vested benefits over 25 years, plus the amount necessary to pay current costs. It is subject to various adjustments and limitations under I.R.C. § 418B.

See REORGANIZATION, TOP-HEAVY/TOP-HEAVY PLAN.

Statutory and Regulatory Reference: I.R.C. §§ 416(c)(2) and 418B(b); Treas. Reg. § 1.416-1, M-1, *et seq.*

Treatise Reference: Tax Mgmt. (BNA), No. 353, *Owner-Dominated Plans—Top-Heavy and H.R. 10 Plans*, and No. 359, *Multiemployer Plans—Special Rules*; *Employee Benefits Law* 730-31 (1991).

minimum coverage rules *See* COVERAGE, AVERAGE BENEFIT PERCENTAGE TEST, RATIO TEST, 70 PERCENT TEST.

minimum funding standard The statutory minimum amount that an employer is required to contribute to qualified defined benefit, money purchase, and target benefit plans to cover all operating costs and PLAN LIABILITIES. Exempt from this standard are governmental plans, nonelecting church plans, and certain other plans. Profit-sharing, stock bonus, and cash or deferred plans, as well as certain insured plans, are not covered under the funding rules of ERISA and the Code. The minimum funding standard is applied to particular employers by means of an accounting system known as the funding standard account. Employers must satisfy the standard in each plan year. Employers failing to meet the minimum funding standard (and thereby incurring an accumulated funding deficiency) are subject to a two-tiered excise tax. Waivers from the minimum funding standard are available from the IRS if the employer demonstrates substantial business hardship.

The amount, under I.R.C. § 404, that an employer may deduct annually in respect of its contributions to money purchase or defined benefit plans is calculated based on the amount necessary to satisfy the minimum funding standard for the year.

See ACCUMULATED FUNDING DEFICIENCY, FUNDING STANDARD ACCOUNT, SUBSTANTIAL BUSINESS HARDSHIP, WAIVED FUNDING DEFICIENCY.

Statutory and Regulatory Reference: ERISA § 302, I.R.C. § 412, Treas. Reg. § 1.412 (general rule); ERISA § 305 and I.R.C. § 412(g) (elective alternative minimum funding standard) and authorities listed under ACCRUAL.

Case and Other Interpretive Reference: Rev. Rul. 79-237, 1979-2 C.B. 190 (application of the minimum funding standard to terminating plans); Rev. Rul. 81-213, 1981-2 C.B. 101 (guidelines for calculating the amortization of experience gains and losses).

Treatise Reference: See Tax Mgmt. (BNA), No. 371, *Employee Plans—Deductions, Contributions, and Funding; see also Employee Benefits Law* 135-42 (1991); D. McGill & D. Grubbs, Jr., *Fundamentals of Private Pensions* 301; 371 (6th ed. 1989).

minimum participation rule A requirement for qualified retirement plans that a plan benefit at least the lesser of: (1) 50 employees; or (2) 40 percent or more of all employees of the employer.

This rule, contained in I.R.C. § 401(a)(26), applies separately to an employer's active employees and its former employees. In addition, to the extent determined by the IRS, it applies separately to certain separate benefit structures, trusts, and other arrangements. Section 401(a)(26) may not be satisfied by aggregating separate plans, even if such plans are identical in all respects or are treated as a single plan for coverage and nondiscrimination purposes and, as such, are treated as providing nondiscriminatory employer contributions or benefits. However, an employer may elect to satisfy the requirement by testing the plans of qualified separate lines of business separately.

The general penalty for failure to comply with I.R.C. § 401(a)(26) (as well as for failure to comply with the coverage requirements of I.R.C. § 410(b)) is plan disqualification. This generally means that the plan's assets will be subject to tax and that the timing of the employer's contribution deduction and the employee's recognition of gross income will be governed by the tax rules applicable to nonqualified plans (I.R.C. §§ 83 and 402(b)), rather than the rules applicable to qualified plans. Under I.R.C. § 402(b)(2), however, if a plan fails to qualify solely because of a failure to satisfy I.R.C. §§ 410(b) and 401(a)(26), nonhighly compensated employees covered by the plan will continue to receive the benefit of the qualified plan rules and thus will only be taxed when benefits are actually distributed to them, rather than upon such benefits becoming vested, as would be the case under I.R.C. §§ 83 and 402(b)(1). Highly compensated participants, by contrast, will be taxed as if their benefits were provided under a nonqualified plan.

See COVERAGE, PARTICIPATION.

Statutory and Regulatory Reference: I.R.C. § 401(a)(26); Prop. Treas. Regs § 1.401(a)(26)-1 *et seq.*

Treatise Reference: Tax Mgmt. (BNA), No. 351, *Pension Plans—Qualification*; *Employee Benefits Law* 103 (1991).

minimum required distribution   A requirement that a qualified retirement plan provide for the payment of benefits, unless the participant elects to the contrary, no later than the 60th day following the close of the PLAN YEAR in which the latest of the following events occurs: (1) the participant attains age 65; (2) the participant completes 10 years of service with the employer; or (3) the participant separates from the employer's service.

Regardless of the participant's election, distributions from a qualified plan must begin no later than April 1 of the calendar year following the calendar year in which the employee reaches age 70½.

The entire interest of the employee must be distributed over the life of the employee, or over the lives of the employee and a designated beneficiary.

Statutory and Regulatory Reference: ERISA § 206, I.R.C. §§ 401(a)(9) and (14), Prop. Treas. Reg. § 1.401(a)(9)-1 (general rules for qualified plans); I.R.C. §§ 408(a)(6) and 408(b)(3) (IRAs); I.R.C. §§ 403(b)(10)-(11) (tax-deferred annuities); I.R.C. § 457(d) (§ 457 plans); and I.R.C. § 4974 (penalty tax on failure to make required distributions).

Treatise Reference: Tax Mgmt. (BNA), No. 370, *Qualified Plans—Taxation of Distributions*; *Employee Benefits Law* 154-57 (1991).

minimum vesting   *See* VESTING, CLIFF VESTING, GRADED VESTING, RULE OF 45 VESTING, TOP-HEAVY.

mistake of fact/mistake of law   A mistake of fact is generally an error consisting of an unawareness of the existence of a fact, or a misunderstanding as to the nature of a fact. Such an error does not include one in which all of the facts are understood, but an incorrect conclusion is reached as to the legal effect of the facts. In contrast, a mistake of law is generally an error in which a party correctly understands the facts, but comes to an incorrect conclusion as to their legal effect.

Under ERISA as originally enacted, excess contributions to a plan could be returned to the employer only within one year of payment and only if the over-contribution was attributable to a "mistake of fact." For this purpose, a mistake of fact generally meant one that was attributable to a clerical error or the employer's mistaken belief that a contract required the contributions. The Multiemployer Pension Plan Amendments Act of 1980 (MPPAA) amended ERISA § 403 with respect to multiemployer plans to allow the return of erroneously paid contributions without regard to whether the mistake was one of law or of fact. Under this standard, however, mistaken contributions to multiemployer plans must be returned within six months of a determination by the PLAN ADMINISTRATOR that the contribution was a mistaken one. For single employer plans to be able to return over-contributions to an employer, the contribution must still be one that is attributable to a mistake of fact, and the contribution must be returned to the employer within one year of the date the contribution was made.

Note that under ERISA §§ 403(c)(2)(B)-(C) and § 403(c)(3), plans may return to the employer contributions that were specifically conditioned on the qualification of the plan under I.R.C. §§ 401 or 403(a) or on their deductibility. Further, a distribution of excess employee deferrals to certain salary reduction plans, such as cash or deferred arrangements under § 401(k), made to enable the plan to comply with I.R.C. § 4979 are permitted. In the case of an excessive payment of withdrawal liability by an employer to a multiemployer plan, ERISA § 403(c)(4) permits the excess to be returned to the employer within six months after the date the payment was determined to be excessive.

See EXCLUSIVE BENEFIT RULE, MPPAA.

Statutory and Regulatory Reference: ERISA § 403(c)(2), I.R.C. § 401(a)(2).

Case and Other Interpretive Reference: For cases interpreting whether a mistake was one of fact or of law, *see Teamsters Local 639 - Employees Health Trust v. Cassidy Trucking Co.,* 646 F.2d 865 (4th Cir. 1981); *Martin v. Hamill,* 608 F.2d 725 (7th Cir. 1979); *Central States, Southeast & Southwest Areas Pension Fund v. Wholesale Produce Supply Co.,* 478 F. Supp. 884 (D. Minn.), *aff'd,* 611 F.2d 694 (8th Cir. 1979).

Treatise Reference: Employee Benefits Law 726-27 (1991).

model amendment   This is a suggested amendment issued by the IRS that, if followed, will comply with the changes to qualified plans required by a particular piece of tax legislation. A set of such model amendments was issued so that employers could conform their plans to the requirements imposed by the Tax Reform Act of 1986.

model SEP   Forms or a prototype plan provided by the IRS that, if used, will comply with the requirements for a simplified employee pension plan. These include IRS Form 5305-SEP (Simplified Employee Pension—Individual Retirement Accounts Contribution Agreement), IRS Form 5305A-SEP (Salary Reduction and Other Elective Simplified Employee Pension—Individual Retirement Accounts Contribution Agreement), and IRS Form 5306-SEP (Application for Approval of Prototype Simplified Employee Pension—SEP).

See SIMPLIFIED EMPLOYEE PENSION PLAN (SEP).

Statutory and Regulatory Reference: See I.R.C. § 408(k).

Treatise Reference: Tax Mgmt. (BNA), No. 355, IRAs and SEPs.

modified endowment contract   A life insurance contract that does not meet the seven-payment test set forth in I.R.C. § 7702A(b) or one that is received in exchange for a contract that does not meet the test. The contract will not meet the seven-payment test if the accumulated amount paid under the contract at any time during the first seven contract years exceeds the sum of the net level premiums that would have been paid on or before such time, if the contract provides for paid-up future benefits after the payment of seven level annual premiums. Withdrawals or loans from the cash value of these policies are treated as being for an annuity. Distributions, for example, withdrawals, loans, and amounts pledged, from a modified endowment contract are classified as ordinary income to the extent of any gain within the contract and thereafter as a return of capital. Also, any amount included in ordinary income generally is subject to a 10 percent penalty tax.

Example: If $500 is the level premium for a seven-pay plan, the first year premium may be $400 and the second year premium may be $600, but the first year premium cannot be $600.

See ENDOWMENT POLICY, LIFE INSURANCE CONTRACT.

Statutory and Regulatory Reference: I.R.C. § 72(e), 7702, 7702A.

Treatise Reference: Tax Mgmt. (BNA), No. 386, *Insurance- Related Compensation.*

money purchase plan   A type of defined contribution pension plan. A money purchase pension plan follows, in most respects, the defined contribution plan model (e.g., it contains individual accounts for each participant) although, for purposes of the Internal Revenue Code's minimum FUNDING rules, these plans are treated as pension plans. The employer under a money purchase plan obligates itself to make annual contributions that are not based on profits. The contributions are divided among participants' accounts according to a formula contained in the plan in the same manner as under a profit-sharing plan. A participant's benefit is the annuity or similar benefit that can be purchased with the account balance upon retirement.

See HYBRID PLAN, MINIMUM FUNDING STANDARD.

Statutory and Regulatory Reference: See generally I.R.C. §§ 401(a) and 414(i); I.R.C. § 401(a)(27)(B) (designation of defined contribution plan as money purchase pension plan); and I.R.C. § 401(a)(22) (employee put option for employer securities).

Treatise Reference: See Tax Mgmt. (BNA), No. 351, *Pension Plans—Qualification; see also Employee Benefits Law* 77-79 (1991).

mortality assumption   An actuarial assumption under a qualified defined benefit plan, concerning the rate at which covered employees are expected to die over a given period.

See ACTUARIAL ASSUMPTIONS.

MPPAA (Multiemployer Pension Plan Amendment Act of 1980)   MPPAA removed multiemployer plans from the plan termination insurance system governing multiple and single-employer plans and substituted a system imposing liability for certain unfunded vested benefits when an employer partially or totally withdrawals from a multiemployer plan. The scheme sets forth a mechanism to guarantee nonforfeitable benefits of multiemployer plans that applies when the plan becomes insolvent, rather than when the plan is terminated as under SEPPAA. Under MPPAA, a multiemployer plan is one in which more than one employer must make a contribution to a plan that is maintained pursuant to a collective bargaining agreement.

MPPAA also amended ERISA and the Internal Revenue Code to enhance the funding requirements for multiemployer pension plans and to provide new rules for financially distressed multiemployer plans.

See COMPLETE WITHDRAWAL, DISTRESS TERMINATION, MULTIEMPLOYER PLAN, PARTIAL WITHDRAWAL, SEPPAA, STANDARD TERMINATION.

Statutory and Regulatory Reference: Pub. L. No. 96-364 (1980). ERISA §§ 3(37)(A), 4041A, 4201(a).

Case and Other Interpretative Reference: PBGC v. R.A. Gray, 467 U.S. 717, 5 EB Cases 1545 (1984) (confirming the constitutionality of MPPAA).

Treatise Reference: Tax Mgmt. (BNA), No. 357, *Plan Terminations and Mergers; Employee Benefits Law* 729-839 (1991).

multiemployer plan   Under ERISA, a multiemployer plan is one that requires contributions from more than one employer and is maintained pursuant to a collective bargaining agreement. They are also known as jointly administered or Taft-Hartley plans. Note that MPPAA made substantial changes to ERISA and the Internal Revenue Code which had the effect of enhancing the funding requirements for multiemployer pension plans, providing new rules for multiemployer plans, and revising the termination insurance provisions applicable to these plans.

See MPPAA, WITHDRAWAL LIABILITY.

Statutory and Regulatory Reference: ERISA §§ 3(37)(A), 4041.

multiple employer plan   A qualified retirement plan maintained by more than one employer. Unlike a multiemployer plan, a multiple employer plan is not collectively bargained. The employers in a multiple employer plan need not be related. Such a plan and its trust will be qualified if all requirements for a qualified plan are satisfied.

Statutory and Regulatory Reference: I.R.C. § 401(a); Treas. Reg. § 1.401-1(d).

Treatise Reference: See Tax Mgmt. (BNA), No. 350, *Plan Selection — Pension and Profit-Sharing Plans; see also Employee Benefits Law* 27 (1991).

multiple employer welfare arrangement (MEWA)   An employee welfare benefit plan, or arrangement, that provides any benefit described under ERISA § 3(1) (defining employee welfare benefit plan or welfare plan) to the employees of two or more employers (including one or more self-employed individuals), or to their beneficiaries, except that the term does not include any plan or arrangement that is established or maintained (1) under or pursuant to one or more collective bargaining agreements, or (2) by a rural electric cooperative. State insurance laws may apply to fully insured MEWAs in some instances through an exemption to the ERISA preemption provisions. MEWAs that are not fully insured may be subject to ERISA Title I provisions and to any state insurance laws.

Statutory and Regulatory Reference: ERISA §§ 3(40), 514(b)(6) (exemption from ERISA's preemption rules); 514(b)(6)(D) (definition of fully insured).

Case and Other Interpretive Reference: See DOL Op. Letter 90-22A (May 15, 1990) (Labor Department declines to exercise authority to prescribe regulations exempting MEWAs from state regulation). *See also* DOL Op. Letter 90-18A (Aug. 16, 1991) (discussing the scope of state regulation).

Treatise Reference: Employee Benefits Law 558-59 (1991).

N

NAIC *See* NATIONAL ASSOCIATION OF IN-
SURANCE COMMISSIONERS

named fiduciary *See* FIDUCIARY/FIDU-
CIARY DUTY.

**National Association of Insurance Com-
missioners (NIAC)** A national organization made up of state insurance regulators to
which insurance companies provide, among
other things, an annual report containing a
detailed statement of what is in their
portfolios. Consumers interested in an
evaluation of the financial condition of an
insurance company may contact this organization.

Treatise Reference: NAIC Publications,
P.O. Box 419038, Department 42, Kansas
City, Missouri 64183-0042.

net unrealized appreciation (NUA)
This term is applied to securities of an
employer corporation that are distributed by
a qualified retirement plan. The amount of
NUA is the market value of the securities at
the time of the distribution minus the plan's
basis in the securities. If employer securities
with NUA are distributed in a total distribution, the recipient can exclude all of the NUA
from income. If the distribution is partial, a
portion of the NUA may be excluded.

Statutory and Regulatory Reference: I.R.C.
§§ 402(a) and (e)(4)(J); Treas. Reg.
§ 1.402(a)-1(b).

no-additional-cost services Services
provided by an employer to an employee for
the personal use of the employee, his or her
spouse or dependent child (or in the case of
air transportation, the employee's parents), at
no charge, at a reduced price, or with total or
partial rebate of the price charged. The Internal Revenue Code provides for an exclusion
from gross income for these amounts
provided: (1) the employer offers the same
service for sale to nonemployee customers in
the ordinary course of a line of business of the
employer; (2) the employee performs substantial services in that same line of business;
and (3) the employer has no substantial additional cost providing the service to the
employee (including foregone revenue).

Example: Eligible for treatment as no-additional-cost services are excess capacity services such as hotel accommodations,
transportation by aircraft, train, or bus, and
so on, and telephone services. Services that
are not eligible for such treatment are nonex-
cess capacity services such as the facilitation

by a stock brokerage firm of the purchase of stock.

Statutory and Regulatory Reference: I.R.C. §§ 132(a)(1), (f), and (i); Treas. Reg. § 1.132-1T and -2T.

Treatise Reference: Tax Mgmt. (BNA), No. 394, *Employee Fringe Benefits*; *Employee Benefits Law* 982 (1991).

noncompliance period For COBRA continuation coverage purposes, with respect to a failure of a group health plan to meet the continuation coverage requirements, the period beginning on the date that the failure first occurs and ending on the earlier of the date the failure is corrected or the date that is six months after the last day in the applicable period of coverage under I.R.C. § 4980B(f) (18 to 36 months depending on the qualifying event). Excise taxes are imposed during this period unless the failure is inadvertent or special grace period rules apply.

See COBRA, CONTINUATION COVERAGE, QUALIFYING EVENT.

Statutory and Regulatory Reference: I.R.C. § 4980B(a)(b)(f).

Treatise Reference: Tax Mgmt. (BNA), No. 389, *Disability and Medical Reimbursement Benefits*; *Employee Benefits Law* 1001 (1991).

noncontributory plan A retirement-type plan that does not require employee contributions as a precondition to participation or benefit accrual.

Treatise Reference: See generally Tax Mgmt. (BNA), No. 351, *Pension Plans—Qualification*, and No. 352, *Profit-Sharing Plans—Qualification*.

nonelective contribution Employer contributions, other than matching contributions, to a § 401(k) plan that the employee may not elect to receive in cash or other benefits instead of being contributed to the plan.

See MATCHING CONTRIBUTION, SECTION 401(k) PLAN.

Statutory and Regulatory Reference: I.R.C. § 401(k); Treas. Reg. § 1.401(k)-1(g)(5).

Treatise Reference: Tax Mgmt. (BNA), No. 358, *Cash or Deferred Arrangements*.

nonforfeitable/nonforfeitable benefit
For federal income tax purposes, a benefit is generally considered nonforfeitable when there is no longer a risk of not receiving it. To be nonforfeitable, the right to receive the benefit must not be conditioned on any subsequent event, subsequent performance, or subsequent forbearance. Benefits under a qualified retirement-type plan must become nonforfeitable in accordance with certain statutory vesting schedules.

Further, upon or attainment of normal retirement age, participants' benefits become vested regardless of what level of vesting the participant is entitled to under the applicable statutory schedule.

For purposes of Title IV of ERISA, ERISA § 4001(a)(8) defines nonforfeitable benefit to mean a benefit for which a participant has satisfied the requirements for entitlement under the plan or under ERISA other than (1) submission of a formal application; (2) retirement; (3) completing a required waiting period; or (4) death (in the case of a plan that returns all or part of a participant's total employee contributions upon the participant's death), regardless of whether the benefit later may be reduced or suspended by plan amendment, the occurrence of a condition, or the operation of ERISA or the Internal Revenue Code.

See VESTING.

Statutory and Regulatory Reference: ERISA § 203(a) and I.R.C. § 411(a)(8) (vesting at normal retirement age); ERISA § 203(a)(3) (minimum vesting rules for non-top-heavy qualified retirement plans); I.R.C. § 411(a)(2); I.R.C. § 411(d)(3) (vesting upon partial or complete termination); I.R.C. § 416(b) (vesting rules for top-heavy plans); Treas. Reg. §§ 1.411(a)-4(a) and 1.411(a)-4T(a).

Treatise Reference: See Tax Mgmt. (BNA), No. 351, *Pension Plans – Qualification*; *Employee Benefits Law* 377 (1991).

nonkey employee   A participant in a qualified retirement-type plan who is not a key employee for purposes of the Internal Revenue Code's top-heavy rules.

See KEY EMPLOYEE, TOP-HEAVY.

Statutory and Regulatory Reference: I.R.C. § 416(i)(2); Treas. Reg. § 1.416-1, Q&A T-12.

Treatise Reference: Tax Mgmt. (BNA), No. 353, *Owner-Dominated Plans – Top-Heavy and H.R. 10 Plans.*

nonlapse restriction   *See*   LAPSE RESTRICTION.

nonqualified cash or deferred arrangement   A cash or deferred arrangement that fails to meet one or more of the requirements for qualification under I.R.C. § 401(k). The primary tax consequence of a nonqualified cash or deferred arrangement is that the employee is taxed on any elective contribution at the time the employee would have received the contribution had it not been contributed to the plan.

See SECTION 401(k) PLAN.

Statutory and Regulatory Reference: I.R.C. § 401(k); Treas. Reg. § 1.401(k)-1(a)(5).

Treatise Reference: Tax Mgmt. (BNA), No. 358, *Cash or Deferred Arrangements.*

nonqualified deferred compensation plan   Any plan in which the employee is not currently taxed on compensation earned but which does not meet one or more of the In-

ternal Revenue Code's requirements for a qualified retirement plan. Such plans include excess benefit plans, nonqualified stock options, top-hat plans, Rabbi trusts, and § 457 plans. A nonqualified plan can be subject to ERISA requirements if it is considered "funded" for ERISA purposes.

In the years since the enactment of ERISA, Congress has generally imposed additional requirements on qualified retirement plans, making it more costly in some cases for employers to maintain qualified plans. These changes have also restricted qualified plans in their ability to direct benefits to highly compensated employees. Nonqualified arrangements, however, can avoid many of these restrictions. For example, nonqualified arrangements generally allow an employer to benefit the employees it chooses in the amounts it chooses, without regard to the nondiscrimination rules applicable to qualified plans. In addition, if the nonqualified arrangement comes within one of the recognized exceptions, such as that provided for top-hat or excess plans, or if the arrangement is not funded, it will be exempt from Title I of ERISA, including the reporting and disclosure rules. Finally, although nonqualified plan assets are not held in a tax-exempt trust (qualified plan assets are), investing in tax-exempt investments such as municipal bonds and variable annuity contracts (where the inside buildup is tax-free) can produce a similar result.

Nonqualified plans also offer employers the advantage of increased flexibility. If the employer uses a funded arrangement, a variety of vehicles are available, including trusts, escrow accounts, time deposits, brokerage accounts, and insurance products. While funded arrangements help secure the employer's promise to pay benefits, unfunded arrangements can also provide attractive benefits. Funded, for this purpose includes arrangements where assets are set aside for employees, whether in a trust, as a bookkeeping account, or otherwise, but, because they are subject to the claims of certain of the employer's creditors, are considered unfunded for purposes of the Code and ERISA.

I.R.C. § 83 governs the deductibility by employers and the inclusion in gross income by employees (and independent contractors) of payments under nonqualified deferred compensation arrangements. Until the time the employer becomes entitled to a deduction and the employee must include the amount involved in income, I.R.C. § 83(a)(1) treats the employer as the owner of the property for tax purposes. Thus, during this period, the income earned by the property will be taxable to the employer.

I.R.C. § 83(a) provides that if, in connection with the performance of services, property is transferred to anyone other than the person to whom such services are rendered, the excess of the transferred property's fair market value at that time over the amount the employee paid for it (if any) is included in the employee's gross income when the property becomes freely transferable by the employee or not subject to a substantial risk of forfeiture.

In determining FAIR MARKET VALUE under I.R.C. § 83, restrictions on the property other than restrictions that, by their terms, will never lapse are disregarded.

For a nonqualified deferred compensation arrangement to be taxed under I.R.C. § 83, it must call for the transfer of property. Property for § 83 purposes includes real and personal property other than money or an unfunded and unsecured promise to pay money or property in the future. Treas. Reg. § 1.83-3(e) provides that property also includes a beneficial interest in assets (including money) which are transferred or set aside from the claims of the employer's creditors.

The regulations cite as examples of property that may be considered set aside from the claims of the employer's creditors property

that has been transferred to a trust or escrow account on behalf of an employee. Not every transfer of property to a trust or escrow arrangement will result in the employer's promise to pay being considered to have been set aside from the employer's creditors, however. In the Rabbi trust area, for instance, property is often transferred into a trust or escrow account with the stipulation that it is to remain subject to the claims of the employer's creditors and that the employee, while the trust or escrow arrangement is in effect, is to have no rights superior to those of a general creditor of the employer. The IRS has treated such arrangements, when appropriately drafted, as being unfunded for tax purposes, and hence not property within the meaning of § 83.

In the case of a life insurance contract, retirement income contract, endowment contract, or other contract providing life insurance protection, only the cash surrender value is considered to be property.

See EXCESS BENEFIT PLAN, FUNDED PLAN, NONQUALIFIED STOCK OPTIONS, QUALIFIED RETIREMENT PLAN, RABBI TRUST, RESTRICTED PROPERTY, TOP-HAT PLAN.

Statutory and Regulatory Reference: ERISA §§ 3(36), 4(b)(5), 201(2), 301(a)(3)(9), and 401(a)(1); I.R.C. §§ 83 and 451; Treas. Reg. § 1.83(a)-1 *et seq.*

Treatise Reference: See Tax Mgmt. (BNA), No. 385, *Deferred Compensation Arrangements*; Tax Mgmt. (BNA), No. 384, *Restricted Property—Section 83. See also Employee Benefits Law* 28-29; 235-38 (1991).

nonqualified stock options   A STOCK OPTION granted to an employee as a part of compensation that does not meet the requirements for qualification under the Internal Revenue Code. If the option has a readily ascertainable market value on the date it is granted, the employee is taxed on the difference between the value of the stock on the date the option is granted and the option price. If the option does not have a readily ascertainable market value on the date it is granted, the employee is not taxed until the option is exercised. At that time, the employee is taxed on the difference between the stock's FAIR MARKET VALUE when the option is exercised, and the option price paid by the employee.

Statutory and Regulatory Reference: See I.R.C. § 83; Treas. Reg. § 1.83-7.

Treatise Reference: Tax Mgmt. (BNA), No. 383, *Nonstatutory Stock Options*.

normal cost   Used in determining the minimum funding for a qualified plan, this is the annual cost of future pension benefits and administrative expenses assigned, under an actuarial cost method, to years subsequent to a particular VALUATION date of the plan. Normal cost must be expressed as (1) a level dollar amount or percentage of pay computed from year to year on an individual or aggregate basis, or (2) an amount equal to the present value of benefits accruing under the method for a particular PLAN YEAR.

See ACTUARIAL COST METHOD, FUNDING.

Statutory and Regulatory Reference: See ERISA § 3(28) (definition); I.R.C. § 412(b)(2)(A); Treas. Reg. § 1.412(c)(3)-1. *See also* ERISA § 302(b)(2)(A) (funding of normal costs).

Treatise Reference: Tax Mgmt. (BNA), No. 371, *Employee Plans – Deductions, Contributions, and Funding*.

normal retirement age (general definition)   Under a qualified retirement plan, the earlier of (a) the age specified in the plan as the normal retirement age, or (b) the later of age 65 or the fifth anniversary of the commencement of an employee's participation in the plan.

See NORMAL RETIREMENT AGE (INTEGRATION DEFINITION).

Statutory and Regulatory Reference: See I.R.C. § 415(b)(8); Treas. Reg. § 1.411(a)-7(b)(1). *See also* the definition in Title I of ERISA (§ 3(24)), which retains the Internal Revenue Code's language as in effect under the Omnibus Budget Reconciliation Act of 1986 (OBRA 1986), Pub. L. No. 99-509.

Case and Other Interpretive Reference: See Rev. Rul. 71-147, 1971-1 C.B. 116 (the NORMAL RETIREMENT AGE in a pension or annuity plan is the lowest age specified in the plan at which the employee has the right to retire without the employer's consent and receive retirement benefits based on service to the date of retirement at the full rate set forth in the plan; while a plan may use a different age than age 65, this is considered the customary age at which employees retire). *See also* Rev. Rul. 80-276, 1980-2 C.B. 131 (profit-sharing plan may provide for a normal retirement age that is less than age 65 and may distribute benefits even though participants have not terminated service at that time); Rev. Rul. 81-211, 1981-2 C.B. 99 (plan providing that participants' employer-derived benefits will become nonforfeitable on a date that occurs after normal retirement age causes plan to fail to satisfy the I.R.C. § 411(a) VESTING rules).

Treatise Reference: See Tax Mgmt. (BNA), No. 351, *Pension Plans – Qualification*, and No. 352, *Profit-Sharing Plans – Qualification*. *See also* D. McGill & D. Grubbs, Jr., *Fundamentals of Private Pensions* 129 (6th ed. 1989).

normal retirement age, Social Security (integration definition)   The age used as an individual's retirement age under § 216(l) of the Social Security Act, except that § 216(l) is applied without regard to the age increase factor, and as if the early retirement age under the Social Security Act were 62.

See INTEGRATION (SOCIAL SECURITY), SOCIAL SECURITY RETIREMENT AGE.

Statutory and Regulatory Reference: I.R.C. § 415(b)(8) and Treas. Reg. § 1.401(l)-1(c)(30).

Treatise Reference: Tax Mgmt. (BNA), No. 356, *Qualified Plans — Integration.*

normal retirement benefit   The periodic benefit payable under a qualified retirement plan upon early retirement (if any) or at normal retirement age, whichever is greater. The normal retirement benefit is determined without regard to medical benefits payable under the plan and without regard to plan disability benefits other than a qualified disability benefit. A qualified disability benefit is one that does not exceed the benefit to which a participant would be entitled if he or she separated from the employer's service at normal retirement age. A plan's normal retirement benefit is also determined without regard to certain Social Security supplements (payments provided under a plan that terminate when the employee becomes eligible to receive Social Security benefits).

Statutory and Regulatory Reference: ERISA § 3(22); I.R.C. § 411(a)(9); Treas. Reg. § 1.401(a)-8.

Treatise Reference: Tax Mgmt. (BNA), No. 351, *Pension Plans — Qualification* and No. 352, *Profit-Sharing Plans — Qualification.*

normal retirement date   The date defined in a plan on which a participant's right to a NORMAL RETIREMENT BENEFIT becomes NONFORFEITABLE. This date may not be later than NORMAL RETIREMENT AGE, since an employee's right to a normal retirement benefit must be nonforfeitable upon attaining normal retirement age.

See NORMAL RETIREMENT AGE.

Statutory and Regulatory Reference: I.R.C. § 411(a); Treas. Reg. § 1.411(a).

Case and Other Interpretive Reference: Rev. Rul. 81-211, 1981-2 C.B. 98.

O

OASDI Old Age Survivors' and Disability Insurance. The largest single component of the Social Security benefit structure, this insurance, funded by Social Security payroll taxes, supplies the retirement-type benefits under Social Security (the other component, hospital insurance, pays for Medicare). Note that, in the formula for determining whether a qualified defined contribution plan integrates with Social Security under the permitted disparity rules, the old age insurance portion of the OASDI tax rate is one component of the testing formula.

See INTEGRATION (SOCIAL SECURITY), SOCIAL SECURITY TAX.

Statutory and Regulatory Reference: I.R.C. § 401(l)(2)(A)(ii)(II).

Treatise Reference: Tax Mgmt. (BNA), No. 356, *Qualified Plans – Integration.*

OCONUS Term meaning outside the continental United States, used for assigning values to certain fringe benefits such as travel and meal allowances.

Statutory and Regulatory Reference: I.R.C. §§ 162 and 274.

Case and Other Interpretive Reference: Rev. Proc. 90-38, 1990-2 C.B. 363.

officer For purposes of the top-heavy and nondiscrimination rules applicable to qualified retirement plans, an executive who is in regular and continued service of the employer who has the level of authority and discretion typically associated with corporate officers. Only individuals performing actual officer functions are considered officers for these purposes, regardless of job title. An example might be the officers of a bank where many individuals have officer titles but do not have the discretionary authority over major corporate matters generally associated with corporate officers. Similarly, an employee who lacks an officer title but performs officer duties will be considered an officer. Officers are not limited to corporations; individuals performing officer functions for unincorporated entities are considered officers.

For top-heavy purposes, officers with annual compensation in excess of 50 percent of the I.R.C. § 415(b)(1)(A) dollar limit applicable to defined benefit plans (this dollar limit is $90,000 as indexed for inflation) are considered key employees. Officers meeting this compensation test in the current PLAN YEAR or the immediately preceding one are also considered highly compensated employees in applying the Internal Revenue Code's nondiscrimination rules.

For both top-heavy and discrimination purposes, the Code limits the number of employees who may be considered officers to no more than (1) 50 employees or, (2) if lesser, the greater of three or 10 percent of employees.

Example: Corporation A has 450 employees, 60 of whom perform officer duties. Under the general 50-employee limit, no more than 50 of these individuals will be considered officers under the top-heavy or nondiscrimination rules. Further, 10 percent of all employees in this case is 45. Since this is less than 50 and greater than three, the second prong of the test also applies. Thus, 45 of the 60 (the greater of 10 percent or three) will be considered officers. The 45 who will be counted will be the 45 earning the highest compensation.

See HIGHLY COMPENSATED EMPLOYEE, KEY EMPLOYEE, TOP-HEAVY.

Statutory and Regulatory Reference: See I.R.C. § 416(i)(1)(A)(i) and Treas. Reg. § 1.416-1, Q&A T-13 (top-heavy definition). *See also* I.R.C. § 414(q)(1)(D) and Treas. Reg. § 1.414(q)-1T (nondiscrimination definition). *See also* I.R.C. § 414(q)(5) and Treas. Reg. § 1.414(q)-1T, Q&A A-10 (nondiscrimination rules); Treas. Reg. § 1.416-1, Q&A T-15 (providing that unincorporated entities may have officers).

Case and Other Interpretive Reference: Rev. Rul. 80-134, 1980-2 C.B. 52 (employee who had an officer title but generally did not perform officer functions not considered an officer for purposes of the general nondiscrimination rule of pre-Tax Reform Act of 1986, I.R.C. § 401(a)(4).

Treatise Reference: Tax Mgmt. (BNA), No. 351, *Pension Plans — Qualification* (nondiscrimination rules), No. 353, *Owner-Dominated Plans — Top-Heavy and H.R. 10 Plans.*

offset plan   A Social Security-integrated defined benefit plan whose benefit formula provides that a portion of an employee's employer-derived benefit will be reduced, or offset, by an offset allowance. This allowance may be an amount specified directly in the plan or a specified percentage of a participant's FINAL AVERAGE COMPENSATION. Note that only defined benefit plans may integrate using the offset method; integrated defined contribution plans must use the excess method.

Example: A defined benefit plan funded solely by employer contributions provides a NORMAL RETIREMENT BENEFIT of 2 percent of a participant's AVERAGE ANNUAL COMPENSATION for each year of credited service, reduced by one-fourth of 1 percent (per year) of his or her final average compensation up to his or her COVERED COMPENSATION.

See DEFINED BENEFIT EXCESS PLAN, DEFINED CONTRIBUTION EXCESS PLAN, INTEGRATION (SOCIAL SECURITY).

Statutory and Regulatory Reference: I.R.C. §§ 401(l)(3)(B) and (4); Prop. Treas. Reg. § 1.401(l)-1(b)(4).

Treatise Reference: Tax Mgmt. (BNA), No. 356, *Qualified Plans — Integration*; *Employee Benefits Law* 120 (1991).

old age insurance   One of the subcomponents of the Old Age Survivors and Disability Insurance (OADSI) portion of the federal Social Security (FICA) tax on employers and employees.

See OASDI.

133¹⁄₃ percent rule   One of three permissible methods of testing a defined benefit plan to determine whether it discriminates in favor of highly compensated employees by excessively backloading benefit accruals (deferring them to the later years of an employee's career). (The other two methods are the fractional and 3 percent rules). A qualified defined benefit plan must pass at least one of the three tests.

The 133⅓ percent rule compares all earlier years of a participant's participation in a plan to all subsequent years to limit excessive backloading. Under this method, a plan must satisfy two requirements: (1) The plan's accrued benefit at NORMAL RETIREMENT AGE must equal the plan's NORMAL RETIREMENT BENEFIT; and (2) The annual rate at which any individual who is, or could be, a participant can accrue retirement benefits payable at normal retirement age must not be more than 133⅓ percent of the annual rate at which the individual can accrue benefits in any prior PLAN YEAR.

Thus, under this test, when a plan's accrual rate increases in a later year, that rate must be compared with all prior years of a participant's participation to see whether the benefit a participant accrued in the later year is more than 133⅓ percent of the benefit in any earlier year. This general rule is subject to certain caveats. These are:

(1) Any plan amendment that is in effect for the current year is treated as having been in effect for all other plan years.

(2) The fact that benefits under the plan may be payable to certain employees before NORMAL RETIREMENT AGE is disregarded.

(3) Any change in a plan's accrual rate that does not apply to any individual who is or could be a participant in the current year is disregarded.

(4) Social Security, compensation, and all other factors used in computing benefits are treated as remaining constant in all future years.

Under the 133⅓ percent method, as under the 3 percent method, deeming compensation to remain constant can result in BACKLOADING due to increases in compensation in the later years of an employee's career. The following example illustrates the application of the 133⅓ percent rule.

Example: A defined benefit plan provides for accruals at a rate of 1.25 percent for the first 15 years, 1.5 percent for the next 15, and 1.75 percent thereafter. Testing the highest possible accrual year against all earlier years will show that the plan, as drafted, would fail the 133⅓ percent test. This is so because 1.25 percent × 1.33 = 1.66 percent, and the plan provides for accruals at a level higher than 1.66 percent of compensation in years 30 and thereafter. If the plan provided a benefit in those years of 1.66 percent of compensation or less, it would pass the test. Note that, if the plan started out by providing 1.25 percent for the first 15 years and 1.5 percent thereafter, but later was amended to provide the benefit structure described above, the amendment increasing benefits would be treated as if it were in effect for all prior years and the plan would pass the test.

See ACCRUAL, BACKLOADING, FRACTIONAL RULE, 3 PERCENT RULE.

Statutory and Regulatory Reference: ERISA § 204(b)(1)(B); I.R.C. § 411(b)(1)(B); Treas. Reg. § 1.411(b)-1(b)(2).

Treatise Reference: See Tax Mgmt. (BNA), No. 351, *Pension Plans — Qualification; see also Employee Benefits Law* 123-24 (1991).

one-year break in service *See* BREAK IN SERVICE.

on-premises athletic facility Employee fitness facilities that are located on the premises of the employer and are operated by the employer. These types of facilities are excludable from the gross income of employees provided that substantially all of the facility's use is by employees.

Statutory and Regulatory Reference: I.R.C. § 132(h)(5).

Treatise Reference: Employee Benefits Law 984 (1991).

opinion letters Letters issued by the Department of Labor in response to inquiries from individuals or organizations that are directly or indirectly affected by ERISA concerning the application of ERISA to certain acts and transactions. These letters may be issued in one of two forms: an information letter, or an advisory opinion.

ERISA Proc. 76-1 defines an information letter as a written statement that does no more than call attention to a well-established interpretation or principle of the Act, without applying it to a specific factual situation.

The same ERISA procedure defines an advisory opinion as "a written statement issued to an individual or organization, or to the authorized representative of such individual or organization ... that interprets and applies the Act to a specific factual situation."

Case and Other Interpretive Reference: ERISA Proc. 76-1, 41 Fed. Reg. 36,281 (Aug. 19, 1976).

Treatise Reference: Employee Benefits Law 450-55 (1991).

owner-employee An employee who (1) owns the entire interest in an unincorporated trade or business; or (2) in a partnership, owns more than 10 percent of either the capital or profits interest. Qualified retirement plans benefiting one or more owner-employees are subject to certain additional qualification requirements, including, e.g., a requirement that benefits provided non-owner employees be no less favorable for those of owner-employees and that plan contributions on behalf of an owner-employee be made only from the individual's trade or business which generated the EARNED INCOME on which the contributions are based.

See KEOGH PLAN, SELF-EMPLOYED INDIVIDUAL.

Statutory and Regulatory Reference: See I.R.C. § 401(c)(3) (definition of owner-employee). *See also* I.R.C. § 401(d) and Treas. Reg. § 1.401-12 (outlining additional qualification requirements). Note, however, that the IRS as of the end of 1990 had not amended the above-referenced regulation to reflect legislative changes enacted by the Tax Equity and Fiscal Responsibility Act of 1982 (TEFRA), Pub. L. No. 97-248 and subsequent legislation.

Case and Other Interpretive Reference: See Rev. Rul. 78-404, 1978-2 C.B. 156 (owner-employee who has reached age 59$1/2$ may roll-over a qualifying lump-sum distribution to an IRA). *See also* Rev. Rul. 81-113, 1981-1 C.B. 176 (premature distribution to owner-employee will not affect qualification of plan as to remaining participants).

Treatise Reference: Tax Mgmt. (BNA), No. 353, *Owner-Dominated Plans — Top-Heavy and H.R. 10 Plans.*

P

parity, rule of For qualified retirement plans, a rule providing that a nonvested (in employer-derived benefits) former participant who returns to employment after a BREAK IN SERVICE need not be credited with prior service if the number of consecutive one-year breaks in service equals or exceeds the greater of five or the participant's total number of years of pre-break service. A qualified plan seeking to use this rule must provide for it in its PLAN DOCUMENT.

Note that any vesting whatsoever in a participant's employer-derived benefit means that a plan may not use the rule of parity to deny an employee credit for his or her pre-break service.

Example: D, a participant in a qualified retirement plan that uses the rule of parity, completes four years of service and then leaves to go to work for another employer. At that time D is not vested employer-derived benefits. D then incurs six consecutive one-year breaks in service before returning to work for the original employer. The original employer's plan need not credit D with pre-break service upon D's return because the greater of five or the number of consecutive years of break (six) equals or exceeds D's total number of years of pre-break service (four).

Statutory and Regulatory Reference: ERISA § 203(b)(3)(C), I.R.C. § 411(a)(6)(D); Treas. Reg. § 1.411(a)-6(c)(iii). Note that the regulation states the rule as it existed before the Retirement Equity Act of 1984 (REA), Pub. L. No. 97-34. REA imposed the five-year component of the statutory formula, effectively requiring that at least five consecutive one-year breaks in service occur before an employee could lose credit for prior service.

Treatise Reference: Tax Mgmt. (BNA), No. 351, *Pension Plans — Qualification*; *Employee Benefits Law* 88-89 (1991).

partial termination The ending of a portion of a qualified plan because of decreases in VESTING, accrual of benefits, or restrictions on ELIGIBILITY for participation. When a partial termination occurs, employees' accrued benefits under the terminated portion of the plan, to the extent funded, must become completely NONFORFEITABLE.

The IRS is to determine whether a partial termination has occurred (and, if so, the time thereof) based on the surrounding facts and circumstances. Under Treasury regulations, these facts and circumstances include: the exclusion, due to a plan amendment or severance by the employer, of a group of employees who have previously been covered by the plan; and plan amendments that adversely affect the rights of employees to vest in their plan benefits.

If a defined benefit plan ceases or decreases future benefit accruals, a partial termination is considered to occur if, as a result of the cessation or decrease, a potential reversion to the employer, or employers, maintaining the plan is created or increased. If no reversion is created or increased, a partial termination is not considered to have occurred due to the cessation or decrease.

A profit-sharing or stock bonus plan may be found to have partially (or completely) terminated due to a complete discontinuance of employer contributions thereto.

See TERMINATION.

Statutory and Regulatory Reference: I.R.C. § 411(d)(3); Treas. Reg. § 1.411(d)-2(a)(1)(b).

Case and Other Interpretive Reference: John Wiley & Sons v. Livingston, 376 U.S. 543 (1964) (parties free to negotiate irrevocable commitments to provide welfare benefits); *Monar v. Wibbelt,* 789 F.2d 422 (3d Cir. 1986) (welfare benefits are not vested as a matter of federal law); *District 29, UMWA v. Royal Coal Co.,* 768 F.2d 588 (4th Cir. 1985) (language of contract unambiguously granted employer right to terminate retiree welfare benefits); Rev. Rul. 81-27, 1981-1 C.B. 228 (partial termination occurred when employer discharged 95 of 165 employees pursuant to the dissolution of one division of its business).

Treatise Reference: Tax Mgmt. (BNA), No. 357, *Plan Terminations and Mergers; Employee Benefits Law* 113; 1360-61 (1991).

partial withdrawal   Under the Multiemployer Pension Plan Amendments Act of 1980 (MPPAA), a partial withdrawal by an employer from a multiemployer plan occurs when there is a 70 percent decline in the employer's contribution base units (CBUs), i.e., the units on which an employers' contribution obligation has been calculated (such as work days over a three-year period). The closing of an employer facility or the termina-

tion of a collective bargaining agreement can result in a partial cessation of the employer's contribution obligation, giving rise to withdrawal liability.

See COMPLETE WITHDRAWAL, CONTRIBUTION BASE UNITS, MPPAA, MULTIEMPLOYER PLAN, WITHDRAWAL LIABILITY.

Statutory and Regulatory Reference: ERISA §§ 205(a)(2), 4001(a)(11), 4205.

Treatise Reference: Tax Mgmt. (BNA), No. 357, *Plan Terminations and Mergers,* and No. 359, *Multiemployer Plans — Special Rules; Employee Benefits Law* 765-68 (1991).

participant   An employee or former employee of an employer, or any member or former member of an employee organization, who is or may become eligible to receive a benefit of any type from an employee benefit plan that covers employees of such employer or members of such organization, or whose beneficiaries may be eligible to receive any such benefits.

See ACTIVE PARTICIPANT, AGE AND SERVICE RULES.

Statutory and Regulatory Reference: ERISA § 3(7).

Treatise Reference: See Tax Mgmt. (BNA), No. 351, *Pension Plans — Qualification. See also* D. McGill & D. Grubbs, Jr., *Fundamentals of Private Pensions* 91 (6th ed. 1989).

participant loan   A participant in a qualified retirement plan may, within two limitations, borrow money from the plan. The first limitation is that a participant loan will be a prohibited transaction unless five conditions are met: (1) the loans must be made available to all participants and beneficiaries on a reasonably equivalent basis; (2) the plan must not discriminate in its loan policy; (3) the PLAN DOCUMENT must contain a provision authorizing participant loans; (4) the loans must bear a reasonable rate of interest; and (5) the loans must be adequately secured.

The second limitation concerns the permissible terms of participant loans. Under this limitation: (1) loans in excess of a maximum amount are treated as distributions to the participant; the maximum amount of aggregate loans to a participant is the lesser of (a) $50,000, reduced by the excess (if any) of (i) the highest outstanding balance of loans from the plan during the one-year period ending on the day before the date on which such loan was made, over (ii) the outstanding balance of loans from the plan on the date on which such loan was made, or (b) the greater of (i) one-half of the participant's vested ACCRUED BENEFIT, or (ii) $10,000; (2) the terms of the loan must provide that it will be repaid within five years, unless the loan is used to acquire a dwelling unit which is to be used within a reasonable time as the participant's principal residence; and (3) payments on the loan must be amortized in level payments over the term of the loan and payments must be made no less frequently than quarterly.

See PROHIBITED TRANSACTION.

Statutory and Regulatory Reference: See I.R.C. § 72(p) (limitations on terms of loan); ERISA § 408(b)(1) and I.R.C. § 4975(d)(1) (prohibited transaction exemption for certain participant loans); *see also* ERISA § 205(c)(4) and I.R.C. § 417(a)(4) (SPOUSAL CONSENT requirement pursuant to the JOINT AND SURVIVOR ANNUITY rules); ERISA §§ 205(e)(3) and (j) and I.R.C. §§ 417(c)(3) and (f)(5) (surviving spouse's rights).

Treatise Reference: See Tax Mgmt. (BNA), No. 370, *Qualified Plans—Taxation of Distributions*; *see also Employee Benefits Law* 174; 305-06; 333 (1991).

participation   Allowing an employee to be covered by a plan, including a qualified retirement plan.

See AGE AND SERVICE RULES, MINIMUM PARTICIPATION RULE, PARTICIPANT.

part-time employees   An employee whose customary employment is less than full time. Such employees must be credited with a proportionate amount of the ACCRUED BENEFIT to which they would have been entitled if they had worked full time. However, a plan does not have to count as a YEAR OF SERVICE any 12-month computation period in which the employee performs less than 1,000 hours of service.

Statutory and Regulatory Reference: I.R.C. §§ 411(b)(4)(B) and (C); Treas. Reg. § 1.411(b).

party in interest   The ERISA term for what the Internal Revenue Code calls a disqualified person, i.e., certain individuals or entities that are prohibited from engaging in certain specified prohibited transactions with a plan. Parties in interest include plan fiduciaries, plan service providers, the sponsoring employer, labor unions whose members are covered by the plan, and certain entities or individuals owning a specified level of interest in such persons and their employees.

ERISA provides for civil enforcement of the prohibited transaction rules, whereas the Code imposes a two-tiered penalty excise tax on such transactions. The first tier is 5 percent of the amount involved. If the transaction is not corrected within a statutory taxable period, the second-tier tax, equal to 100 percent of the amount involved, applies.

See PROHIBITED TRANSACTION.

Statutory and Regulatory Reference: ERISA §§ 3(14)(A)-(I); I.R.C. § 4975(e)(2)(a)-(I) (containing the parallel definition of disqualified person). The first and second-tier excise taxes are imposed by I.R.C. §§ 4975(a) and (b), respectively. The definition for taxable period is found at I.R.C. § 49759(f)(2); I.R.C. § 4975(f)(4) defines amount involved.

Treatise Reference: Tax Mgmt. (BNA), No. 351, *Pension Plans—Qualification*; *Employee Benefits Law* 301-03 (1991).

past service liabilities   The amount of employer liability for benefits under a qualified defined benefit plan or money purchase plan subject to the Internal Revenue Code's minimum funding standard that is attributable to benefits earned, or compensation received, before the employer established the plan. Past service costs are one type of supplemental liability that is charged to such a plan's funding standard account. A plan may provide credit for past service either in its initial document or by later plan amendment, but credit for past service is not mandatory.

See FUNDING STANDARD ACCOUNT, MINIMUM FUNDING STANDARD, SUPPLEMENTAL LIABILITY.

Statutory and Regulatory Reference: ERISA §§ 302(b)(2)(B)(ii)-(iii) and (b)(3)(B)(i); I.R.C. §§ 412(b)(2)(B)(ii), (b)(3)(B)(i), and 412(l).

Case and Other Interpretive Reference: Rev. Rul. 81-248, 1981-2 C.B. 91 (plan basing benefits solely on past service discriminates in operation where effect of this provision is to disproportionately direct benefits in favor of the prohibited group).

Treatise Reference: Tax Mgmt. (BNA), No. 371, *Employee Plans—Deductions, Contributions, and Funding*.

payroll-based tax credit ESOP (PAYSOP)   Under former law, a type of employee stock ownership plan under which employers could get a credit against their federal income tax liability for their plan contributions. This tax credit was based on the amount of compensation received by employees. Although such plans may still exist, the credit was repealed.

See ESOP.

Statutory and Regulatory Reference: I.R.C. § 409 (qualification requirements for a PAYSOP) and former I.R.C. § 41 (providing for the credit).

Treatise Reference: Tax Mgmt. (BNA), No. 354, *ESOPs*.

PBGC   The Pension Benefit Guaranty Corporation is a corporation operated under the Department of Labor to administer the pension plan termination insurance program established pursuant to Title IV of ERISA. The PBGC charges covered single-employer and multiemployer defined benefit plans an annual per participant premium that provides the funds for insuring unfunded plan benefits in the event of plan termination.

The PBGC is a corporation, capable of suing and being sued. It is governed by a Board of Directors. Directors include the Secretary of Labor (who acts as chairman) as well as the Secretaries of Commerce and Treasury. The Secretary of Labor appoints an Executive Director who is responsible for the PBGC's operation. The PBGC has the authority to issue regulations. Key regulations issued by the PBGC include ones governing plan funding and the valuation of plan benefits.

The corporation consists of 10 departments: (1) office of the general counsel; (2) communications and public affairs; (3) corporate budget; (4) financial operations; (5) corporate policy and research; (6) human resources and support services; (7) information resources management; (8) insurance operations; (9) office of the inspector general; and (10) participant and employer appeals.

The PBGC operates seven revolving funds. Four of the seven funds relate to specific guaranteed benefits under ERISA. These funds cover: (1) basic benefits under ERISA § 4002; (2) nonbasic benefits under ERISA § 4022; (3) basic benefits under ERISA § 4022A; and (4) nonbasic benefits under ERISA § 4022A; (5) reimbursement of uncollectible withdrawal liability under ERISA § 4222; (6) the supplemental benefit guaranty program of ERISA § 4022A(g)(2); and (7) risk-related premiums. These funds pay benefits that are guaranteed under ERISA, purchase the assets of plans that the PBGC has terminated, repay amounts borrowed, pay the administrative expenses of maintaining the funds, and pay guaranteed benefits of insolvent or abandoned plans.

See MULTIEMPLOYER PLAN, PARTIAL TERMINATION, TERMINATION, WITHDRAWAL LIABILITY.

Statutory and Regulatory Reference: See generally ERISA § 4002.

Treatise Reference: See Tax Mgmt. (BNA), No. 357, *Plan Terminations and Mergers*; *see also Employee Benefits Law* 45-49; 472-80 (1991).

pension plan, qualified   A written qualified retirement plan providing for definitely determinable retirement benefits for the livelihood of employees or their beneficiaries that meets the requirements imposed by I.R.C. § 401(a).

The regulations provide the following definition of a qualified pension plan:

"A pension plan within the meaning of § 401(a) is a plan established and maintained by an employer to provide systematically for the payment of definitely determinable benefits over a period of years, usually for life, after retirement. Retirement benefits are usually measured by, and based on, such factors as years of service and compensation received by employees. The determination of the amount of retirement benefits and the contribution to provide such benefits are not dependent on profits."

See DEFINED BENEFIT PLAN, DEFINITELY DETERMINABLE BENEFIT REQUIREMENT, MONEY PURCHASE PLAN.

Statutory and Regulatory Reference: Treas. Reg. § 1.401-1(b)(1)(i). Note that, for purposes of ERISA's labor title, ERISA § 3(2)(A) provides, in general, that a pension plan (qualified or otherwise) means any plan, fund, or program established or maintained by an employer, an EMPLOYEE ORGANIZATION, or both to the extent that it (1) provides retirement income to employees, or (2) results in income deferral by employees for periods extending to the TERMINATION of covered employment or beyond.

Case and Other Interpretive Reference: Rev. Rul. 81-162, 1981-1 C.B. 169 (plan that funds benefits solely with ordinary life insurance contracts which are converted to life annuities at retirement is not a pension plan within the meaning of I.R.C. § 401).

Treatise Reference: See Tax Mgmt. (BNA), No. 351, *Pension Plans—Qualification*; *see also Employee Benefits Law* 17-32 (1991).

Pension Benefit Guaranty Corporation
See PBGC.

percentage test   *See* 70 PERCENT TEST.

per diem allowance   A payment under a reimbursement plan or other expense allowance arrangement that meets the requirements of Treas. Reg. § 1.62-2T(c)(1), which requires (1) a business connection, substantiation, and return of amounts in excess of expenses, or (2) that the amount must be paid with respect to ordinary and necessary business expenses incurred by an employee for lodging or meals in connection with the performance of services as an employee, and (3) that the amount is reasonably calculated not to exceed the expenses and is paid at the applicable federal per diem rate, a flat rate, or a rate determined according to a stated schedule.

Statutory and Regulatory Reference: I.R.C. § 62; Treas. Reg. § 1.62-2T(c)(1); 41 C.F.R. Part 301-07.

Case and Other Interpretive Reference: Rev. Proc. 89-67, 1989-52 I.R.B. 17.

periodic payment   Regular payments that are made at predetermined intervals, e.g., monthly or yearly. Periodic benefit payments under qualified retirement plans are typically taxed to recipients under the tax law rules for annuities.

Statutory and Regulatory Reference: See generally I.R.C. §§ 72 and 402(a) and the regulations promulgated thereunder.

Treatise Reference: Tax Mgmt. (BNA), No. 134, *Annuities, and No. 370, Qualified Plans — Taxation of Distributions.*

PERK   Generally used to refer to I.R.C. § 132 fringe benefits, i.e., the nonstatutory or incidental fringe benefits. E.g., airline employees' right to free passage. These are not welfare benefits nor are they employee benefits.

See NO-ADDITIONAL-COST FRINGE BENE-FITS, DE MINIMIS FRINGE BENEFITS, ON-PREMISES ATHLETIC FACILITY, QUALIFIED EMPLOYEE DISCOUNT, WORKING CONDITION FRINGE BENEFITS.

Statutory and Regulatory Reference: I.R.C. § 132; Treas. Reg. §§ 1.132-1 to -8.

Treatise Reference: Tax Mgmt. (BNA), No. 394, *Employee Fringe Benefits; Employee Benefits Law* 982-85 (1991).

permanence (of qualified plan)   A requirement that a qualified retirement plan, at its inception, be intended to be a permanent program or arrangement.

The regulations explain as follows:

"Thus, although the employer may reserve the right to change or terminate the plan and to discontinue contributions thereunder, the abandonment of the plan for any reason other than business necessity within a few years after it has taken effect will be evidence that the plan, from its inception was not a bona fide program for the exclusive benefit of employees in general. Especially will this be true if, e.g., a pension plan is abandoned soon after pensions have been fully funded for persons in favor of whom discrimination is prohibited under § 401(a)."

The permanency of the plan will be indicated by the surrounding facts and circumstances, including the likelihood of the employer's ability to continue contributions as provided under the plan. In other words, when the plan is established, the employer must have a present intent to establish a permanent program or arrangement. Only unforeseen business occurrences, such as bankruptcy, casualty loss or recession, will enable the employer to overcome the presumption that the plan was not intended to be permanent where a plan terminates within a few years of its adoption. The regulations make it clear, however, that, in a profit-sharing plan, this does not mean that the employer must contribute every year.

Statutory and Regulatory Reference: I.R.C. § 401(a); Treas. Reg. § 1.401-1(b)(2).

Treatise Reference: Tax Mgmt. (BNA), No. 351, *Pension Plans — Qualification.*

permanent and total disability   An individual is permanently and totally disabled if unable to engage in any substantial gainful activity by reason of a medically determinable physical or mental impairment that can be expected to result in death or that has lasted or can be expected to last for a continuous period of not less than 12 months. An individual will not be considered permanently and totally disabled unless he or she furnishes proof of the disability.

See DISABILITY RETIREMENT INCOME, SECTION 22 AMOUNT.

Statutory and Regulatory Reference: I.R.C. § 22(e).

permissive aggregation group *See* AGGREGATION GROUP.

permitted disparity See INTEGRATION (SOCIAL SECURITY).

phantom stock plan An incentive plan in which employees are awarded hypothetical shares of employer stock. At a specified future date, such as retirement or termination of employment, the employee is entitled to receive an amount equal to the excess (if any) of the FAIR MARKET VALUE of all phantom shares as of that date over the fair market value of those shares at the time they were credited to the employee's account. In a variation of this plan, the employee's account is also credited from time to time with amounts equal to the dividends that would have been paid on the phantom stock if it had been actual stock. In either variant, the employee has no TAXABLE INCOME until actually receiving amounts under the plan; the crediting of his or her account with phantom shares or dividends does not give rise to income.

Treatise Reference: Tax Mgmt. (BNA), No. 385, *Deferred Compensation Arrangements,* and No. 60, *S Corporations.*

plan administrator The individual or firm responsible for performing duties incidental to the maintenance of an ongoing welfare or retirement-type plan, such as determining ELIGIBILITY for benefits, processing benefit claims, and so on. For purposes of ERISA's labor title, ERISA § 16(A) provides:

"The term 'administrator' means —

"(i) the person specifically so designated by the terms of the instrument under which the plan is operated,

"(ii) if an administrator is not so designated, the plan sponsor, or

"(iii) in the case of a plan for which an administrator is not designated and a plan sponsor cannot be identified, such other person as the Secretary [of Labor] may by regulation prescribe."

ERISA § 3(21)(A) imposes fiduciary status on anyone having discretionary authority or control with respect to the administration of a plan.

See FIDUCIARY, INVESTMENT MANAGER, QUALIFIED PLAN ASSET MANAGER (QPAM).

Treatise Reference: Tax Mgmt. (BNA), No. 351, *Pension Plans — Qualification.*

plan assets The investment holdings of an employee benefit plan that are held for the benefit of participants and beneficiaries. The characterization of property as a plan asset has several important implications. For instance, ERISA § 403(a) requires that the assets of a covered employee benefit plan be held in trust by one or more trustees and ERISA's prohibited transaction rules are phrased in terms of a prohibition on a party-in-interest or disqualified person engaging in certain transactions with respect to plan assets. Also, I.R.C. § 401(a)(2), the exclusive benefit rule, requires that plan assets be managed, and the plan maintained, for the exclusive benefit of participants and their beneficiaries. Thus, a party in interest/disqualified person's dealings with plan assets could, in addition to violating the fiduciary rules, violate this qualification requirement. In that case, in addition to possible civil (and criminal) sanctions, the plan could be disqualified.

Note that generally, under ERISA, the trustee has exclusive authority to manage and control the assets of an employee benefit plan unless: (1) the plan provides that the trustee is subject to the direction of a nontrustee fiduciary; or (2) authority to manage the plan's assets has been delegated to one or more investment managers pursuant to ERISA § 402(c)(3).

The Labor Department has promulgated regulations defining what constitutes a plan asset for purposes of ERISA's labor title. Under those regulations, generally, when a plan invests in another entity, its assets include its investment, but do not, solely by reason of the investment, include any of the entity's underlying assets. However, where the plan invests in an equity interest of an entity that is neither a publicly offered security nor a security issued by an investment company registered under the Investment Company Act of 1940, its assets include both the equity interest and an undivided interest in each of the underlying assets of the entity, unless: (1) the entity is an operating company, or (2) equity participation in the entity by benefit plan investors is not significant.

Therefore, any person who exercises authority or control over the management or disposition of such underlying assets, and anyone who provides investment advice concerning those assets for a fee (direct or indirect), is a fiduciary of the investing plan.

The regulations define an equity interest as any interest in an entity other than an instrument that is treated as indebtedness under applicable local law and which has no substantial equity features. The regulations cite as examples of an equity interest a profits interest in a partnership, an undivided ownership interest in property, and a beneficial interest in a trust.

For purposes of the first exception, above, the regulations define an operating company as an entity that is primarily engaged, directly or through a majority-owned subsidiary or subsidiaries, in the production or sale of a product or service other than the investment of capital. An operating company also includes a venture capital operating company or a real estate operating company.

The regulations treat equity participation in an entity by benefit plan investors as significant on any date if, immediately after the most recent acquisition of any equity interest in the entity, benefit plan investors hold 25 percent or more of the value of any class of equity interests in it.

A benefit plan investor is: (1) an employee benefit plan within the meaning of ERISA § 3(3) (regardless of whether it is subject to Title I); (2) a plan described in I.R.C. § 4975(e)(1); and (3) any entity whose underlying assets include plan assets by reason of a plan's investment in the entity.

Where a plan jointly owns property with others, or where the value of a plan's equity interest in an entity relates solely to identified property of the entity, the property is treated as the sole property of a separate entity.

Under a look-through exception to the general rule, the regulations provide that, except where the entity is an investment company registered under the Investment Company Act of 1940, when a plan acquires or holds an interest in any of the following entities its assets include its investment and an undivided interest in each of the entity's underlying assets: (1) certain I.R.C. § 501(a) tax-exempt group trusts; and (2) bank common or collective trust funds; and certain separate accounts of insurance companies.

Further, when a plan acquires or holds an interest in any entity (other than an insurance company) that is established or maintained to offer or provide any benefit described in ERISA §§ 3(1) or (2) to participants or beneficiaries of the investing plan, its assets will include its investment and an undivided interest in the entity's underlying assets.

Finally, when a plan or a related group of plans owns all of the outstanding equity interests (other than directors' qualifying shares) in an entity, its assets generally include those equity interests and all of the entity's underlying assets.

Plan assets also include amounts (other than union dues) that a participant or beneficiary pays to an employer, or amounts that a participant has withheld from his wages by an employer, for contribution to the plan. These amounts become plan assets as of the earliest date on which they can reasonably be segregated from the employer's general assets. This period, however, may not exceed 90 days from the date on which such amounts are received by the employer (for amounts that a participant or beneficiary pays to an employer) or the date on which such amounts would otherwise have been payable to the participant in cash (for amounts withheld by an employer from a participant's wages).

See EXCLUSIVE BENEFIT RULE, FIDUCIARY, PROHIBITED TRANSACTION.

Statutory and Regulatory Reference: 29 C.F.R. §§ 2510.3-101 through -102.

Treatise Reference: Employee Benefits Law 255 (1991).

plan liabilities   The legal obligations of a welfare or retirement plan, usually for the payment of benefits to employees or beneficiaries who are entitled to such payments under the plan's terms; also includes plan administrative costs.

Statutory and Regulatory Reference: For retirement plans, *see* Treas. Reg. § 1.401-1(b). *See also* I.R.C. § 401(a)(2), providing that qualified plans must first use their assets to satisfy all liabilities to employees and their beneficiaries before they may be diverted to any other purpose (the exclusive benefit rule).

plan loan   *See* PARTICIPANT LOAN.

plan/plan document   For purposes of qualified retirement plans, a definite written program maintained by an employer for the benefit of employees or beneficiaries that is intended to be permanent and is communi-

cated to employees. The Conference Report to ERISA states: "[a] written plan is to be required in order that every employee may, on examining the plan documents, determine exactly what his rights and obligations are under the plan. Also, a written plan is required so the employees may know who is responsible for operating the plan." *See* H.R. CONF. REP. NO. 1280, 93d Cong., 2d Sess 297 (1974).

Note that ERISA's written plan instrument rule does not determine if a plan will be subject to ERISA. For this purpose, a plan will be considered to exist, even without a written document, if it has the characteristics of an employee benefit plan within the meaning of ERISA §§ 3(1) and (3).

See EMPLOYEE BENEFIT PLAN.

Statutory and Regulatory Reference: ERISA §§ 3(3) (definition), 402(a)(1), and 403(a) (requirement that plan's terms be embodied in a written plan document). The requirement that the plan be communicated to employees is contained in ERISA § 102(a)(1). *See also* Treas. Reg. § 1.401-1(a)(1) (general description of requirements of a qualified plan); (a)(2)(i) (detailing additional requirements particular to pension plans); (a)(2)(ii) (requirements for profit-sharing plans); and (a)(2)(iii) (stock bonus plans).

Case and Other Interpretive Reference: For cases on the issue of whether, based on the attendant facts and circumstances, a plan existed notwithstanding the absence of a formal plan document, *see Scott v. Gulf Oil Corp.,* 754 F.2d 1499 (9th Cir. 1985); *Blau v. Del Monte Corp.,* 748 F.2d 1348 (9th Cir. 1984), *cert. denied,* 474 U.S. 865 (1985); *Donovan v. Dillingham,* 688 F.2d 1367 (11th Cir. 1982) (*en banc*).

Treatise Reference: Employee Benefits Law 245; 253 (1991).

plan sponsor   For federal income tax purposes, generally the employer that establishes and maintains a welfare or retirement plan that provides benefits to employees.

For purposes of ERISA's labor title, ERISA § 3(16)(B) provides:

"(B) The term 'plan sponsor' means (i) the employer in the case of an employee benefit plan established or maintained by a single employer, (ii) the employee organization in the case of a plan established or maintained by an employee organization, or (iii) in the case of a plan established or maintained by two or more employers or jointly by one or more employers and one or more employee organizations, the association, committee, joint board of trustees, or other similar group of representatives of the parties who establish or maintain the plan."

Statutory and Regulatory Reference: See I.R.C. § 401(a) (flush language) and Treas. Reg. § 1.401-1(a)(3)(i). *See also* Treas. Reg. § 1.401-1(d), which provides that a qualified retirement plan may also be sponsored jointly by more than one employer.

Treatise Reference: Tax Mgmt. (BNA), No. 351, *Pension Plans – Qualification.*

plan year   Any period of 12 consecutive months chosen for keeping the records of the plan. This period need not coincide with the employer's taxable year, but, in practice, often does for ease of administration.

See TAXABLE YEAR.

Statutory and Regulatory Reference: ERISA § 3(39).

Treatise Reference: See generally Tax Mgmt. (BNA), No. 351, *Pension Plans – Qualification.*

portability (of retirement benefits)   The ability of participants, upon leaving the service of their employer, or ending participation in a particular retirement plan to take their benefits with them to their new employers or new plans either in cash or in kind or by means of a system of reciprocal credits. One type of pension portability is the ability of an employee who receives a qualifying distribution from a retirement plan to ROLLOVER that distribution, tax-free, into the plan of a new employer or into an IRA.

Case and Other Interpretive Reference: Rev. Rul. 78-406, 1978-2 C.B. 157 (providing that certain transfers from one IRA trustee to another of IRA funds are TRUSTEE-TO-TRUSTEE TRANSFERS and not rollovers within the meaning of I.R.C. § 408(d).

Treatise Reference: See generally Tax Mgmt. (BNA), No. 355, *IRAs and SEPs.*

postretirement cost of living adjustment (COLA)   A pension plan is permitted to provide for automatic periodic increases in retirement benefits to reflect increases in the cost of living. Such provisions must, however, take into account the annual dollar limitation on benefits that can be paid by a qualified plan. Thus, the annual increases cannot make the retirement benefits exceed the annual benefit limit; a cost of living adjustment (COLA) to a benefit that is already at the limit can become effective no sooner than the annual adjustment is made to the benefit limit.

In determining the dollar value of the benefits received by a participant for purposes of the annual limit, the value of the cost of living feature is not taken into account, as long as the actual benefits paid do not exceed the annual limit.

See LIMITATION ON ANNUAL BENEFITS.

Statutory and Regulatory Reference: I.R.C. § 415; Treas. Reg. §§ 1.415-5(c) and-3(c) (2)(iii).

Treatise Reference: Tax Mgmt. (BNA), No. 351, *Pension Plans – Qualification.*

PPO   *See* PREFERRED PROVIDER ORGANIZATION.

postretirement medical benefits Medical benefits offered by an employer to retired employees either through the employer's group medical plan covering current employees or through a medical plan designed particularly for retirees. Unlike standard medical benefits that generally are terminable at the will of the employer, in some instances retiree medical benefits may not be terminable, or even subject to modification.

Employers must give postretirement benefits special consideration regarding their coordination with Medicare and also their treatment under FASB #106 that requires employers to recognize currently the liability to pay these obligations to retirees at some point in the future.

The benefits generally are excluded from the employee's income. Employer contributions are subject to the deduction and taxation rules associated with the particular mechanism used to fund the benefits (e.g., they may be subject to the VEBA rules if so funded, but where not funded through a qualified retirement plan or WELFARE BENEFIT FUND, employer contributions generally are treated as if furnished under a NONQUALIFIED DEFERRED COMPENSATION PLAN and are deductible when the benefits are taxed to the retiree upon actual or CONSTRUCTIVE RECEIPT.

Statutory and Regulatory Reference: I.R.C. §§ 105, 106, 404, 419.

Case and Other Interpretive Reference: See Peterson v. Grand Trunk Western Railroad, 683 F. Supp. 649, 9 EB Cases 2085 (1988) (where employer increased retirees' premium contributions for health insurance, employer could unilaterally reduce or even eliminate benefits unless bound by contractual obligation because welfare benefit plans are exempt from ERISA vesting requirements). *See also Musto v. American Gen. Corp.,* 801 F.2d 897, 10 EB Cases 1441 (6th Cir. 1988), *cert. denied,* 490 U.S. 1020 (1989); Moore v. Metropolitan Life Insurance Co.,

856 F.2d 488, 9 E.B. Cases 2658 (2d Cir. 1988); *Howe v. Variety Corp.,* 896 F.2d 1107, 11 EB Cases 2585 (8th Cir. 1990); *Auto Workers v. Cadillac Malleable Iron,* 728 F.2d 807, 11 EB Cases 2242 (6th Cir. 1989) (where employer terminated retiree life and health benefits after expiration of collective bargaining agreement, court found that bargaining history and exit interviews with prospective retirees demonstrated employer's intent to provide lifetime benefits).

Treatise Reference: Measuring and Funding Corporate Liabilities For Retiree Health Benefits (Employee Benefit Research Institute, 1987); Akresh, et al., *Retiree Health Benefits: How to Cope with the Accounting, Actuarial, and Management Issues* (Montvale, N.J.: National Association of Accountants, 1989); *Employee Benefits Law* 873-80; 1056-58 (1991).

preexisting condition limitation A limitation included in a health care plan which generally provides that coverage will not be extended to an already existing condition until the covered individual has completed 90 days without treatment for the condition or has been covered under the plan for 12 months, whichever occurs first (either of these periods may be increased or decreased subject to insurance company requirements). A preexisting condition generally is a condition for which the individual has received treatment within the 90 days prior to coverage under the plan (although the look-back period can be longer than 90 days).

Treatise Reference: Tax Mgmt. (BNA), No. 389, *Disability and Medical Reimbursement Benefits;* J. V. Nackley, *Primer on Workers' Compensation* (2d ed. 1989).

preferred provider organization (PPO) An alternative health care delivery system, combining fee-for-service with some of the utilization controls found in HMOs. Devised as a cost containment system, a health care plan with a PPO feature encourages employees to seek care from preferred providers, who generally furnish health care services at contractually discounted rates, thus creating a cost savings to the employer. The preferred providers benefit from the prompt payment arrangements and continuous referrals of patients. PPOs may be formed to provide a comprehensive range of health care services or may be limited to a specific health care speciality.

Example: A physician PPO offers to serve employees and dependents covered by a company health plan at a 15 percent discount from its usual physicians' fees, on the basis of having half of the health plan's usual 20 percent cost-sharing waived whenever one of the preferred physicians is used.

Treatise Reference: J. Mamorsky, *Employee Benefits Handbook* (1987).

prefunding of benefits   The contribution of funds, generally by an employer, to a welfare or retirement-type plan, on an actuarially estimated basis, before the time when the plan is obligated to pay such amounts in the form of benefits to participants or beneficiaries. Certain welfare and qualified retirement plans may be prefunded, with the contributing employer being allowed to take a tax DEDUCTION at the time the funds are contributed to the plan, rather than waiting until such amounts are payable.

Statutory and Regulatory Reference: I.R.C. § 404(a) and Treas. Reg. § 1.404(a)-1 *et seq.* (retirement plans); I.R.C. §§ 419, 419A, and Treas. Reg. § 1.419-1T (certain welfare plans).

Treatise Reference: Tax Mgmt. (BNA), No. 371, *Employee Plans — Deductions, Contributions, and Funding* (retirement plans), and No. 395, *Section 501(c)(9) and Self-Funded Employee Benefits* (certain welfare plans).

premature distribution   Any distribution from a qualified retirement plan that is not: (1) made after the participant attains age 59½; (2) on account of the death or disability of the participant; (3) in annuity form for the participant's life; (4) to a participant following a separation from the employer's service after reaching age 55; (5) from dividend distributions from an ESOP under I.R.C. § 404(k); (6) used for medical expenses that do not exceed the DEDUCTION allowable under I.R.C. § 213 for such expenses; (7) certain pre-1990 distributions from ESOPs; or (8) payments to alternate payees under QUALIFIED DOMESTIC RELATIONS ORDERS (QDROS). A premature distribution is subject to a 10 percent penalty tax under the Internal Revenue Code. This tax applies in addition to any federal income tax that may be due with respect to the disposition.

See LUMP-SUM DISTRIBUTION, MINIMUM REQUIRED DISTRIBUTION.

Statutory and Regulatory Reference: I.R.C. § 72(t)(q); and I.R.C. § 402(g)(2)(C) (premature distribution tax on excess deferrals).

Case and Other Interpretive Reference: Rev. Rul. 81-113, 1981-1 C.B. 176 (PREMATURE DISTRIBUTION to owner-employee will not affect qualification of plan as to remaining participants).

Treatise Reference: See Tax Mgmt. (BNA), No. 370, *Qualified Plans — Taxation of Distributions; see also Employee Benefits Law* 188-91 (1991).

preretirement death benefit   A benefit provided by a qualified pension plan that is in the form of life, health, or accident insurance and is payable before retirement. Such a benefit, if excessive, can disqualify a plan, since the principal purpose of a pension plan must be to provide pensions to employees at retirement. Thus, any preretirement death benefit must be incidental to the plan.

Generally, in a pension or annuity plan funded with insurance contracts, a preretirement death benefit is incidental if the amount of the benefit is no greater than 100 times the monthly annuity benefit provided under the plan.

See INCIDENTAL DEATH BENEFITS, PRERETIREMENT SURVIVOR ANNUITY, QUALIFIED JOINT AND SURVIVOR ANNUITY (QJSA).

Case and Other Interpretive Reference: IRS Publication 778, *Guides for Qualification of Pension, Profit-Sharing, and Stock Bonus Plans.*

Treatise Reference: Tax Mgmt. (BNA), No. 351, *Pension Plans — Qualification.*

preretirement survivor annuity A benefit under a qualified plan that is payable as an ANNUITY for the life of the participant's spouse in the event the participant does not survive to retirement.

In general, qualified retirement plans to which I.R.C. § 401(a)(11) applies must provide married vested participants who retire under the plan with benefit payments in the form of a qualified joint and survivor annuity. If a vested participant dies before his or her ANNUITY STARTING DATE and has a surviving spouse, the plan, if covered by § 401(a)(11), must provide the spouse with a "qualified preretirement survivor annuity," unless the participant makes an election to the contrary and that election is accompanied by a written consent thereto by the participant's spouse that meets certain requirements.

A qualified preretirement survivor annuity is a survivor annuity for the life of the participant's surviving spouse that satisfies certain conditions. First, the payments to the spouse must not be less than the amounts that would be payable as a survivor annuity under the plan's qualified joint and survivor annuity (or the actuarial equivalent thereof) if certain criteria were met. These criteria are as follows:

(1) If a participant dies after attaining the plan's earliest retirement age, the annuity must be as great as the survivor annuity that would have been payable to the spouse under the plan's joint and survivor annuity if the participant had retired with an immediate qualified joint and survivor annuity on the date of death.

(2) If a participant dies on or before the date he would have attained the plan's earliest retirement age, the annuity must be as great as the survivor portion of the plan's joint and survivor annuity if the participant had (a) separated from the employer's service on his date of death; (b) survived to the plan's earliest retirement age; (c) retired with an immediate qualified joint and survivor annuity at the plan's earliest retirement age; and (d) died on the day after the day on which he would have attained the plan's earliest retirement age.

In addition, the earliest period for which a surviving spouse may receive a payment under the preretirement survivor annuity must not be later than the month in which the participant would have attained the earliest retirement age under the plan.

See QUALIFIED JOINT AND SURVIVOR ANNUITY (QJSA), QUALIFIED PRERETIREMENT SURVIVOR ANNUITY (QPSA).

Statutory and Regulatory Reference: ERISA § 205(d); I.R.C. § 417 and the regulations promulgated thereunder.

Case and Other Interpretive Reference: Rev. Rul. 85-15, 1985-1 C.B. 132 (guidance on how plans may satisfy the INCIDENTAL DEATH BENEFIT rule after being amended solely to provide for the preretirement survivor annuity provisions enacted by the Retirement Equity Act of 1984 (REA), Pub. L. No. 98-397).

Treatise Reference: Tax Mgmt. (BNA), No. 370, *Qualified Plans — Taxation of Distributions.*

present value   The amount of money that would be needed on a particular day to produce a specified stream of income over some future period at some assumed rate of interest. For purposes of ERISA, the present value of a liability means the value adjusted to reflect anticipated events.

Statutory and Regulatory Reference: ERISA § 3(27).

primary insurance amount (PIA)   A figure used to compute how much Social Security a person is to receive upon reaching Social Security retirement age. It is based on the individual's wages, compensation, self-employment income, and deemed military wage credits for years after 1950.

Statutory and Regulatory Reference: I.R.C. § 401(l); 20 C.F.R. § 404.211(b)(1).

Treatise Reference: Tax Mgmt. (BNA), No. 356, *Qualified Plans—Integration.*

private letter ruling (PLR)   A ruling given by the IRS in response to a request by a taxpayer for the IRS's view of the tax consequences of a proposed transaction. The ruling applies to the specific fact situation provided by the taxpaycr in the request, and is binding on the IRS only with respect to the facts supplied by the taxpayer as they affect that particular taxpayer. A PLR can, however, be cited as substantial authority for purposes of avoiding the penalty for substantial understatement of tax.

See GENERAL COUNSEL MEMORANDUM, REVENUE RULING, TECHNICAL ADVICE MEMORANDUM.

profit-sharing plan   A qualified retirement plan designed to enable employees and their beneficiaries to participate in the profits of the employer's business.

Treas. Reg. § 1.401-1(a)(2) defines a profit-sharing plan as:

"a definite written program and arrangement which is communicated to the employees and which is established and maintained by an employer...to enable employees or their beneficiaries to participate in the profits of the employer's trade or business, or in the profits of an affiliated employer who is entitled to deduct his or her contributions to the plan under § 404(a)(3)(B), pursuant to a definite written formula for allocating the contributions and for distributing the funds accumulated under the plan...."

Treas. Reg. § 1.401-1(b)(1)(ii) adds:

"A profit-sharing plan is a plan established and maintained by an employer to provide for the participation in his or her profits by his or her employees or their beneficiaries. The plan must provide a definite predetermined formula for allocating the contributions made to the plan among participants and for distributing the funds accumulated under the plan for a fixed number of years, the attainment of a stated age, or upon prior occurrence of some event such as layoff, illness, disability, retirement, death, or severance of employment."

The Tax Reform Act of 1986 (TRA 1986), Pub. L. No. 99-514, added I.R.C. § 401(a)(27), which provides that a profit-sharing plan that satisfies the other qualification requirements of § 401(a) shall not fail to qualify merely because the employer does not have current or accumulated earnings and profits or because the employer is tax-exempt.

See DEFINED BENEFIT PLAN/DEFINED CONTRIBUTION PLAN.

Statutory and Regulatory Reference: I.R.C. § 401(a); Treas. Reg. § 1.401-1.

Treatise Reference: See Tax Mgmt. (BNA), No. 352, *Profit-Sharing Plans—Qualification; see also Employee Benefits Law* 25; 77-79 (1991); D. McGill & D. Grubbs, Jr., *Fundamentals of Private Pensions* 645 (6th ed. 1989).

prohibited group   Under the law as it existed before the Tax Reform Act of 1986 (TRA 1986), Pub. L. No. 99-514, the group of employees in whose favor qualified plans could not discriminate. The group included highly compensated employees, officers, and owners of the employer. The TRA 1986 replaced this group with highly compensated employees; however, in practice, the two terms are often used interchangeably when referring to either pre- or post- TRA 1986 law.

See HIGHLY COMPENSATED EMPLOYEE.

Statutory and Regulatory Reference: I.R.C. § 401(a)(4) both before and after amendment by TRA 1986; Treas. Reg. § 1.401-4(a) (reflecting pre-1986 law); and Treas. Reg. § 1.401(a)(4)-1-13 (reflecting post-1986 law).

Treatise Reference: Tax Mgmt. (BNA), No. 351, *Pension Plans — Qualification*.

prohibited transaction   A transaction that is not allowed between a PARTY IN INTEREST (the term used in ERISA) or a DISQUALIFIED PERSON (the term used in the parallel provisions of the Internal Revenue Code and used herein for ease of reference) and an employee benefit plan. For purposes of the tax definition, the term plan includes a qualified plan, § 403 annuity, individual retirement account, or an individual retirement annuity. For purposes of ERISA's labor title, it means a plan subject to ERISA. The labor provisions are enforceable by means of civil sanctions, whereas the Code's parallel rules are enforceable through a two-tiered penalty excise tax (*see* explanation of the tax in the definition of party in interest).

The types of transactions that are prohibited include: (a) the sale, exchange or leasing of property between the plan and a disqualified person; (b) the lending of money between the plan and a disqualified person; (c) the furnishing of goods, services or facilities between the plan and a disqualified person; (d) the use by a disqualified person of plan income or assets; (e) dealing by the plan's FIDUCIARY for his or her own account with plan income or assets; and (f) the receipt of consideration for his or her personal account by the fiduciary in connection with a transaction involving the income or assets of the plan.

Various statutory exceptions to the general prohibited transaction rules apply; plans may also apply to the Labor Department for an exemption of a particular transaction from the prohibited transaction rules. Exemptions are granted on either a class or an individual basis and apply only to the conditions described in the exemption.

See PARTY IN INTEREST.

Statutory and Regulatory Reference: ERISA § 406(a), I.R.C. § 4975(f)(3) (definition); ERISA §§ 406(c) and 407 (employer real property and employer securities rules); I.R.C. §§ 4975(a)-(b) (excise tax); ERISA § 408 and I.R.C. § 4975(d) (exemptions to the prohibited transactions rules) and the regulations promulgated thereunder.

Treatise Reference: See Tax Mgmt. (BNA), No. 351, *Pension Plans — Qualification; see also Employee Benefits Law* 301-40 (1991).

projected benefit liability   The amount of benefits that a plan is expected to have to pay in the future. The figure is based on ACTUARIAL ASSUMPTIONS, and affects the level of FUNDING required for the plan.

See FUNDING STANDARD ACCOUNT.

Treatise Reference: Tax Mgmt. (BNA), No. 371, *Employee Plans — Deductions, Contributions, and Funding*.

proration/pro rata   Apportionment of amounts among several persons in accordance with their allocable shares.

prototype plan   Another term for a master plan. *See* MASTER PLAN.

PS 58 rates   Rates contained in IRS Table PS 58 used in computing the cost of pure TERM LIFE INSURANCE protection that is taxable to an employee on whose life the insurance is purchased under qualified retirement plans, SPLIT-DOLLAR PLANS, and SECTION 403(B) PLANS. The Table sets forth premiums for one-year of term coverage for $1,000 of life insurance protection at various ages. The rate at the insured's attained age is then applied to the excess of the amount payable at death over the cash value of the policy at the end of the year, in order to calculate the amount taxed to the employee.

Case and Other Interpretive Reference: Rev. Rul. 55-747, 1955-2 C.B. 228; Rev. Rul. 66-110, 1966-1 C.B. 12.

Treatise Reference: Tax Mgmt. (BNA), No. 386, *Insurance-Related Compensation.*

pyramiding   A technique in which the holder of an employer STOCK OPTION uses the gain from selling the stock back to the employer to exercise options to purchase additional employer stock. By alternately exercising options and selling back the stock, the holder can theoretically increase his or her stock holdings in the employer in a geometric progression at minimal cost.

Treatise Reference: See Tax Mgmt. (BNA), No. 383, *Nonstatutory Stock Options.*

Q

QPAM   A qualified plan asset manager (also known as a qualified professional asset manager) is a bank, insurance company, or investment adviser registered under the Investment Advisers Act of 1940 (15 U.S.C. § 80a-1 *et seq.*). A QPAM that is a bank or insurance company must be subject to State and/or federal regulation, and a QPAM that is an investment manager must be registered under the Investment Advisers Act of 1940 and must satisfy requirements with respect to equity capital, net worth, and assets under management. The QPAM distinction is particularly important since such a classification permits the manager to pursue a QPAM exemption, that permits pension plans to engage in various transactions otherwise prohibited under ERISA's prohibited transaction restrictions.

Statutory and Regulatory Reference: ERISA §§ 406 and 408; PTE 84-14, 49 Fed. Reg. 9494 (Mar. 14, 1984), amended by 50 Fed. Reg. 41,430 (Oct. 10, 1988).

qualified asset account   An account set up to hold assets set aside for the payment of disability benefits, medical benefits, SUB or severance pay benefits, or life insurance benefits. Within certain limitations, employers may deduct amounts contributed to a qualified asset account for these pur-

poses. The limitations are such that an employer cannot contribute an amount that exceeds the account limit, which is either calculated actuarially or with regard to specific safe harbors provided in the Internal Revenue Code.

Statutory Reference: I.R.C. §§ 419 and 419A. JOINT COMMITTEE ON TAXATION, GENERAL EXPLANATION OF THE TAX REFORM ACT OF 1986, at 786 (1987) (DEFRA)(explaining safe harbor and actuarial methods for determining account limits).

Treatise Reference: R.A. Kladder & P.J. Routh, *Welfare Benefits Guide,* 1990-1991 §§ 8.09 through 8.11 (1990); *Employee Benefits Law* 1006-09 (1991).

qualified beneficiaries   Individuals eligible for COBRA health care continuation coverage. A qualified beneficiary is an employee, an employee's spouse, or dependents, covered under the employer's group health care plan on the day before a qualifying event. In this context, the term employee includes former employees, such as retirees, as well as sole proprietors, partners, directors, and independent contractors, if they are covered under a plan that also covers employees. Employee does not include, however, nonresident aliens with no U.S.-source income.

Example: X voluntarily terminates employment and properly elects COBRA coverage under a group health plan. Under the plan, a covered employee who marries can choose to have the spouse covered under the plan as of the date of marriage. One month after electing COBRA coverage, X marries Y and chooses to cover Y under the group health plan. If X dies during the period of continuation coverage, the plan does not have to offer Y the opportunity to elect COBRA coverage since Y is not a qualified beneficiary.

See COBRA, CONTINUATION COVERAGE, QUALIFYING EVENT.

Statutory and Regulatory Reference: See ERISA § 607(3); I.R.C. § 4980B; Prop. Treas. Reg. §§ 1.106-1, 1.162-26, Q&As 15-17.

Treatise Reference: Tax Mgmt. (BNA), No. 389, *Disability and Medical Reimbursement Benefits*; *Employee Benefits Law* 992-93 (1991).

qualified costs   In the case of a funded welfare benefit plan, such as a VEBA, the sum of the qualified direct costs for the year and the additions to the qualified asset account for the year.

See QUALIFIED DIRECT COSTS, QUALIFIED ASSET ACCOUNT, VEBA.

Statutory and Regulatory Reference: I.R.C. §§ 419(c) and 419A.

qualified direct costs   In the case of a funded welfare benefit plan, such as a VEBA, these costs are the sum of the administrative expenses (e.g., accounting and legal fees) and benefits paid to participants by the VEBA for that year (rather than the amount the employer contributed that year).

Example: Employer X contributes $200,000 to a VEBA in 1992 for purposes of making payments to employees for medical

and disability benefits. In 1992, X pays out $50,000 in disability benefits and $100,000 in medical benefits and has $10,000 of administrative expenses. The qualified direct costs for the VEBA for 1992 are $160,000.

Statutory and Regulatory Reference: I.R.C. § 419(c).

Treatise Reference: R.A. Kladder & P.J. Routh, *Welfare Benefits Guide,* 1990-1991 §§ 8.09 through 8.11 (1990); *Employee Benefits Law* 1006 (1991).

qualified domestic relations order (QDRO)   A domestic relations order is a judgment, decree, or order (including approval of a property settlement agreement) that relates to the provision of child support or alimony payment, or the marital property rights of a spouse, child, or other dependent of a plan participant. A QDRO is an exception to the general rule that a participant's benefit cannot be assigned or alienated prior to distribution. It is an order issued by a court recognizing the existence of an alternate payee's right to receive all, or part, of the benefits payable with respect to a participant under a plan. The order must be made pursuant to a state domestic relations law. To be a QDRO, a domestic relations order must contain: (1) the name and last known mailing address of the participant and each alternate payee covered by the order; (2) the amount or percentage of the participant's benefits to be paid by the plan to each alternate payee or the manner by which that amount or percentage is to be determined; (3) the number of payments, or the period to which the order applies; and (4) each plan to which the order applies.

See ALTERNATE PAYEE.

Statutory and Regulatory Reference: ERISA §§ 206(d)(3)(B) (definition and rules for compliance) and 206(d)(3)(F) (survivor benefits under qualified domestic relations orders); I.R.C. §§ 401(a)(11) (taxation of alternate payee), 401(a)(13)(B), and 414(p); Treas. Reg. § 1.401(a)-13(g).

Case and Other Interpretive Reference: See Taylor v. Taylor, 11 EB Cases 1513 (Ohio 1989) (Ohio law permitting court-ordered withholding of governmental pension benefits for payment of support authorizes domestic relations courts to issue QDROs withholding benefits from private, ERISA-covered pension plans). *See also* I.R.S. Notice 89-25, 1990-1 C.B. 662 (child support orders can create rights in a participant's pension).

Treatise Reference: Tax Mgmt. (BNA), No. 370, *Qualified Plans—Taxation of Distributions; see also Employee Benefits Law* 171 (1991).

qualified employee discount   A discount offered by an employer to an employee with respect to property or services for personal use of the employee, the employee's spouse, dependent child, or, in the case of air transportation, the employee's parents. If the discount qualifies as a qualified employee discount, the employee need not recognize gross income with respect to the provision of the benefit for federal income tax purposes. For this purpose, an employee discount: (1) must be with respect to services or property (however, the property may not consist of property which is other than real property or tangible or intangible personal property of a kind commonly held for investment, whether or not the employee is purchasing the property for investment); and (2) must involve property or services offered by the employer for sale to nonemployee customers in the ordinary course of a line of business of the employer (and the employee must perform substantial services in that same line of business). The employee discount is the amount by which the customer price of the offered property or service exceeds the price at which the property or service is provided by the employer to the employee.

A discount will constitute a qualified employee discount, to the extent that it does not exceed: (1) in the case of property, the gross profit percentage at which the property is being offered by the employer to customers; or (2) in the case of services, 20 percent of the price at which the services are being offered by the employer to customers. The gross profit percentage is computed by taking the amount by which the total sales price of the property for customers exceeds the total cost of the property to the employer and dividing it by the total sale price of the property.

Example: An employer in a wholesale business offers property for sale to two customers groups at different prices. During the prior year, 70 percent of the employer's gross sales were made at a 15 percent discount and 30 percent of sales were made at no discount. The current undiscounted price at which the property is being offered by the employer for sale to customers may be reduced for employees by the 15 percent discount, which can be treated as a qualified employee discount.

See EMPLOYEE, PERK, WORKING CONDITION FRINGE BENEFITS.

Statutory and Regulatory Reference: I.R.C. §§ 132(a)(2), (c), and (f); Treas. Reg. §§ 1.132-1T and -3.

Treatise Reference: Tax Mgmt. (BNA), No. 394, *Employee Fringe Benefits; Employee Benefits Law* 982-83 (1991).

qualified joint and survivor annuity (QJSA)   An annuity payable under a qualified retirement plan, effective if the participant survives to retirement, for the life of the participant with a survivor annuity for the life of the participant's surviving spouse. To constitute a qualified joint and survivor annuity, the payments to the surviving spouse must be between 50 and 100 percent of the amounts payable during both spouses' joint lives. A qualified joint and survivor annuity must be at least the actuarial equivalent of the normal form of life annuity or, if greater, of any optional form of life annuity offered under the plan. Most qualified retirement plans must provide that the mode of benefit payment for a married participant who retires on or after the plan's NORMAL RETIREMENT AGE will be a QUALIFIED JOINT AND SURVIVOR ANNUITY, absent an election by the participant to the contrary accompanied by a written consent thereto executed by the participant's spouse.

Specifically, the Internal Revenue Code requires that, where a qualified plan provides benefits in the form of a life annuity, the plan must presume, where the participant and the participant's spouse have been married for at least one year on the annuity starting date that, absent an election to the contrary by the participant, accompanied by written consent thereto by the participant's spouse, normal retirement benefits will be provided in a form having the effect of a qualified joint and survivor annuity. In the case of an unmarried participant, the presumptive mode of benefit payment in this situation is a life annuity for the participant's life.

The definition also encompasses any annuity which, in form, has the effect of a qualified joint and survivor annuity. An annuity is not a qualified joint and survivor annuity if payments to the spouse of a deceased participant are terminated or reduced because the spouse remarries.

A "life annuity," for this purpose, is defined as an annuity that provides retirement payments and requires the survival of the participant or the participant's spouse as one of the conditions for any payment or possible payment under the annuity. Thus, an annuity that provides payments for 10 years or until death, whichever occurs sooner, or whichever occurs later, would, in either case, be a life annuity. A provision allowing a plan to involuntarily CASH-OUT annuity benefits having a present value not in excess of $3,500, how-

ever, will not violate the joint and survivor or preretirement survivor annuity rules. Thus, under I.R.C. § 417(f), qualified retirement plans may distribute benefits in a lump sum to a participant if the present value of such benefits do not exceed $3,500. Benefits in excess of this amount may be cashed out only with the participant's consent. In determining present value under this rule, if the benefit is under $25,000, the interest rate to be used in calculating the value of the benefit is the rate used by the PBGC in calculating the value of lump-sum distributions upon plan termination. If the vested benefit exceeds $25,000 the interest rate to be used in calculating present value may not exceed 120 percent of such PBGC rate.

The qualified joint and survivor annuity requirement applies to the following:

(1) Any qualified defined benefit plan;

(2) Any qualified defined contribution plan that is subject to the MINIMUM FUNDING STANDARD of I.R.C. § 412, e.g., a MONEY PURCHASE PENSION PLAN; and

(3) In the case of a defined contribution plan, to any participant in such plan unless (a) the plan provides that the participant's nonforfeitable accrued benefit is payable in full on the participant's death to the participant's surviving spouse; (b) the participant does not elect to receive benefits in life annuity form; and (c) with respect to the participant, the defined contribution plan is not a direct or indirect transferee of a defined benefit plan or a defined contribution plan subject to the minimum funding standard of I.R.C. § 412.

Certain Employee Stock Ownership Plan (ESOP) benefits are also excepted from the qualified joint and survivor annuity requirement. The ESOP exception applies to certain tax-credit ESOPs as defined in I.R.C. § 409(a), and ESOPs as defined in I.R.C. § 4975(e)(7). For such plans, the qualified joint and survivor annuity requirement does not apply to that portion of an employee's accrued benefit to which the requirements of I.R.C. § 409(h) (relating to an employee's right to demand benefit distributions in the form of employer securities) apply, provided the other requirements of (3), above, are met.

Plans subject to the qualified joint and survivor annuity requirement are also subject, in the case of a vested participant who dies before his or her annuity starting date, to the qualified preretirement survivor annuity requirement.

See QUALIFIED PRERETIREMENT SURVIVOR ANNUITY (QPSA).

Statutory and Regulatory Reference: ERISA § 205(d); I.R.C. §§ 401(a)(11) and 417(b); Treas. Reg. §§ 1.401(a)-11 *et seq.*

Treatise Reference: See Tax Mgmt. (BNA), No. 370, *Qualified Plans — Taxation of Distributions; see also Employee Benefits Law* 161-68 (1991). *See also* D. McGill & D. Grubbs, Jr., *Fundamentals of Private Pensions* 164 (6th ed. 1989).

qualified nonelective contributions   In
a SECTION 401(K) PLAN, employer contributions other than elective contributions and matching contributions. Under the § 401(k) regulations, these contributions may be counted to help a plan pass the actual deferral percentage test of § 401(k), or the actual contribution percentage test of § 401(m), provided certain nondiscrimination requirements are met.

Statutory and Regulatory Reference: I.R.C. § 401(k); Treas. Reg. § 1.401(k)-1.

Treatise Reference: See Tax Mgmt. (BNA), No. 358, *Cash or Deferred Arrangements; Employee Benefits Law* 212 (1991).

qualified nonguaranteed insurance contract   An insurance contract (including a reasonable premium stabilization reserve) where there is no contractual guarantee of renewal and where, other than insurance protection, only nonguaranteed, experience-

rated refunds or policy dividends are payable to the employer or employee. Experience-rated refunds or policy dividends must be determined by factors other than the amount of welfare benefits paid to or on behalf of the employees or their beneficiaries. Such contracts are not categorized as welfare benefit funds and thus are not subject to the welfare benefit fund limitations of I.R.C. §§ 419 and 419A.

See WELFARE BENEFIT FUND.

Statutory and Regulatory Reference: I.R.C. §§ 419(e); 419A.

Treatise Reference: Tax Mgmt. (BNA), No. 395, *Section 501(c)(9) and Self-Funded Employee Benefits.*

qualified preretirement survivor annuity (QPSA)   For retirement plans to which I.R.C. § 401(a)(11) applies (generally all qualified plans except for certain defined contribution plans as listed in the QUALIFIED JOINT AND SURVIVOR ANNUITY entry) QPSA must be provided for a participant's surviving spouse if the participant has some level of VESTING in his or her plan benefit but does not survive to retirement. Such an annuity generally must be the equivalent of the survivor annuity the spouse would have received under the qualified joint and survivor annuity rules if the participant had survived until retirement and died immediately thereafter. To waive this form of benefit, the participant must file an election in writing with the plan, accompanied by a written consent to the waiver by the participant's spouse.

The survivor annuity for the life of the participant's surviving spouse must satisfy certain conditions. First, the payments to the spouse must not be less than the amounts that would be payable as a survivor annuity under the plan's joint and survivor annuity rules (or the actuarial equivalent thereof) if certain criteria were met. These criteria are:

(1) If a participant dies after attaining the plan's earliest retirement age, the annuity must be as great as the survivor annuity that would have been payable to the spouse under the plan's joint and survivor annuity if the participant had retired with an immediate qualified joint and survivor annuity on the date of death.

(2) If a participant dies on or before the date he would have attained the plan's earliest retirement age, the annuity must be as great as the survivor portion of the plan's joint and survivor annuity if the participant had (a) separated from the employer's service on his date of death; (b) survived to the plan's earliest retirement age; (c) retired with an immediate qualified joint and survivor annuity at the plan's earliest retirement age; and (d) died on the day after the day on which he would have attained the plan's earliest retirement age.

In addition, the earliest period for which a surviving spouse may receive a payment under a qualified preretirement survivor annuity must not be later than the month in which the participant would have attained the earliest retirement age under the plan.

In a defined contribution plan, however, the plan must permit the surviving spouse to direct the commencement of benefit payments within a reasonable time following the participant's death.

See QUALIFIED JOINT AND SURVIVOR ANNUITY (QJSA).

Statutory and Regulatory Reference: See I.R.C. §§ 401(a)(11) and 417; Treas. Reg. §§ 1.401(a)-11 *et seq.*

Treatise Reference: See Tax Mgmt. (BNA), No. 370, *Qualified Plans — Taxation of Distributions; see also Employee Benefits Law* 163-64 (1991); D. McGill & D. Grubbs, Jr., *Fundamentals of Private Pensions* 165 (6th ed. 1989).

qualified retirement plan   A retirement-type plan that meets the requirements of the Internal Revenue Code for such plans, including the requirements of I.R.C. § 401(a) and therefore receives favorable federal income tax treatment.

The Code provides many advantages to qualified plans. In contrast to nonqualified arrangements, where the employer may not deduct its contributions until the employee takes the benefits into income, an employer may deduct contributions to a qualified plan in the year they are made, subject to the limits of I.R.C. § 404. Employees for whom contributions are made, however, do not recognize income until their benefits are actually distributed. In addition, the assets of a qualified plan, while held in the plan's trust, grow tax-free.

One way of viewing the advantages afforded by a qualified plan is to think in terms of the time value of money. In a nonqualified arrangement, the employer cannot take a compensation deduction until the employee includes the compensation in income. By permitting the employer to deduct contributions when paid, the resulting tax savings frees funds for the employer to invest. From the employee's standpoint, in addition to the benefits of tax deferral and tax-free compounding, I.R.C. § 402(e) provides favorable federal income tax treatment to lump-sum distributions under qualified plans that may reduce the employee's tax on retirement benefits.

The favorable income tax treatment accorded qualified plans is not without its price, however. Qualified plans must satisfy standards concerning coverage, participation, vesting, benefit accrual, and funding. These rules seek to prevent qualified plans from discriminating in favor of highly compensated employees.

I.R.C. § 401(a)(4) contains the general antidiscrimination rule. Under this rule, a plan will not qualify if it discriminates as to benefits or contributions in favor of highly compensated employees. Various other rules imposed by the Code also attempt to insure that a qualified retirement plan will not discriminate, either on its face or in operation, in favor of highly compensated employees.

See DEFINED BENEFIT PLAN, DEFINED CONTRIBUTION PLAN, NONQUALIFIED DEFERRED COMPENSATION PLAN.

Statutory and Regulatory Reference: See I.R.C. §§ 401(a) (plan qualification requirements), 402 (rules governing the taxation of distributions from qualified plans), and 501(a) (conferring tax-exempt status on a qualified plan's trust) and the regulations promulgated thereunder.

Case and Other Interpretive Reference: See Pulver Roofing Co. v. Commissioner, 70 T.C. 1001 (1978) (IRS may disqualify a plan for failure to comply with the I.R.C. § 401(a) requirements retroactively). *But see Boggs v. Commissioner*, 784 F.2d 1166 (4th Cir. 1986) (IRS may not revoke a favorable determination letter retroactively if the plan and the law in question had not been changed since the initial letter was issued).

Treatise Reference: See Tax Mgmt. (BNA), No. 351, *Pension Plans – Qualification*, and No. 352, *Profit-Sharing Plans – Qualification*; *see also Employee Benefits Law* 23-32 (1991).

qualified stock option   An option granted generally before May 21, 1976, under a plan that permits an employee to purchase employer stock within five years at a price equal to or greater than the stock's FAIR MARKET VALUE as of the date the option was granted. These options were the historical predecessor to incentive stock options (ISOs) and received similarly favorable tax treatment.

See INCENTIVE STOCK OPTION (ISO).

Statutory and Regulatory Reference: See generally I.R.C. § 421-25.

Treatise Reference: See Tax Mgmt. (BNA), No. 7, *Stock Options (Statutory) – Qualification*.

qualified total distribution   Any distribution or series of distributions either (1) made within one TAXABLE YEAR of the employee on account of the TERMINATION of a qualified plan or the complete discontinuance of contributions to a profit-sharing or stock bonus plan; (2) constituting a lump-sum distribution; or (3) constituting a distribution of qualified voluntary employee contributions.

The recipient of a qualified total distribution can rollover to an eligible retirement plan the entire FAIR MARKET VALUE of the property received in the distribution, less employee contributions other than qualified voluntary employee contributions.

See LUMP-SUM DISTRIBUTION, QUALIFIED VOLUNTARY EMPLOYEE CONTRIBUTIONS, ROLLOVER.

Statutory and Regulatory Reference: I.R.C. § 402(a)(5)(e)(i) (definition); I.R.C. § 401(a)(20) (permitting such distributions under qualified plans).

Treatise Reference: See Tax Mgmt. (BNA), No. 370, *Qualified Plans – Taxation of Distributions*.

qualified transportation   Transportation in a commuter highway vehicle (a highway vehicle with seating capacity of at least eight adults, not including the driver) where at least 80 percent of the mileage can reasonably be expected to be for purposes of transporting employees between their residence and place of employment. The number of employees transported for these purposes must be at least one-half the adult seating capacity of the vehicle (not including the driver). The qualified transportation must be provided pursuant to a separate written plan that does not discriminate in favor of officers, shareholders, or highly compensated employees. For years beginning before January 1, 1986, employees did not have to include the value of this qualified transportation in gross income.

Statutory and Regulatory Reference: See I.R.C. §§ 46(c)(6)(B) and 124.

Treatise Reference: See Tax Mgmt. (BNA), No. 394, *Employee Fringe Benefits*.

qualified trust   A trust forming part of a tax-qualified retirement plan that holds the plan's assets. Income earned on the assets in such a trust are not subject to federal income tax.

See QUALIFIED RETIREMENT PLAN.

Statutory and Regulatory Reference: See ERISA § 403(a); I.R.C. §§ 401(a) (trust requirement for qualified plans) and 501(a) (tax exemption for trusts that are a part of a qualified plan.

Treatise Reference: See Tax Mgmt. (BNA), No. 351, *Pension Plans—Qualification*, and No. 352, *Profit-Sharing Plans—Qualification*.

qualified voluntary employee contributions (QVECs)   For 1982-86, amounts that employees were allowed to contribute, on a tax-deductible basis, to a qualified retirement plan, in lieu of making deductible IRA contributions. Such contributions were also referred to as deductible employee contributions. The Tax Reform Act of 1986 (TRA 1986), Pub. L. No. 99-514, repealed the rules that allowed employees to make such contributions. The repeal was effective as of December 31, 1986. Qualified plans, however, may still hold some assets attributable to these types of contributions, and special IRA restrictions apply to such a plan's handling of these amounts.

Statutory and Regulatory Reference: See former I.R.C. §§ 72(o) and 219(e).

Treatise Reference: See Tax Mgmt. (BNA), No. 355, *IRAs and SEPs*.

qualifying employer real property
Parcels of EMPLOYER REAL PROPERTY are considered qualifying employer real property (1) if a substantial number of the parcels are dispersed geographically; (2) if each parcel of real property and the improvements on it are suitable (or adaptable without excessive cost) for more than one use; (3) even if all of the property is leased to more than one lessee; and (4) if the acquisition or retention of the property otherwise meets the requirements of Title IV of ERISA (other than the diversification requirements). A sponsoring employer's plan that is not an individual account plan cannot hold qualifying employer real property exceeding 10 percent of the FAIR MARKET VALUE of its assets.

Statutory and Regulatory Reference: See ERISA § 407(d)(4); 29 C.F.R. § 2550.407a-2(b).

Case and Other Interpretive Reference: See Rutland v. Commissioner, U.S.T.C., 12/8/87, 9 EB Cases 1147 (1987)(company sale of real property to employee retirement plan and plan's subsequent lease of the property to employer were prohibited transactions because transaction did not involve qualifying real property; property was concentrated in one geographic area). *See also Lambos v. Commissioner*, 88 T.C. 1440, 8 EB Cases 1853 (1987) (parcels of property leased to the plan's employer-sponsor held not geographically dispersed even though each parcel reflected distinct and disparate market conditions).

Treatise Reference: Employee Benefits Law 310-12 (1991).

qualifying employer security   An EMPLOYER SECURITY that is stock or a marketable obligation (e.g., a bond, debenture, note or certificate acquired on a market) issued by an employer whose employees are covered by the plan or an affiliate of such employer. Stock fits the definition only if, immediately following the acquisition of the stock, (1) no more than 25 percent of the aggregate amount of stock of the same class issued and outstanding at the time of the acquisition is held by the plan, and (2) at least 50 percent of the aggregate amount of stock of the same class issued and outstanding at the time of acquisition is held by persons independent of the issuer. A sponsoring employer's plan that is not an individual account plan cannot hold qualifying employer securities exceeding 10 percent of the FAIR MARKET VALUE of its assets.

Statutory and Regulatory Reference: See ERISA §§ 407(d)(5) and 407(d)(1).

Treatise Reference: Employee Benefits Law 310-12 (1991).

qualifying event   For purposes of the health care continuation coverage rules under COBRA, one of the following events that causes an individual to lose coverage under the employer's group health plan: (1) the death of the employee; (2) the termination of the employee's employment (other than for gross misconduct) or a reduction in the employee's hours; (3) the divorce or legal separation of the employee from his or her spouse; (4) the employee's entitlement to Medicare; (5) a dependent child ceasing to be a dependent under the plan. For these purposes, termination includes a strike, layoff, or walkout that results in loss of coverage. Commencement of bankruptcy proceedings that substantially eliminate retirees' health coverage within one year before or after such proceedings commence also will be considered a qualifying event. The occurrence of any of these events ending health care coverage triggers the employer's duty to give notice of continuation coverage.

Example: X is a covered employee who is married to Y. Both are covered under the health plan maintained by X's employer. X and Y are divorced, and under the terms of the health plan, Y will lose coverage. The divorce is a qualifying event. If Y elects COBRA coverage and then remarries during the period of coverage, Y's new spouse might become covered under X's employer's group health plan.

See COBRA, CONTINUATION COVERAGE, QUALIFIED BENEFICIARY.

Statutory and Regulatory Reference: See I.R.C. § 4980B(f)(3); Prop. Treas. Reg. § 1.162-26, Q&As 18-21, Q&A 31.

Case and Other Interpretive Reference: See Paris v. F. Korbel & Bros., Inc., 13 EB Cases 2489 (1990) (California federal district court found that disclosing a confidential statement made by a company executive did not constitute gross misconduct for COBRA continuation coverage purposes).

Treatise Reference: See Tax Mgmt. (BNA), No. 389, *Disability and Medical Reimbursement Benefits. See Also Employee Benefits Law* 993-97 (1991).

R

Rabbi trust A nonqualified deferred compensation plan, typically for the benefit of an employer's key executives, in which the employer places funds for the employee's retirement in a trust that remains under the employer's control and subject to the claims of the employer's creditors. A properly drafted Rabbi trust will result in the employer being treated as the owner of the trust property for tax purposes until the employee actually receives a distribution of the plan's assets.

See NONQUALIFIED DEFERRED COMPENSATION PLAN.

Statutory and Regulatory Reference: See generally I.R.C. §§ 83, 451, 671, and 677. Treas Reg. §§ 1.451-2, 1.671-3, and 1.677(a)-1.

Case and Other Interpretive Reference: PLR 8113107 (first Rabbi trust ruling); PLR 8634031 (first postmoratorium Rabbi trust ruling); PLRs 8804023, 8834015, and 8952037 (regarding the direction of asset investment); PLRs 8843045, 8845007, and 8844020 (regarding hardship withdrawals); PLR 9041052 (regarding assets that can be transferred into a Rabbi trust); PLRs 8735047, 8844031, and 9119052 (regarding the acceleration of distributions).

Treatise Reference: See Tax Mgmt. (BNA), No. 385, *Deferred Compensation Arrangements*.

rate making A statistical method by which insurance companies determine the price of an insurance contract, using mortality tables to determine the probability of a death and thereby forecasting when the applicant will die. A basic rate is computed by determining the costs the insurance company will bear for pure risk protection and the probability that the company will have to pay the death benefit. This basic protection is called one-year term and the calculation gives the cost of one-year term stated as a cost per thousand dollars worth of insurance at a given age. The method is also used to determine annuity rates.

Case and Other Interpretive Reference: See 1980 Commissioner's Standard Ordinary Mortality Tables.

ratio test One of three alternative tests for determining the adequacy of COVERAGE of employees by a qualified retirement plan (a plan must satisfy at least one of the three). This test requires that the plan benefit a classification of employees that does not allow more than a specified difference between the percentage of an employer's highly compensated employees who are covered and a similarly computed percentage for nonhighly compensated employees. For this purpose, the maximum allowable difference is a 70 percent ratio.

Example: A qualified plan covers certain of the employees of an employer. Its terms extend coverage to 80 percent of the employer's highly compensated employees and 60 percent of its nonhighly compensated employees. The plan will pass the ratio test because 60 is more than 70 percent of 80.

See AVERAGE BENEFIT PERCENTAGE TEST, 70 PERCENT TEST.

Statutory and Regulatory Reference: I.R.C. § 410(b)(1)(B); Treas. Reg. § 1.410(b)-2(b)(2).

Treatise Reference: See Tax Mgmt. (BNA), No. 351, *Pension Plans – Qualification*; *Employee Benefits Law* 96 (1991).

reasonable compensation   The amount paid to an employee or independent contractor for services that would be paid by a like enterprise under like circumstances if the parties were dealing at arm's length.

The Internal Revenue Code allows an employer to deduct all the ordinary and necessary expenses incurred in carrying on its trade or business. This includes a reasonable allowance for salaries and other compensation for personal services. The regulations, however, deny a DEDUCTION for any amount paid in the form of compensation which is not in fact related to the purchase price of services.

Statutory and Regulatory Reference: I.R.C. § 162(a)(1); Treas. Reg. § 1.162-7.

Treatise Reference: Tax Mgmt. (BNA), No. 390, *Reasonable Compensation*.

recharacterization   Excess contributions to a Section 401(k) plan can be recharacterized as elective contributions within two and one-half months after the end of plan year to which the recharacterization relates. Recharacterized contributions must be reported as income by the affected employees for the year in which they would have been taken into income if the employees had not initially elected to have them contributed to the plan. The amount of contributions recharacterized cannot exceed the amount of elective contributions made by highly compensated employees for the year.

The purpose of recharacterization is to allow the plan to meet the actual deferral percentage (ADP) test. To this end, the excess contributions of the highly compensated employee with the highest actual deferral ratio are recharacterized first to the extent necessary for the plan to meet the ADP test or to reduce that employee's actual deferral ratio to equal the ratio of the highly compensated employee with the next highest actual deferral ratio. If the plan still does not meet the test, this process is repeated until either the plan meets the test or there are no more excess contributions to be recharacterized.

See ACTUAL CONTRIBUTION PERCENTAGE (ACP), ACTUAL DEFERRAL PERCENTAGE (ADP), EXCESS CONTRIBUTIONS.

Statutory and Regulatory Reference: I.R.C. § 401(k); Treas. Reg. § 1.401(k)-1(f).

Treatise Reference: Tax Mgmt. (BNA), No. 358, *Cash or Deferred Arrangements*.

recovery ratio   *See* ANNUITY EXCLUSION RATIO RULE.

reduction in force (RIF)   An employer program to reduce its work force. The reductions are subject to the Age Discrimination in Employment Act (ADEA) rules if they allow for a window period during which older workers can qualify for early retirement. Thus, early retirement caused by a RIF must be wholly voluntary.

See AGE DISCRIMINATION IN EMPLOYMENT ACT (ADEA), WINDOW PLAN/WINDOW PERIOD.

Case and Other Interpretive Reference: EEOC v. Sandia Corp., 639 F.2d 600, 12 EB

Cases 1689 (10th Cir. 1980) (use of statistical evidence showing termination of disproportionately large number of older employees established a prima facie violation of ADEA); *McCorstin v. U.S. Steel Corp.*, 621 F.2d 749 (5th Cir. 1980) (availability of permissive early retirement programs could not be used as a factor in terminating an employee during a RIF).

Treatise Reference: Tax Mgmt. (BNA), No. 363, *Age and Sex Discrimination and Employee Benefit Plans*; *Employee Benefits Law* 913-41 (1991).

registration-class of securities   For purposes of a tax credit ESOP, any class of securities that is required to be registered under § 12 of the Securities Exchange Act of 1934, and any class of securities that would be required to be registered under that section except for the exemption in § 12(g)(2)(H) of the Securities Exchange Act of 1934.

Statutory and Regulatory Reference: I.R.C. § 409(e)(4).

Treatise Reference: Tax Mgmt. (BNA), No. 354, *ESOPs.*

remedial amendment period   The period during which a retirement plan seeking qualified status under I.R.C. § 401(a) may make amendments to remedy any deficiencies that constitute disqualifying provisions (i.e., ones that would cause the plan to not qualify).

Under I.R.C. § 401(b), a stock bonus, pension, profit-sharing, or annuity plan will qualify from the date it was put into effect, or for the period beginning with the earlier of the date on which there was adopted or put into effect any amendment that caused the plan to fail to satisfy I.R.C. § 401(a), and ending with the time prescribed by law for filing the employer's tax return for the taxable year in which the amendment was adopted (including extensions), if the appropriate corrective amendments are made within this period. All

provisions of the plan that are needed to satisfy § 401(a) must be in effect by the end of the above period and must have been made effective for the entire period.

Statutory and Regulatory Reference: I.R.C. § 401(b); Treas. Reg. § 1.401(b).

Case and Other Interpretive Reference: See Rev. Rul. 79-227 for the application of the remedial amendment period to the plans of employers that are not required to file federal income tax returns. *See also* Rev. Rul. 82-66, 1982-1 C.B. 61 (IRS will permit a retroactive amendment to qualify a plan for prior years after the remedial amendments period has expired if two conditions are met: (1) the plan is retroactively amended to comply with the qualification requirements as of the time the defect in the plan arose; and (2) employee benefit rights are restored retroactively to the levels they would have been had the plan been in compliance with the qualification requirements from the date the defect arose).

required aggregation group   *See* AGGREGATION GROUP.

required distribution   The amount that a qualified plan must distribute to an employee or beneficiary. In general, the Internal Revenue Code requires such distributions to begin no later than the April 1 following the year the employee reaches age 70½ and that they be paid over a period not extending beyond the life or LIFE EXPECTANCY of the employee or the combined lives or life expectancies of the employee and a designated beneficiary. Special rules apply if the employee or beneficiary dies before all distributable amounts have been distributed.

Statutory and Regulatory Reference: I.R.C. § 401(a)(9); Prop. Treas. Reg. § 1.401(a)(9).

Treatise Reference: Tax Mgmt. (BNA), No. 370, *Qualified Plans—Taxation of Distributions*; *Employee Benefits Law* 155-57 (1991).

reserves *See* QUALIFIED ASSET ACCOUNT (QAA).

restricted property Property, other than money, transferred to an employee or independent contractor by the employer or an owner of the employer in respect of services rendered or to be rendered. Such property often takes the form of nonqualified deferred compensation.

See LAPSE RESTRICTION, NONQUALIFIED DEFERRED COMPENSATION PLAN.

Statutory and Regulatory Reference: See generally I.R.C. § 83; Treas. Reg. § 1.83-1 *et seq.*

Treatise Reference: Tax Mgmt. (BNA), No. 384, *Restricted Property—Section 83.*

restricted stock option An option granted an employee to purchase the stock of his or her employer, which was granted generally before January 1, 1964, under a plan that permits an employee to purchase employer stock within 10 years at a price equal to 85 percent of the FAIR MARKET VALUE of the stock as of the date the option was granted. These options were the historical antecedents of qualified stock options and incentive stock options in receiving favorable federal income tax treatment.

Statutory and Regulatory Reference: I.R.C. § 424.

Treatise Reference: See Tax Mgmt. (BNA), No. 7, *Stock Options (Statutory)—Qualification.*

retired lives reserves (RLR) insurance An insurance arrangement that combines a flexible retirement annuity (or similar investment) with a group-term life insurance policy in order to provide a means to continue group-term coverage of employees after retirement. Part of each premium is used to purchase current group-term life insurance

coverage and part is deposited in an accumulation fund of the insurer. The amount is actuarially determined to ensure that the accumulated fund will be sufficient to maintain group-term coverage during the employee's postretirement years. The employee has no interest in the fund before retirement. An RLR is considered a welfare benefit fund, and the deductibility of contributions and taxation of benefits are subject to the limitations set forth for welfare benefit funds.

See GROUP-TERM LIFE INSURANCE, WELFARE BENEFIT FUND.

Statutory and Regulatory Reference: I.R.C. §§ 79, 419(e)(3), 419, and 419A and the regulations promulgated thereunder.

Treatise Reference: See Tax Mgmt. (BNA), No. 386, *Insurance-Related Compensation.*

retirement age *See* ACTUAL RETIREMENT AGE, EARLY RETIREMENT AGE, NORMAL RETIREMENT AGE.

retirement plan A written arrangement, whether or not tax-qualified, that provides for the retirement income needs of employees. Retirement plans may be funded by employer or employee contributions or a combination of both.

See QUALIFIED RETIREMENT PLAN.

Statutory and Regulatory Reference: I.R.C. § 401(a) and the regulations promulgated thereunder.

Treatise Reference: See Tax Mgmt. (BNA), No. 351, *Pension Plans—Qualification,* and No. 352, *Profit-Sharing Plans—Qualification; Employee Benefits Law* 17-34 (1991).

revenue procedure Internal practices and procedures of the IRS. Procedures give guidance on subjects of interest to taxpayers, such as how the IRS will apply certain rules or how certain tax computations should be made. Revenue Procedures are published weekly in the Internal Revenue Bulletin, and are cumulated semi-annually in the Cumulative Bulletin.

revenue ruling An official pronouncement of the IRS showing how the IRS would apply the federal tax laws to a hypothetical set of facts. Revenue rulings are typically issued in areas where the law is unclear and the IRS has received numerous PRIVATE LETTER RULING requests concerning the appropriate tax treatment of a transaction. Revenue rulings are published in the IRS' weekly Internal Revenue Bulletin and are cumulated twice annually in the IRS' Cumulative Bulletin.

reverse split-dollar insurance An employer-sponsored insurance arrangement whereby an employee purchases a life insurance policy for which the employer pays the premiums at the PS 58 cost, and the employee pays the remaining premium. The employee owns the equity in the policy, and the employer owns the protection element of the policy. The policy generally terminates after a specific number of years when the employee owns the entire policy with no premium payment due. However, if the employee dies before this turnover, the employer receives the stated death benefit, with any remaining amount passing to the employee's beneficiary.

See SPLIT-DOLLAR INSURANCE.

Statutory and Regulatory Reference: I.R.C. § 264 and the regulations promulgated thereunder.

Case and Other Interpretive Reference: See Rev. Rul. 64-328, 1964-22 C.B. 11 (defining split-dollar life); Rev. Rul. 78-420, 1978-2 C.B. 67 (treatment of third-party split-dollar); Rev. Rul., 79-50, 1979-1 C.B. 138 (treatment of shareholder split-dollar). *See also Genshaft v. Commissioner*, 64 T.C. 282 (1975)

(employer pay-all split dollar treated as split dollar).

Treatise Reference: See Tax Mgmt., (BNA), No. 386, *Insurance-Related Compensation*; Richey, *Evaluating and Designing Split-Dollar Life Insurance*, Sixth Annual Notre Dame Estate Planning Institute (1981).

reversion The return to an employer of the portion of its contributions to a retirement plan in excess of the amount needed to satisfy all fixed and contingent liabilities of the plan, usually on account of the plan's TERMINATION. To be entitled to receive a reversion from a terminated plan, the plan administrator must show that the plan's assets are sufficient to pay all plan benefits (whether or not vested), distribute all assets needed to pay such benefits, and distribute all excess assets that are attributable to employee contributions. Further, the plan must provide for such reversions upon termination and the provision must have been adopted at least five calendar years before plan termination. The Internal Revenue Code imposes a penalty excise tax on qualified PLAN ASSET reversions equal to either 20 percent or 50 percent of the amount involved, depending on the circumstances.

Statutory and Regulatory Reference: See ERISA § 4044 enumerating the priority categories of PLAN LIABILITIES that must be satisfied before an employer may receive a reversion from a defined benefit plan subject to Title IV of ERISA and I.R.C. § 401(a)(2), limiting the extent to which an employer may obtain a reversion under a qualified plan); I.R.C. § 4980 (excise tax on reversions). *See also* Treas. Reg. § 1.401-2(b)(2) (definition of liabilities to include fixed liabilities (those that are nonforfeitable prior to termination) and contingent liabilities (those not forfeitable prior to termination).

Case and Other Interpretive Reference: See Rev. Rul. 77-200, 1977-1 C.B. 98 (examining the circumstances under which a qualified plan may allow the reversion of employer contributions without adversely affecting the plan's qualified status); Rev. Rul. 83-52, 1983-1 C.B. 87 (interpreting liabilities that may be satisfied under Treas. Reg. § 1.401-2(b)(2); Rev. Rul. 85-6, 1985-1 C.B. 133 (liabilities for accrued early retirement subsidies must be satisfied before employer may recover excess assets). *See also C.D. Moyer Pension Trust,* 441 F. Supp. 1128 (E.D. Pa. 1977), *aff'd mem.,* 582 F.2d 1273 (3d Cir. 1978) (general exclusive benefit language in plan does not prevent it from later being amended before it is terminated to permit the employer to receive a reversion of its surplus assets; *Blessit v. Retirement Plan for Employees of Dixie Engine Co.,* 848 F.2d 1164 (11th Cir. 1987) (*en banc*) (while, in the case of a retirement-type subsidy, the plan must pay benefit liabilities accrued as of the date of the plan's termination with respect to employees who, at that time, qualify for the subsidy, the plan need not pay for benefits that would be expected to accrue in future years not yet worked).

Treatise Reference: See Tax Mgmt. (BNA), No. 357, *Plan Terminations and Mergers; see also Employee Benefits Law* 395; 419-32 (1991).

RIF   *See* REDUCTION IN FORCE.

RLR Insurance   *See* RETIRED LIVES RESERVE INSURANCE.

rollover   The reinvestment in a qualified plan, IRA, or Keogh plan of money or property received in a nonrequired distribution from another qualified plan that meets certain requirements. If the reinvestment is made within 60 days of the distribution, federal income tax on the distribution is deferred until the benefits involved are finally distributed from the recipient plan.

Statutory and Regulatory Reference: I.R.C. § 401(a)(20) (requirement that employer

notify PBGC upon qualifying total distribution upon plan termination); I.R.C. § 402(a)(5)-(6) (rollover rules for distributions from qualified plans); I.R.C. § 402(a)(5)(F)(ii) (restrictions on rollovers in the case of a key employee); I.R.C. §§ 402(a)(6)(H) and 408(d)(3)(F) (frozen deposits); I.R.C. § 402(a)(7) (rollover rules for distributions to participant's surviving spouse); I.R.C. § 402(f) (notice to recipient of ELIGIBILITY for rollover treatment on a distribution); I.R.C. § 403(a)(4) (§ 403(a) annuity plans); I.R.C. § 403(b)(8) (tax-deferred annuities); and I.R.C. § 408(d)(3) and Treas. Reg. § 1.408-4 (rollover rules for distributions from INDIVIDUAL RETIREMENT ARRANGEMENTS).

Case and Other Interpretive Reference: See Rev. Rul. 81-275, 1981-2 C.B. 92 (life insurance contract may not be rolled over to an IRA and its value, when distributed, is taxable to the employee); Rev. Rul. 82-153, 1982-2 C.B. 86 (individual may rollover qualifying distribution to an IRA after age 70½, but distributions in accordance with the MINIMUM REQUIRED DISTRIBUTION for IRAs must begin by the close of the taxable year in which the rollover occurred); Rev. Rul. 87-77, 1987-2 C.B. 115 (contribution to an IRA of cash representing the fair market value of property received by a participant does not qualify for rollover treatment — participant must either rollover cash or the actual proceeds from the sale of in-kind property — not an amount deemed to represent its fair market value); Rev. Rul. 89-50, 1989-1 C.B. 112, (transfer to an IRA of amounts distributed from a § 403(b) plan are not eligible for rollover treatment to the extent they were attributable to amounts contributed by the employer in excess of the exclusion allowance of § 403(b)(2). *See also Baetens v. Commissioner,* 777 F.2d 1160 (6th Cir. 1985) (distribution from a plan that has been disqualified is not eligible to be rolled over tax-free to an IRA).

Treatise Reference: See Tax Mgmt. (BNA), No. 355, *IRAs and SEPs; see also Employee Benefits Law* 184 (1991); D. McGill & D. Grubbs, Jr., *Fundamentals of Private Pensions* 722 (6th ed. 1989).

rule of 45 vesting   An alternative regular vesting schedule that qualified plans could satisfy for plan years beginning before January 1, 1989. Also known as age related vesting, this was the only schedule that took into account both a participant's age and length of service with the employer in determining his or her level of vesting in employer-derived benefits. This type of vesting was repealed by the Tax Reform Act of 1986 (TRA 1986), Pub. L. No. 99-514.

See VESTING.

Statutory and Regulatory Reference: See former I.R.C. § 411(b)(2)(C).

Treatise Reference: Tax Mgmt. (BNA), No. 351, *Pension Plans — Qualification*, and No. 352, *Profit-Sharing Plans — Qualification*.

rule of parity   *See* PARITY, RULE OF.

S

salary reduction arrangement An employer-sponsored arrangement in which an employee may elect to have some portion of his or her salary, instead of being paid to the employee directly, contributed to a qualified plan on the employee's behalf. Types of salary reduction arrangements include § 401(k) plans, salary reduction SEPs (SARSEPs), and § 403(b) plans.

See SALARY REDUCTION SEP (SARSEP), SECTION 401(k) PLAN, SECTION 403(b) PLAN.

Statutory and Regulatory Reference: I.R.C. § 401(k) and the final and proposed Treasury regulations promulgated thereunder (CODAs); I.R.C. § 403(b) and Treas. Reg. § 1.403(b) (TDAs); I.R.C. § 408(k)(6) (SARSEPs).

Treatise Reference: Tax Mgmt. (BNA), No. 355, *IRAs and SEPs*, No. 358, *Cash or Deferred Arrangements*, and No. 388, *Tax-Deferred Annuities — Section* 403(b).

salary reduction SEP (SARSEP) A simplified employee pension (SEP) maintained by certain qualifying small employers, to which employees may make salary reduction contributions on a pre-tax basis. An employer can only maintain a SARSEP if at no time during the preceding year it had more than 25 employees and if 50 percent or more of its employees elect to make salary reduction contributions. Certain nondiscrimination rules, similar to those that apply to § 401(k) plans, also apply.

See SALARY REDUCTION ARRANGEMENT, SIMPLIFIED EMPLOYEE PENSION (SEP).

Statutory and Regulatory Reference: I.R.C. § 408(k) and the regulations promulgated thereunder.

Treatise Reference: See Tax Mgmt. (BNA), No. 355, *IRAs and SEPs*.

savings plan *See* THRIFT PLAN.

seasonal employees Employees in an industry where the customary period of employment is less than 1,000 hours during a calendar year. In such cases, participation in qualified plans and VESTING and ACCRUAL of benefits are to be determined by regulations prescribed by the Secretary of Labor.

Statutory and Regulatory Reference: See ERISA § 202(a)(3)(B) and I.R.C. § 410(a)(3)(B) (participation); ERISA § 203(b)(2)(C) and I.R.C. § 411(a)(5)(C) (vesting); ERISA § 204(b)(3)(D) and I.R.C. § 411(b)(4)(D) (benefit accrual). *See also* 29 C.F.R. Part 2530.

Treatise Reference: Tax Mgmt., (BNA), No. 351, *Pension Plans — Qualification*, and No. 352, *Profit-Sharing Plans — Qualification*.

Section 22 amount A federal income tax credit available to certain disabled individuals. With respect to disability retirement benefits, a qualified individual may take a credit equal to 15 percent of the individual's § 22 amount for the taxable year. A qualified individual is any individual (1) who has attained age 65 before the close of the taxable year, or (2) who retired on disability before the close of the taxable year and who, upon retirement, was permanently and totally disabled. The § 22 amount is the qualified individual's initial amount, subject to certain reductions. The initial amount is (1) $5,000 for a single individual or where there is a joint return and only one spouse is a qualified individual, (2) $7,500 for a joint return where both spouses are qualified individuals, and (3) $3,750 for a married individual filing separately.

Example: Various reductions apply to the initial amount: for married individuals filing jointly, where both spouses have not attained age 65 before the close of the year, the initial amount may not exceed the sum of the spouses' disability income (the aggregate amount included in gross income for the year under I.R.C. §§ 72 or 105(a) to the extent the amount constitutes wages for the period during which the individual is absent from work on account of total and permanent disability).

See DISABILITY RETIREMENT BENEFITS, PERMANENT AND TOTAL DISABILITY.

Statutory and Regulatory Reference: See I.R.C. §§ 22, 105, and the regulations promulgated thereunder.

Treatise Reference: See Tax Mgmt. (BNA), No. 389, *Disability and Medical Reimbursement Benefits.*

Section 89 This section of the Internal Revenue Code contained the WELFARE BENEFIT PLAN nondiscrimination rules. Initially passed in the Tax Reform Act of 1986, it was repealed in 1989 by the Debt Limit Extension Act, so that it never actually took effect. Section 89 mandatorily applied qualification and complex nondiscrimination testing to health or accident plans and group-term life insurance plans. Employers also could elect to have § 89 apply to group legal service plans, educational assistance plans, and dependent care assistance programs. The various tests conditioned tax-free treatment of these employee benefits on satisfaction of a set of uniform nondiscrimination rules to protect against discrimination in favor of highly compensated employees. The basic concept was that if one of the enumerated benefit plans discriminated in favor of highly compensated employees, the excess benefit was taxable to the favored employees. The excess benefit of the highly compensated employees was the excess of the employees' employer-provided benefit over the highest permitted benefit. The highest permitted benefit was the benefit determined by reducing the nontaxable benefit of the highly compensated employees until the plan would not be considered discriminatory.

Statutory and Regulatory Reference: I.R.C. §§ 79, 89, 105, 120, 127, 129 and the regulations promulgated thereunder.

Treatise Reference: See Tax Mgmt., (BNA), No. 394, *Employee Fringe Benefits*; Hevener, *Employer's Handbook, A Practical Guide to Section 89 Compliance* (1989).

Section 132 benefits *See* PERK, WORKING CONDITION FRINGE BENEFITS.

Section 162 plan *See* EXECUTIVE BONUS PENSION PLAN.

Section 401(h) account An account set up under a pension or annuity plan to provide for the payment of benefits for sickness, accident, hospitalization, and medical expenses of retired employees, their spouses and dependents, with these restrictions: (1) the benefits must be subordinate to the retirement benefits provided by the pension or annuity plan; (2) a separate account must be established and maintained for the benefits; (3) amounts cannot possibly be diverted from the account for other purposes; (4) after satisfaction of all liabilities to provide the medical and other benefits, amounts remaining in the separate account must be returned to the employer. The Revenue Reconciliation Act of 1990, Pub. L. No. 191-508, added a provision temporarily allowing qualified transfers of excess pension assets from non-multiemployer defined benefit pension plans to a health benefits account (defined as an account established and maintained as a § 401(h) account) that is part of the plan.

Statutory and Regulatory Reference: I.R.C. §§ 401(h), and 420; Treas. Reg. § 1.401-14(c)(explaining when nonretirement benefits are treated as subordinate).

Case and Other Interpretive Reference: GCM 39,785 (contributions to a § 401(h) account maintained within a qualified plan to fund retiree medical benefits can be based on actual plan costs rather than actual contributions to the plan; this position was reversed in part by the Omnibus Budget Reconciliation Act of 1989 (OBRA 1989), Pub. L. No. 101-239, with amendment to § 401(h)).

Treatise Reference: Tax Mgmt. (BNA), No. 351, *Pension Plans—Qualification*.

Section 401(k) plan   Stock bonus or profit-sharing plans that contain features allowing employees to elect to defer part of their compensation on a pretax basis into the plan's tax-exempt trust. These plans, also known as cash or deferred arrangements, are subject to special nondiscrimination rules that limit the amount of money highly compensated employees may defer based on the amount deferred by nonhighly compensated employees. In general, only a qualified profit-sharing plan or stock bonus plan can contain a § 401(k) cash or deferred arrangement.

Section 401(k) plans were given tax-favored status by the 1978 Revenue Act. To qualify as a § 401(k) plan, the plan must be an arrangement under which a covered employee may elect to have the employer make annual payments to the plan's trust or to receive those amounts in cash.

As indicated above, § 401(k) plans must pass at least one of two actual deferral percentage (ADP) tests designed to prevent discrimination in favor of highly compensated employees within the meaning of IRC § 414(q). (The actual deferral percentage is the amount deferred by an employee for the year, expressed as a percentage of that employee's compensation).

Under the first test, the ADP of highly compensated employees as a group cannot exceed that of nonhighly compensated employees (also as a group) by more than 125 percent. Under the second test (also applied on a group basis), the ADP of the highly compensated group may not exceed that of nonhighly compensated employees by more than 200 percent and the difference between the ADP of the highly compensated group and that of the nonhighly compensated group may not exceed two percentage points.

A § 401(k) plan will not be disqualified for failure to satisfy the ADP tests for a plan year if, with respect to highly compensated employees having excess deferrals, before the close of the following plan year: (1) the excess and any income thereon is distributed to the employees involved; (2) the employer makes correcting contributions to the plan; or (3) to the extent permitted by the plan, the highly compensated employees are treated as having received a distribution equal to the amount of the excess and then as having recontributed the distributed amounts to the plan on an after-tax basis.

Notwithstanding the fact that the employer distributes an excess deferral and the income thereon in time to avoid plan disqualification, the employer will be subject to the 10 percent penalty excise tax on excess deferrals imposed by I.R.C. § 4979 unless it meets the requirements of that section. To avoid this tax, the plan must distribute the excess amounts to the employees involved within two and one half months following the close of the plan year. Amounts distributed in such a correcting distribution are not subject to the I.R.C. § 72(t) penalty tax on premature distributions.

Where there are excess deferrals, the permissible deferral percentage of the highly compensated employee with the highest ADP is reduced first.

Aside from correcting distributions, a § 401(k) plan may distribute amounts held in the plan's trust that are attributable to salary reduction contributions to participants or beneficiaries no earlier than:

(1) Separation from service, death, or disability;

(2) Termination of the plan without the establishment of a successor plan;

(3) The date of sale by a corporation of substantially all of its assets used in its trade or business with respect to an employee who continues to work for the corporation that acquires the assets;

(4) The date of the sale by a corporation of its interest in a subsidiary, with respect to an employee who continues employment with the subsidiary;

(5) In the case of § 401(k) plans forming part of a profit-sharing or stock bonus plan, attaining age 59½ or upon the hardship of an employee.

In addition, a § 401(k) plan cannot impose a participation requirement that exceeds one year and any employer-provided benefit other than employer matching contributions may not be made contingent on an employee's election to defer.

Note that the Tax Reform Act of 1986 (TRA 1986), Pub. L. No. 99-514, prohibited tax-exempt organizations and state and local governments from establishing § 401(k) plans. Such organizations that already had CODAs in effect, however (for governments on May 6, 1986, and for tax-exempts on July 2, 1986), were allowed to continue to maintain those plans.

See ACTUAL CONTRIBUTION PERCENTAGE (ACP), ACTUAL DEFERRAL PERCENTAGE (ADP), QUALIFIED NONELECTIVE CONTRIBUTIONS.

Statutory and Regulatory Reference: I.R.C. § 401(k); Treas. Reg. § 1.401(k)-1.

Treatise Reference: Tax Mgmt (BNA), No. 358, *Cash or Deferred Arrangements.*

Section 403(b) plan An annuity plan granted tax-favored status by the Internal Revenue Code to help provide retirement benefits for employees of certain tax-exempt organizations and public schools. These plans are also known as tax-sheltered annuities (TSAs) or tax-deferred annuities (TDAs). They may be funded with employer contributions, employee contributions, or a combination of both. Employee salary reduction contributions to such plans are generally limited to $9,500 per year and certain other special limits apply. Tax-deferred annuities are, for certain purposes, considered money purchase plans.

See CATCH-UP ELECTION, MONEY PURCHASE PLAN.

Statutory and Regulatory Reference: I.R.C. § 403(b); Treas. Reg. § 1.403(b)-1.

Case and Other Interpretive Reference: Rev. Rul. 82-102, 1982-1 C.B. 62 (arrangement whereby educational organization contributes to a nonforfeitable share account in credit union on behalf of its employees does not qualify as a § 403(b) plan); Rev. Rul. 84-149, 1984-2 C.B. 97 (illustrating the computation of the exclusion allowance with respect to employer contributions); Rev. Rul. 87-114, 1987-2 C.B. 116 (continuing SALARY REDUCTION AGREEMENT with respect to a § 403(b) plan for a year does not preclude the employee from entering into a new salary reduction agreement at any time during the employee's current taxable year); Rev. Rul. 89-50, 1989-1 C.B. 112 (transfer to an IRA of amounts distributed from a § 403(b) plan are not eligible for ROLLOVER treatment to the extent they were attributable to amounts contributed by the employer in excess of the exclusion allowance of § 403(b)(2)); Rev. Rul. 90-24, 1990-11 I.R.B. 6 (circumstances under which certain transfers between or among § 403(b)(1) annuities and § 403(b)(7) custodial accounts will not be considered to constitute a distribution).

Treatise Reference: See Tax Mgmt. (BNA), No. 388, *Deferred Annuities — Section* 403(b); *see also Employee Benefits Law* 32; 216-21 (1991).

self-directed account   An account in a defined contribution plan where the employee is allowed to select how his or her benefit funds will be invested, e.g., a self-directed IRA or a self-directed account in a qualified profit-sharing plan. A participant is not, by virtue of this right, considered a FIDUCIARY with respect to the plan, but the plan's fiduciaries will be relieved of certain duties with respect to the assets over which the right of self-direction is exercised. Labor Department regulations detail how many investment options, and of what nature, must be provided under a self-directed plan.

Statutory and Regulatory Reference: ERISA § 404(c); 29 C.F.R. § 2550.404c *et seq.*

Treatise Reference: See Tax Mgmt. (BNA), No. 351, *Pension Plans — Qualification; Employee Benefits Law* 293 (1991).

self-employed individual   An individual who, for the current or the immediately

preceding TAXABLE YEAR, has net earned income (gross earned income less applicable deductions) from self-employment within the meaning of I.R.C. § 401(c)(2), or someone who would have such income except for the fact that the relevant trade or business did not have a profit for the year.

Example: Examples of self-employed individuals include sole proprietors, partners in partnerships, and (for some purposes), S corporation shareholders. Certain special restrictions apply to qualified plans benefiting self-employed individuals (*see* discussion under owner-employee).

See EARNED INCOME, KEOGH PLAN, OWNER-EMPLOYEE.

Statutory and Regulatory Reference: I.R.C. § 401(c)(1) and Treas. Reg. § 1.401-10.

Treatise Reference: See Tax Mgmt. (BNA), No. 353, *Owner-Dominated Plans — Top-Heavy and H.R. 10 Plans.*

separate line of business (SLOB)   The separate line of business exception permits electing businesses that are part of a controlled group to ignore affiliates when testing retirement and dependent care plans for nondiscrimination, thereby treating each business as a stand-alone company for these purposes. Under the proposed regulations, a line of business is organized and operated separately only if it complies with five criteria during that testing year: separate organizational unit, separate financial accountability, separate employee work force, separate management, separate tangible assets. A line of business must have 50 employees to be treated as separate.

See LINE OF BUSINESS, NONDISCRIMINATION.

Statutory and Regulatory Reference: I.R.C. § 414(r); Prop. Treas. Reg. § 1.414(r).

Case and Other Interpretative Reference: Fujinon Optical, Inc. v. Commissioner, 76 T.C. 499 (1981) (SLOB exception would permit sophisticated medical optics company and retail film-distribution company owned by common parent to be tested for nondiscrimination purposes as separate lines of business).

separation from service   A termination of employment for any reason other than a quit, discharge, retirement, or death, regardless of the duration of such absence.

Example: If an employee is laid off for a period of time, the employee is deemed to be separated from service during that period for purposes of entering into participation in any qualified plan of the employer.

See SEVERANCE FROM SERVICE.

Statutory and Regulatory Reference: I.R.C. § 410; Treas. Reg. § 1.410(a)-7(c)(3)(ii).

SEPPAA (Single-Employer Pension Plan Amendments Act of 1986)   The statute that applies to voluntary defined benefit plan terminations initiated on or after January 1, 1986. SEPPAA changed the PBGC rules for single-employer plan terminations and insurance premiums and set up the standard and distress termination procedures currently followed by the PBGC.

See PBGC, STANDARD TERMINATION, DISTRESS TERMINATION, MPPAA.

Statutory and Regulatory Reference: Pub. L. No. 99-272.

Treatise Reference: Tax Mgmt. (BNA), No. 357, *Plan Terminations and Mergers*; *Employee Benefits Law* 391-411 (1991).

70 percent test   One of three minimum COVERAGE tests (the others are the average benefits percentage test and the ratio test) imposed by I.R.C. § 410(b) (qualified plans must pass at least one). This test requires a plan to benefit 70 percent or more of all of the employer's nonhighly compensated employees. For this purpose, all eligible

employees are considered to benefit under a plan. In a § 401(k) plan, or a plan to which employees may voluntarily contribute or may receive employer matching contributions, all employees eligible to contribute will be considered to benefit in that portion of the plan.

See AVERAGE BENEFIT PERCENTAGE TEST, RATIO TEST.

Statutory and Regulatory Reference: I.R.C. § 410(b)(1)(A). Treas. Reg. § 1.410(b)-2(b)(2) combines both the ratio test and the 70 percent test into what it terms the ratio percentage test, because any plan that passes the 70 percent test will automatically pass the ratio test.

Treatise Reference: Tax Mgmt. (BNA), No. 351, *Pension Plans — Qualification*; *Employee Benefits Law* 95-99 (1991).

severance from service   In the elapsed time method of crediting service, severance from service occurs on the earlier of: (1) the date on which an employee quits, retires, is discharged or dies, or (2) the first anniversary of the first date of a period in which an employee remains absent from service (with or without pay) for any other reason, such as vacation, holiday, sickness, DISABILITY, leave of absence, or layoff.

See ELAPSED TIME METHOD.

Statutory and Regulatory Reference: I.R.C. § 410(a); Treas. Reg. § 1.410(a)-7(b)(2).

simplified employee pension (SEP)   A retirement plan in which, in effect, the employer establishes individual retirement accounts (IRAs) for eligible employees. A SEP is treated as a defined contribution plan but, unlike I.R.C. § 401(a) plans, SEPs are subject to certain simplified qualification requirements that make them easier to administer, although somewhat less flexible, than § 401(a) plans. SEPs are often maintained under model arrangements between employers and banks or similar institutions.

See INDIVIDUAL RETIREMENT ARRANGEMENT, SARSEP.

Statutory and Regulatory Reference: I.R.C. § 408(k); Prop. Treas. Reg. §§ 1.408-7 and -8.

Treatise Reference: See Tax Mgmt. (BNA), No. 355, *IRAs and SEPs*; *see also Employee Benefits Law* 31; 222-32 (1991).

simplified split-dollar insurance   A split-dollar insurance arrangement under which the employer and employee enter into an agreement as to how much the employee's beneficiary will receive upon the employee's death. If the policy is surrendered before the employee's death, the standard split-dollar rules apply, and the employer recovers the cash value or at least the amount equal to the premiums paid by the employer.

See SPLIT-DOLLAR LIFE INSURANCE.

Statutory and Regulatory Reference: I.R.C. § 264 and the regulations promulgated thereunder.

Case and Other Interpretive Reference: Rev. Rul. 64-328, 1964-22 C.B. 11 (defining split-dollar life); Rev. Rul. 78-420, 1978-2 C.B. 67 (treatment of third-party split-dollar); Rev. Rul. 79-50, 1979-1 C.B. 138 (treatment of shareholder split-dollar). *See also Genshaft v. Commissioner,* 64 T.C. 282 (1975) (employer pay-all split dollar treated as split dollar).

Treatise Reference: See Tax Mgmt. (BNA), No. 386, *Insurance Related Compensation*; Richey, *Evaluating and Designing Split-Dollar Life Insurance*, Sixth Annual Notre Dame Estate Planning Institute (1981).

Single-Employer Pension Plan Amendments Act of 1986   *See* SEPPAA.

single-employer plan   Any employee benefit plan other than a multiemployer plan.

See EMPLOYEE BENEFIT PLAN, MULTIEMPLOYER PLAN.

Statutory and Regulatory Reference: ERISA §§ 3(41) and 4001(a)(15).

single-premium life insurance   A life insurance product that magnifies the cash value rather than the death benefit of life insurance. The policy generally is paid with one to four premiums. There are two types of single-premium policies, whole life and variable life. For single-premium whole life insurance, there generally is a fixed return for a fixed duration and the insurer invests amounts in bonds and mortgages. For variable life single-premium insurance, the cash value is invested in funds the policyholder selects, for example, a stock fund or a real estate fund. Single-premium policies once were used as a means of building cash values that could be borrowed, but after the Tax Reform Act of 1986 (TRA 1986), Pub. L. No. 99-514, loans are treated as taxable distributions. These policies also may be subject to the modified endowment contract limitations.

See LIFE INSURANCE CONTRACT, MODIFIED ENDOWMENT CONTRACT, VARIABLE LIFE INSURANCE, WHOLE LIFE INSURANCE.

Statutory and Regulatory Reference: I.R.C. § 72(c), 7702(f)(7) and the regulations promulgated thereunder.

Treatise Reference: Tax Mgmt. (BNA), No. 386, *Insurance-Related Compensation.*

SLOB   *See* SEPARATE LINE OF BUSINESS.

Social Security   The system of social insurance maintained by the federal government and supported by various excise taxes on employers and employees to fund its two components: Old Age Survivors' and Disability Insurance (OADSI) and Medicare.

See INTEGRATION (SOCIAL SECURITY), OASDI, SOCIAL SECURITY TAX, AND SOCIAL SECURITY TAXABLE WAGE BASE.

Statutory and Regulatory Reference: Social Security Act, 42 U.S.C. § 301 (commonly known as FICA).

Social Security integration   *See* INTEGRATION (SOCIAL SECURITY).

Social Security retirement age   For qualified plan purposes, the age used as the retirement age under § 216(l) of the Social Security Act, determined without regard to the age increase factor used in that Act and as if the early retirement age under Act § 216(l)(2) were age 62. This age is used in determining the maximum benefit payable under a qualified defined benefit plan and in applying the Social Security integration rules.

See EARLY RETIREMENT AGE.

Statutory and Regulatory Reference: I.R.C. § 415(b)(8) (general rule) and Prop. Treas. Reg. § 1.401(l)-1(c)(30) (integration definition).

Treatise Reference: Tax Mgmt. (BNA), No. 392, *Withholding, Social Security and Unemployment Taxes on Compensation.*

Social Security supplement   A benefit under a qualified retirement plan payable to an employee who retires before becoming eligible to receive Social Security benefits. The plan will provide the employee with a benefit equivalent to part or all of the benefit he or she will ultimately receive from Social Security until Social Security payments begin.

See SOCIAL SECURITY.

Treatise Reference: Tax Mgmt. (BNA), No. 351, *Pension Plans – Qualification*, and No. 352, *Profit-Sharing Plans – Qualification.*

Social Security tax   Also known as FICA (Federal Insurance Contribution Act). FICA taxes are imposed on wages paid to employees. The revenues derived therefrom go to fund Social Security benefits for employees. Both the employer and the employee must pay FICA tax at a rate of 7.65 percent on an employee's annual wages from the employer up to the Social Security taxable wage base.

Both the employer and employee portions of the FICA tax are divided into two components or "premiums." The Old Age, Survivors and Disability Insurance (OASDI) premium is the largest component of the FICA tax. It is imposed at a 6.2 percent rate. The other element or premium is the "hospital insurance" premium (Medicare), imposed at a 1.45 percent rate.

See INTEGRATION (SOCIAL SECURITY), SOCIAL SECURITY TAXABLE WAGE BASE, UNEMPLOYMENT TAXES.

Statutory and Regulatory Reference: See generally I.R.C. §§ 3101-3111 and the regulations promulgated thereunder.

Treatise Reference: Tax Mgmt. (BNA), No. 392, *Withholding, Social Security and Unemployment Taxes on Compensation.*

Social Security taxable wage base   The level of an employee's annual wages on which FICA taxes are imposed and on which Social Security benefits are based. This amount is established annually under § 230 of the Social Security Act. This wage base is also used in the Social Security integration (permitted disparity) rules for qualified plans in determining a plan's proper integration level.

See INTEGRATION LEVEL.

Statutory and Regulatory Reference: I.R.C. § 401(l)(5)(A); Treas. Reg. § 1.401(l)-1(c)(32).

Treatise Reference: Tax Mgmt. (BNA), No. 356, *Qualified Plans – Integration*, and No. 392, *Withholding, Social Security and Unemployment Taxes on Compensation.*

spinoff   *See* MERGED PLAN/MERGER.

split-dollar life insurance   An insurance plan used to finance premium pay-

ments on a WHOLE LIFE INSURANCE policy. It is arranged as an insurance agreement whereby an employer and an employee split both the insurance premium on the employee's life and the cash values and death benefits. The employee and employer combine to purchase life insurance for the employee with a substantial investment element (this precludes the use of term insurance policies; the most common type of insurance used for these purposes is whole life insurance with a cash value feature). Generally, the employer pays an annual premium equal to the increase in the policy's cash surrender value for the year and the balance of the annual premium is paid by the employee. When the employee dies, the employer receives from the policy's proceeds an amount equal to the cash surrender value of the policy and the balance of the proceeds are paid to the employee's beneficiary. Split-dollar policies generally are of two types: (1) the endorsement system (the employer owns the policy and pays the premiums; the employee then reimburses the employer for his or her portion of the premium); and (2) collateral assignment system (the employee owns the policy and pays the premium, and the employer makes annual loans without or at a low interest rate to the employee equal to the yearly increase in the cash surrender value of the policy. The employee assigns the policy to the employer as collateral for the loans, which are payable when the employee terminates employment or dies).

Statutory and Regulatory Reference: I.R.C. § 264 and the regulations promulgated thereunder.

Case and Other Interpretive Reference: Rev. Rul. 64-328, 1964-22 C.B. 11 (defining split-dollar life); Rev. Rul. 78-420, 1978-2 C.B. 67 (treatment of third-party split-dollar); Rev. Rul. 79-50, 1979-1 C.B. 138 (treatment of shareholder split-dollar). *See also Genshaft v. Commissioner,* 64 T.C. 282 (1975) (employer pay-all split dollar treated as split dollar).

Treatise Reference: Tax Mgmt. (BNA), No. 386, *Insurance-Related Compensation;* Richey, *Evaluating and Designing Split-Dollar Life Insurance,* Sixth Annual Notre Dame Estate Planning Institute (1981).

split funding A method of funding a pension plan in which part of the retirement benefits are funded through insurance contracts that are converted to annuities at retirement and the remaining retirement benefits are funded through assets held in a trust.

See FULLY INSURED PLAN.

Treatise Reference: Tax Mgmt. (BNA), No. 371, *Employee Plans—Deductions, Contributions, and Funding.*

spousal consent The consent required before a benefit under a qualified plan can be paid in a form other than a qualified joint and survivor annuity or, in the case of preretirement death benefits, a qualified preretirement survivor annuity. Consent need not be obtained if the participant and the spouse have been married for less than one year before the earlier of the ANNUITY STARTING DATE or the participant's death. Spousal consent is also required before a participant's ACCRUED BENEFIT can be used as security for a loan.

See QUALIFIED JOINT AND SURVIVOR ANNUITY (QJSA), QUALIFIED PRERETIREMENT SURVIVOR ANNUITY (QPSA).

Statutory and Regulatory Reference: See ERISA §§ 205(a)(c)(2); *see also* I.R.C. §§ 401(a)(11) and 417(a)(2) and the regulations promulgated thereunder.

Treatise Reference: See Tax Mgmt. (BNA), No. 370, *Qualified Plans—Taxation of Distributions; see also Employee Benefits Law* 164-65 (1991).

spousal IRA Where one spouse has compensation and the other does not (or elects to be treated as if he or she does not), the spouse with compensation can contribute an amount to an IRA for the other. The maximum total DEDUCTION for both spouses is $2,250 for the year. No particular mix is required for the payments to the IRAs of the couple, but neither can have deductible contributions of more than $2,000.

See INDIVIDUAL RETIREMENT ARRANGEMENT, IRA.

Statutory and Regulatory Reference: I.R.C. § 219 and the regulations promulgated thereunder.

Treatise Reference: Tax Mgmt. (BNA), No. 355, *IRAs and SEPs.*

standard termination   Under SEPPAA, a voluntary TERMINATION of a single-employer defined benefit plan where the plan has sufficient assets to cover all benefit liabilities. A plan may be terminated under a standard termination only if: (1) the plan administrator provides 60-days' advance notice of intent to terminate to affected parties; (2) appropriate notice is given to the PBGC, participants, and beneficiaries of benefit liabilities; (3) the PBGC does not issue a notice of noncompliance; and (4) when the final distribution of assets occurs, the plan is sufficient for benefit liabilities (all fixed and contingent obligations, both vested and non-vested, as of the date of termination).

See DEFINED BENEFIT PLAN, DISTRESS TERMINATION, INVOLUNTARY TERMINATION, SEPPAA (SINGLE-EMPLOYER PENSION PLAN AMENDMENTS ACT OF 1986).

Statutory and Regulatory Reference: See ERISA §§ 4001(a)(16) (defining benefit liabilities by reference to I.R.C. § 401(a)(2)) and 4041(b) (standard termination of single-employer plan); I.R.C. § 401(a)(2)(defining benefit liability); Treas. Reg. § 1.401-2 (defining benefit liabilities to include fixed and contingent, vested and nonvested, as of date of plan termination). *See also* PBGC Proposed Regulations: Distress Terminations of Single-Employer Plans and Standard Terminations of Single-Employer Plans, 52 Fed. Reg. 33,318 (Sept. 2, 1987); PBGC Notice of Interim Procedures, Single-Employer Plan Terminations under The Single-Employer Pension Plan Amendments Act of 1986, 51 Fed. Reg. 12,491 (April 10, 1986); PBGC Notice of Revised Termination Rules, 53 Fed. Reg. 1904 (Jan. 22, 1984); PBGC Notice of Issuance of New Termination Forms, 54 Fed. Reg. 52,904 (Dec. 22, 1989). IRS Notice 87-57, 1987-35 I.R.B. (Aug. 31, 1987) (plans terminated after the effective date of the Tax Reform Act of 1986, but prior to the date of retroactive plan amendments that are required to be adopted, must be amended no later than the date of termination).

Case and Other Interpretive Reference: See GCM 39,310 (April 4, 1984) (participants in defined contribution plans must be paid their otherwise nonvested benefits, to the extent funded, if the plan terminated prior to their incurring breaks in service). *See also Mead Corp. v. Tilley*, 815 F.2d 989, 8 EB Cases 2134 (4th Cir. 1987), *rev'd,* 490 U.S. 714, 10 EB Cases 2569 (1989) (ERISA does not require plan administrator to pay plan participants unreduced early retirement benefits provided under plan before residual assets may revert to employer since ERISA § 4044 does not confer right upon participants to recover unaccrued benefits); *Blessit v. Retirement Plan for Employees of Dixie Engine Co.,* 848 F.2d 1164 (11th Cir. 1987)(*en banc*) (no statutory requirement that upon termination plan must pay benefits based on future years of service not yet worked); *Anderson v. Emergency Medicine Associates,* 860 F.2d 987, 10 EB Cases 1414 (10th Cir. 1988) (pension plan did not partially terminate when two of plan's four participants voluntarily left employer; voluntary employee decisions to leave employer are not employee terminations requisite to trigger partial plan termination).

Treatise Reference: Tax Mgmt. (BNA), No. 357, *Plan Terminations and Mergers*; *Employee Benefits Law* 391-411 (1991).

statutorily excludable employees   Under a qualified retirement plan, employees who need not be counted in determining whether the plan meets the MINIMUM COVERAGE RULES of I.R.C. § 410(b). These employees are: (1) those covered by a collective bargaining agreement where retirement benefits have been the subject of good faith bargaining; (2) certain employees who perform their duties aboard an aircraft in flight; (3) nonresident aliens who have no EARNED INCOME from the year from United States sources; and (4) employees who do not satisfy the plan's minimum age and service requirements (provided that such requirements comply with the Internal Revenue Code).

See QUALIFIED RETIREMENT PLAN.

Statutory and Regulatory Reference: I.R.C. § 410(b)(3)(A)-(C); Treas. Reg. § 1.410(b)-1(c).

Treatise Reference: Tax Mgmt. (BNA), No. 351, *Pension Plans—Qualification*, and No. 352, *Profit-Sharing Plans—Qualification*.

step-rate/step-rate excess plan   A qualified retirement plan that integrates with Social Security by providing a higher level of benefits for compensation above the INTEGRATION LEVEL, and that provides at least some level of benefits both above and below the integration level. The plan is required to satisfy rules limiting the amount of the disparity between benefits above the integration level and benefits below the integration level.

Example: A defined contribution plan's integration level is the Social Security taxable wage base. The plan provides for an allocation of employer contributions to each participant's plan account equal to 5 percent of his or her compensation for the year up to the integration level. For compensation in excess of the integration level, the allocation increases to 8 percent.

See EXCESS BENEFIT PLAN, INTEGRATION (SOCIAL SECURITY).

Statutory and Regulatory Reference: I.R.C. §§ 401(a)(5) and 401(l) and the regulations promulgated thereunder.

Treatise Reference: Tax Mgmt. (BNA), No. 356, *Qualified Plans—Integration*.

stock appreciation rights (SARs)   A nonqualified employee incentive compensation arrangement, usually for an employer's executives and key employees, in which employees receive a contractual right to employer stock or cash equal to the APPRECIATION in value of the stock between the date the right is granted and a future specified date. The employee is not taxed on receipt of the contractual right, since such a right is not considered property within the meaning of I.R.C. § 83. The employee is taxed when he or she receives the cash or stock on the amount of the cash or the FAIR MARKET VALUE of the stock.

See INCENTIVE STOCK OPTION (ISO), NON-QUALIFIED DEFERRED COMPENSATION PLAN, RESTRICTED PROPERTY.

Statutory and Regulatory Reference: See I.R.C. § 83 and the regulations promulgated thereunder.

Treatise Reference: See Tax Mgmt. (BNA), No. 383, *Nonstatutory Stock Options*.

stock bonus plan   A type of qualified defined contribution plan established and maintained by an employer to provide benefits similar to a profit-sharing plan, except that benefits are generally paid in the form of the employer's stock and the level of employer contributions does not necessarily depend on profits. An Employee Stock Ownership Plan (ESOP) may take the form, in whole or part, of a stock bonus plan, as may a § 401(k) plan.

Statutory and Regulatory Reference: See I.R.C. § 401(a), Treas. Reg. § 1.401-1(a)(2)(iii) (definition); I.R.C. §§ 401(a)(22) and 409(e) (voting rights pass-through); I.R.C. §§ 401(a)(23), 409(h) and (o) (special put option and distribution requirements, respectively).

Treatise Reference: See Tax Mgmt. (BNA), No. 352, *Profit-Sharing Plans — Qualification*, and No. 354, *ESOPs*; *see also Employee Benefits Law* 25-26 (1991); D. McGill & D. Grubbs, Jr., *Fundamentals of Private Pensions* 674 (6th ed. 1989).

stock option (compensatory) The right of an employee, in payment for services rendered or to be rendered, to purchase the securities of the employer or a related employer during a specified period for a predetermined price.

See INCENTIVE STOCK OPTION (ISO), QUALIFIED STOCK OPTION, RESTRICTED PROPERTY, RESTRICTED STOCK OPTION.

Statutory and Regulatory Reference: See generally I.R.C. § 83; Treas. Reg. § 1.83-7 (rules for taxation of nonstatutory options); *see also* I.R.C. §§ 421-25 and the regulations promulgated thereunder (rules governing different types of statutory (tax-favored) stock options.

Treatise Reference: Tax Mgmt. (BNA), No. 7, *Stock Options (Statutory) — Qualification*, No. 383, *Nonstatutory Stock Options*, and No. 384, *Restricted Property — Section* 83.

stop-loss reinsurance A term for one of several forms of insurance coverage whereby there is a separate insurance contract under which the insurer agrees to reimburse the company (as policyholder) for a portion of incurred (or paid) claims that exceed a predetermined amount in exchange for an insurance premium. This type of coverage is generally purchased by self-insured programs that want a level of security from catastrophic or excessive claim losses, thereby stabilizing expected claim costs and reducing the financial impact of year-to-year fluctuations in claims.

Treatise Reference: J. Mamorsky, *Employee Benefits Handbook* (1987); J.F. Dobbyn, *Insurance Law in a Nutshell* (2d ed. 1989).

stock purchase plan *See* EMPLOYEE STOCK PURCHASE PLAN.

SUB plan *See* SUPPLEMENTAL UNEMPLOYMENT BENEFIT PLAN.

substantial risk of forfeiture In relation to restricted property (generally property other than cash, qualified plan benefits, or fringe benefits transferred in exchange for the performance of services), a significant possibility that the employee's rights to full enjoyment of the property may never fully vest due to some contingency, such as the performance of substantial future services. Such a contingency may take the form of a positive requirement (e.g., the employee will be entitled to full vesting in the property upon completing five years of service) or a negative forfeiture condition (e.g., the employee has the right to the property now, but will forfeit it if he or she quits before five years have passed). When the employee's rights in the property are either no longer subject to a substantial risk of forfeiture or are transferable, the employee will have to recognize gross income equal to the property's FAIR MARKET VALUE and the employer may take an offsetting compensation deduction.

See RESTRICTED PROPERTY, VESTING.

Statutory and Regulatory Reference: I.R.C. § 83(c)(1); Treas. Reg. § 1.83-3(c)(1).

Treatise Reference: See Tax Mgmt. (BNA), No. 384, *Restricted Property — Section* 83.

success tax   A 15 percent excise tax imposed on certain distributions from and accumulations in qualified plans and IRAs. The excise tax generally applies to excess retirement accumulations which exist at the death of the participant.

See EXCESS DISTRIBUTION.

Statutory and Regulatory Reference: See I.R.C. § 4980A; Temp. and Prop. Treas. Reg. § 1.4980A-1.

Treatise Reference: See Tax Mgmt. (BNA), No. 370, *Qualified Plans—Taxation of Distributions.*

super top-heavy plan   *See* MAXIMUM BENEFITS.

supplemental benefits   Benefits payable by a pension plan other than retirement benefits. A qualified pension plan can provide for payment of a pension due to disability and can provide for payment of incidental death benefits. It cannot, however, provide for payment of benefits not customarily included in a pension plan, such as layoff benefits or benefits for sickness, accident, hospitalization, or medical expenses (except medical expenses for retired employees and their spouses and dependents).

See INCIDENTAL DEATH BENEFITS.

Statutory and Regulatory Reference: I.R.C. § 401(a); Treas. Reg. § 1.401-1(b)(1)(i).

Treatise Reference: Tax Mgmt. (BNA), No. 351, *Pension Plans—Qualification,* and No. 352, *Profit-Sharing Plans—Qualification.*

supplemental cost   *See* FUNDING STANDARD ACCOUNT, NORMAL COST.

supplemental executive retirement plan (SERP)   A nonqualified deferred compensation plan used to provide highly compensated employees with retirement benefits. A SERP would be used by an employer who wishes to provide certain executives with benefits greater than those permitted by the limitations on the amount of benefits that can be paid by qualified plans.

See NONQUALIFIED DEFERRED COMPENSATION PLAN, TOP-HAT PLAN.

supplemental liability   Any cost or reduction in cost of funding a qualified defined benefit plan subject to the minimum funding standard of I.R.C. § 412 that is not spread out over the future service of the employees as part of normal cost. Instead, it is amortized over a statutorily specified period of years. A supplemental liability can result from past service costs or from changes in costs resulting from experience gains and losses, changes in ACTUARIAL ASSUMPTIONS, or a switch from one actuarial method to another.

See DEFINED BENEFIT PLAN, EXPERIENCE GAINS AND LOSSES, FUNDING STANDARD ACCOUNT, MINIMUM FUNDING STANDARD, NORMAL COST, PAST SERVICE LIABILITIES.

Statutory and Regulatory Reference: I.R.C. § 412 and the regulations promulgated thereunder.

Treatise Reference: Tax Mgmt. (BNA), No. 371, *Employee Plans—Deductions, Contributions, and Funding.*

supplemental unemployment benefit plan   An employee benefit plan that provides benefits in the event of involuntary separation from service (temporary or permanent), if the separation results directly from a reduction in force (RIF), the discontinuance of a plant or operation, or other similar conditions, including separations resulting from cyclical or seasonal causes. The plan is generally funded through the use of a VEBA or a § 501(c)(17) SUB trust.

See SEVERANCE PAY, VEBA.

T

Taft-Hartley Act plan A jointly administered (union and employer) pension plan regulated under § 302 of the Labor Management Relations Act (Taft-Hartley Act). Such plans are also subject to ERISA, including the requirements imposed by ERISA's multiemployer plan provisions.

See MULTIEMPLOYER PLAN.

Statutory and Regulatory Reference: Labor-Management Relations Act § 302(c)(5); ERISA §§ 3(37)(A), 4041A, 4201A.

Treatise Reference: See Tax Mgmt. (BNA), No. 3595, *Multiemployer Plans – Special Rules; Employee Benefits Law* 692-840 (1991).

target benefit plan A type of qualified retirement plan under which the amount of each year's employer contribution is determined by reference to the plan's original actuarial assumptions rather than on assumptions that are adjusted periodically to reflect experience (as is the case for defined benefit plans). Such a plan is treated as a defined contribution plan for purposes of certain of the limits imposed by the Internal Revenue Code.

See ACTUARIAL ASSUMPTIONS, DEFINED BENEFIT PLAN/DEFINED CONTRIBUTION PLAN, QUALIFIED RETIREMENT PLAN.

Statutory and Regulatory Reference: I.R.C. § 411(b)(2)(C) (benefit accrual rules for target benefit plans).

Case and Other Interpretive Reference: Rev. Rul. 76-464, 1976-2 C.B. 115, which provides guidelines for determining whether a target benefit plan discriminates within the meaning of I.R.C. § 401(a)(4). (Note that the version of § 401(a)(4) described in this ruling is the one that existed before the Tax Reform Act of 1986 (TRA 1986), Pub. L. No. 99-514, modified the definition of the PROHIBITED GROUP in whose favor DISCRIMINATION is prohibited).

Treatise Reference: Tax Mgmt. (BNA), No. 351, *Pension Plans – Qualification*, No. 352, *Profit-Sharing Plans – Qualification,* and No. 371, *Employee Plans – Deductions, Contributions, and Funding.*

taxable income For federal income tax purposes, the amount of annual income on which a taxpayer is subject to federal income tax. Taxable income is computed by determining a taxpayer's gross income, then subtracting any applicable deductions.

See DEDUCTIONS.

Statutory and Regulatory Reference: I.R.C. § 63(a).

taxable wage base   *See* SOCIAL SECURITY TAXABLE WAGE BASE.

taxable year   The calendar year, or the fiscal year ending during such calendar year, on the basis of which a taxpayer's TAXABLE INCOME is computed for federal income tax purposes. Such a year is generally a 12-consecutive-month period except where Treasury regulations allow a fraction of a year (known as a short taxable year) to be used. Short-year returns are generally available only for the first or last year of a taxpayer's existence or for a year in which the taxpayer changes to a different taxable year than the one it had previously.

Statutory and Regulatory Reference: I.R.C. § 7701(a)(23).

tax-deferred annuity   An annuity used to fund retirement plans of colleges and universities, hospitals, and other tax-exempt employers or to fund the retirement savings of employees of those organizations.

See SECTION 403(b) PLAN.

Statutory and Regulatory Reference: I.R.C. § 403(b) and the regulations promulgated thereunder.

Treatise Reference: No. 388 Tax Mgmt. (BNA), *Tax-Deferred Annuities—Section 403(b); Employee Benefits Law* 32; 216-21 (1991).

tax-qualified plan   *See* QUALIFIED RETIREMENT PLAN.

technical advice memorandum (TAM)   A ruling letter in the nature of a private letter ruling that is issued by the IRS' National Office (unlike regular private letter rulings, which are issued by local IRS district offices) explaining how the IRS will apply federal tax law to a given set of facts. TAMs typically originate as private letter ruling requests from taxpayers that are referred to the National

Office by either the taxpayer or the IRS district office because of their uniqueness or complexity. While they do not constitute precedent except as to the taxpayer to whom they are issued, they constitute important evidence of how the IRS will treat a particular transaction and taxpayers may cite them as persuasive authority in cases before the IRS.

See PRIVATE LETTER RULING (PLR), REVENUE RULING, REVENUE PROCEDURE.

10-or-more employer plan   A welfare benefit fund to which more than one employer contributes and to which no employer normally contributes more than 10 percent of the total contributions made under the plan by all employers. These multiple employer welfare funds are excepted from the account limitations under I.R.C. § 419 for welfare benefit funds.

See VEBA, WELFARE BENEFIT FUND.

Statutory and Regulatory Reference: I.R.C. §§ 419, 419A(f), and 501(c)(9).

Treatise Reference: Tax Mgmt. (BNA), No. 395, *Section 501(c)(9) and Self-Funded Employee Benefits*.

termination   The ending of a pension plan by decision of the employer or by force of circumstances (such as bankruptcy) or the ending of a profit-sharing plan by complete discontinuance of contributions.

Title IV of ERISA provides that in the case of single-employer and multiple-employer plan terminations, certain benefits will be paid to the participants even where the plan lacks adequate assets to make such payments. Subject to certain limits, the Pension Benefit Guaranty Corporation (PBGC) guarantees the payment of nonforfeitable benefits under defined benefit, single-employer plans covered by PBGC termination insurance.

A defined benefit plan may be voluntarily terminated only in a standard termination or a distress termination. In addition, the PBGC may initiate an involuntary plan termination, if the employer's financial condition demands this to prevent further losses. In both a standard and a distress termination the plan must have sufficient assets to cover benefit liabilities and guaranteed benefits.

See DISTRESS TERMINATION, INVOLUNTARY TERMINATION, STANDARD TERMINATION.

Statutory and Regulatory Reference: See ERISA §§ 4041-42. *See also* ERISA § 203(c)(2) and I.R.C. § 411(d)(2) (rule restricting distributions to an employer's 25 most highly compensated employees in the event of certain early terminations); I.R.C. § 411(d)(3) (VESTING requirement upon plan termination); ERISA § 403(d) and 4044 (allocation of plan assets among certain priority categories upon plan termination); ERISA §§ 4041A, 4048, 4070, 4261, and 4281 (rules regarding the termination of multiemployer plans); PBGC Notice of Interim Procedures, 51 Fed. Reg. 12,491 (April 10, 1986); PBGC Proposed Regulations, 52 Fed. Reg. 33,318 (Sept. 2, 1987); PBGC Revised Termination Rules, 54 Fed. Reg. 52,904 (Dec. 22, 1989).

Case and Other Interpretive Reference: See Rev. Rul. 80-229, 1980-2 C.B. 133 (rules for determining whether the allocation of assets upon termination of a defined benefit plan causes discrimination under I.R.C. § 401(a)(4)).

Treatise Reference: See Tax Mgmt. (BNA), No. 357, *Plan Terminations and Mergers*; *see also Employee Benefits Law* 47; 391-411 (1991); D. McGill & D. Grubbs, Jr., *Fundamentals of Private Pensions* 577 (6th ed. 1989).

term life insurance   Insurance designed to cover the life of the insured during a particular period or term. Annual renewable term insurance is generally the most basic pure risk coverage available combining the pure risk protection of term insurance with an option to renew each year, up to a maximum age, at a specific price.

Statutory and Regulatory Reference: See I.R.C. §§ 72, 79, and 101 and the regulations promulgated thereunder.

Treatise Reference: See Tax Mgmt. (BNA), *Financial Planning*, Para. 425, *Insurance Planning* (1991).

3 percent rule   One of three accrual rules that a qualified defined benefit plan may satisfy, designed to prevent excessive BACKLOADING of benefits. (The others are the fractional rule and the $133^{1}/_{3}$ percent rule; qualified defined benefit plans must satisfy at least one). This rule requires that participants accrue at least 3 percent of their NORMAL RETIREMENT BENEFIT under the plan for each year of credited service they perform. Thus, an employee with two years of credited service would have to have accrued at least 6 percent of his or her NORMAL RETIREMENT BENEFIT. Under the rule, at separation from service, an employee's benefit must not be less than:

(1) 3 percent of the normal retirement benefit to which the participant would be entitled if he or she began participation at the earliest possible entry age under the plan (where there is no minimum age requirement, the earliest possible entry age is deemed to be zero) and worked continuously until the earlier of age 65 or the plan's normal retirement age, multiplied by

(2) the number of years (not to exceed $33^{1}/_{3}$) of the individual's participation in the plan.

Basically, the 3 percent method takes the maximum benefit that a participant could accrue if he or she entered the plan at the plan's earliest possible entry age and remained in the employer's service until the earlier of age 65 or the plan's NORMAL RETIREMENT AGE.

Example 1: If a plan had an entry age of 20 and a normal retirement age of 60, the rule would have to be tested over a theoretical working career that spanned this period. Since the rule requires that only 33⅓ years be counted, however, only the first 33⅓ years would be taken into account. To pass this test, the plan must be able to satisfy the 3 percent test at any point in time with respect to any theoretical participant. Thus, after six years of service, a participant would have to have accrued at least 18 percent of his or her normal retirement benefit, after seven years, at least 21 percent, and so on.

In applying the 3 percent test, possible future adjustments to the plan's benefit formula, such as a change in Social Security benefits (in the case of an integrated plan) and changes in the consumer price index (in the case of a plan that is indexed to the CPI) are ignored. These benefits are treated as remaining constant from the year being tested to all future years. Further, if the plan provides a benefit that is based on compensation, the number of years of compensation that is considered in applying the 3 percent method cannot exceed the 10 consecutive years in a participant's career for which his or her compensation was the highest. This prevents a plan from reducing the benefit to which a participant is entitled by considering only compensation from the participant's early (low compensation) years of service. The example below illustrates the application of the 3 percent method:

Example 2: Defined benefit plan H has an entry age of 20 and a normal retirement age of 60. Under the plan, a participant accrues a benefit equal to 1.25 percent of compensation for the first 15 years of service. In years 16-30, the annual accrual increases to 1.5 percent of compensation. After the 30th year, the participant accrues benefits at the rate of 1.75 percent of compensation per year. The following computational steps show why this plan would fail the 3 percent test:

Step (1): Determine the Normal Retirement Benefit for Purposes of the 3 Percent Test:

$$
\begin{aligned}
&\;(1.25 \text{ percent} \times 15 \text{ years} =) & 18.75 \text{ percent} \\
+ &\;(1.50 \text{ percent} \times 15 \text{ years} =) & 22.50 \text{ percent} \\
+ &\;(1.75 \text{ percent} \times 3\tfrac{1}{3} \text{ years} =) & 5.83 \text{ percent} \\
\hline
& + & 47.08 \text{ percent}
\end{aligned}
$$

(normal retirement benefit for purposes of the 3 percent test);

Step (2): Multiply the Result of Step (1) by 3 Percent and Compare With Plan's Benefit Formula:

47.08 percent $\times$ .03 = 1.41 percent.

Because the plan fails to provide a benefit of at least 1.41 percent of compensation in years before the 15th year, it will fail the 3 percent test. If the plan had provided a benefit of at least 1.41 percent of compensation in all possible years during the first 33⅓ years, it would have passed the test. Note that the normal retirement benefit for purposes of this test, 47.08 percent of compensation, is less than the normal retirement benefit that a participant could accrue under the plan if he or she started at the earliest entry age, 20, and worked until normal retirement age, 60, because only the first 33⅓ years are considered.

See ACCRUAL, BACKLOADING, FRACTIONAL RULE, 133⅓ PERCENT RULE.

Statutory and Regulatory Reference: ERISA § 204(b)(1)(A)(ii); I.R.C. § 411(b)(1)(A); Treas. Reg. § 1.411(b)-1(b)(1).

Treatise Reference: See Tax Mgmt. (BNA), No. 351, *Pension Plans — Qualification; see also Employee Benefits Law* 123 (1991)

thrift plan　A plan similar to a profit-sharing plan in which the employer makes contributions to match mandatory employee contributions. Voluntary employee contributions may also be permitted. A thrift plan is subject to the Internal Revenue Code's nondiscrimination rules.

See DISCRIMINATION, SECTION 401(k) PLAN.

Statutory and Regulatory Reference: See I.R.C. §§ 401(k) and (m) and the regulations promulgated thereunder.

Treatise Reference: Tax Mgmt. (BNA), No. 352, *Profit-Sharing Plans—Qualification,* and No. 358, *Cash or Deferred Arrangements.*

top-hat plan   An unfunded nonqualified deferred compensation arrangement for the benefit of a select group of an employer's key management employees. Such plans are exempt from most of ERISA's requirements, such as the reporting and disclosure rules and the VESTING and participation rules.

See NONQUALIFIED DEFERRED COMPENSATION PLAN, RABBI TRUST.

Statutory and Regulatory Reference: ERISA § 201(2).

Treatise Reference: See Tax Mgmt. (BNA), No. 385, *Deferred Compensation Arrangements.*

top heavy/top-heavy plan   A qualified retirement plan that allocates an excessive portion of its benefits (more than 60 percent) to certain executives of the employer known as key employees. Such plans must use a faster VESTING schedule than non-top heavy plans and must give nonkey employees at least a specified minimum level of benefits. The Tax Equity and Fiscal Responsibility Act of 1982 (TEFRA), Pub. L. No. 97-248, made satisfaction of the top-heavy rules a qualification requirement for all I.R.C. § 401(a) plans.

A top-heavy plan must satisfy certain minimum vesting, and minimum benefit/contribution requirements. The top-heavy vesting rules require that, for any top-heavy plan year, the plan either provide for: (1) 100 percent vesting after an employee has completed three years of service; or (2) vesting in 20 percent annual increments over six years, with the first increment being in an employee's second year of service. These alternatives are known as three-year cliff vesting and six-year graded vesting.

The minimum contribution/benefit rules require that a top-heavy defined contribution plan provide each nonkey employee with a benefit equal to 3 percent of annual compensation or such lesser percentage as may be provided the key employee who receives the highest percentage of compensation as an employer contribution to his plan account for the plan year. A top-heavy defined benefit plan must provide each nonkey employee with an accrued benefit equal to 2 percent of such employee's compensation earned during a statutory testing period, not to exceed 20 percent of such testing period compensation with respect to any nonkey employee for all top-heavy plan years.

If a nonkey employee ceases employment before a plan becomes top-heavy, it need not provide him with minimum accruals, contributions, or vesting unless the employee returns to work for the employer.

Finally, if a plan is top-heavy, the combined plan limit on the accrual of benefits by an employee who participates in one or more defined benefit and one or more defined contribution plans maintained by the same employer is decreased.

See ACCRUAL, AGGREGATION GROUP, COMBINED PLAN LIMIT, DETERMINATION DATE, KEY EMPLOYEE, NONKEY EMPLOYEE, QUALIFIED RETIREMENT PLAN.

Statutory and Regulatory Reference: I.R.C. §§ 401(a)(10)(B) and 416; Treas. Reg. § 1.416-1 *et seq.*

Treatise Reference: See Tax Mgmt. (BNA), No. 353, *Owner-Dominated Plans—Top-Heavy and H.R. 10 Plans; see also Employee Benefits Law* 114-17 (1991); D. McGill & D. Grubbs, Jr., *Fundamentals of Private Pensions* 122 (6th ed. 1989).

top-heavy group   *See* AGGREGATION GROUP.

top-paid group   An employee is in the top-paid group of employees for the year for purposes of determining whether he or she is a highly compensated employee if the employee is among the top 20 percent of employees as ranked on the basis of compensation paid during the year.

See DISCRIMINATION, HIGHLY COMPENSATED EMPLOYEE.

Statutory and Regulatory Reference: I.R.C. § 414(q)(4) and the regulations promulgated thereunder.

Treatise Reference: Tax Mgmt. (BNA), No. 351, *Pension Plans—Qualification*, and No. 352, *Profit-Sharing Plans—Qualification*.

transferability restriction A condition applicable to restricted property (property transferred in exchange for services) on the employee's right to freely transfer the property. If restricted property becomes either not subject to a substantial risk of forfeiture or transferable, it will be taxed to the employee at its FAIR MARKET VALUE and the employer may take an offsetting compensation deduction.

See NONQUALIFIED DEFERRED COMPENSATION PLAN, RESTRICTED PROPERTY, SUBSTANTIAL RISK OF FORFEITURE.

Statutory and Regulatory Reference: I.R.C. § 83(a)(1); Treas. Reg. § 1.83-3.

Treatise Reference: Tax Mgmt. (BNA), No. 384, *Restricted Property—Section 83*.

trusteed plan A welfare or retirement-type plan the assets of which are held in a trust, administered by a trustee.

See NONQUALIFIED DEFERRED COMPENSATION PLAN, QUALIFIED RETIREMENT PLAN, WELFARE PLAN.

Treatise Reference: Tax Mgmt. (BNA), No. 351, *Pension Plans—Qualification*, No. 352, *Profit-Sharing Plans— Qualification*, and No. 394, *Employee Fringe Benefits*.

trustee-to-trustee transfer A transfer of assets directly from one trust to another upon TERMINATION of a plan or of an individual's participation in a plan.

See ROLLOVER, TERMINATION.

Statutory and Regulatory Reference: ERISA §§ 208, 4234, and 4321 (multiemployer plans); I.R.C. §§ 401(a)(12), 414(l) (single-employer plans).

Treatise Reference: Tax Mgmt. (BNA), No. 357, *Plan Terminations and Mergers*.

turnover rate/turnover assumption An assumption used by the actuary for a defined benefit pension plan as to the rate at which plan participants will leave the employer's service for reasons other than death or retirement.

See ACTUARIAL ASSUMPTIONS, FUNDING STANDARD ACCOUNT, MINIMUM FUNDING STANDARD.

Statutory and Regulatory Reference: I.R.C. § 412 and the regulations promulgated thereunder.

Treatise Reference: Tax Mgmt. (BNA), No. 351, *Pension Plans—Qualification*, and No. 371, *Employee Plans—Deductions, Contributions, and Funding*.

U

UBIT *See* UNRELATED BUSINESS TAX-ABLE INCOME.

unemployment tax (FUTA) An excise tax imposed on employers under the Federal Unemployment Tax Act (FUTA). The tax is equal to a percentage of the wages paid to employees. Contributions to state unemployment funds are generally creditable against the FUTA tax.

See SOCIAL SECURITY TAX.

Statutory and Regulatory Reference: I.R.C. §§ 3301-11 and the regulations promulgated thereunder.

Treatise Reference: Tax Mgmt. (BNA), No. 392, *Withholding, Social Security and Unemployment Taxes on Compensation.*

unfunded deferred compensation plan A nonqualified arrangement for deferred compensation in which the employer merely promises to pay an amount to the employee at a future time. The employer can set aside assets to pay for future payments, but the plan will be unfunded only if the assets remain subject to the claims of the employer's general creditors. If the arrangement satisfies certain requirements, the employee will not be taxed on his or her benefit until it becomes funded and no longer subject to a substantial risk of forfeiture.

See FUNDING, NONQUALIFIED DEFERRED COMPENSATION PLAN, RABBI TRUST, RESTRICTED PROPERTY, SUBSTANTIAL RISK OF FORFEITURE.

Treatise Reference: Tax Mgmt. (BNA), No. 384, *Restricted Property — Section 83*, and No. 385, *Deferred Compensation Arrangements.*

unit-benefit excess plan A defined benefit pension plan that is integrated with Social Security by providing an increased employer contribution for compensation above the plan's integration level.

Example: A defined benefit plan is integrated with Social Security. Its integration level is a participant's covered compensation. Under the plan's benefit formula, a participant accrues a benefit of 1 percent of covered compensation per year. With respect to a participant's compensation in excess of covered compensation, the plan provides benefit accruals at the rate of 1.25 percent per year.

See DEFINED BENEFIT EXCESS PLAN, INTEGRATION LEVEL, INTEGRATION (SOCIAL SECURITY), UNIT BENEFIT PLAN.

Statutory and Regulatory Reference: I.R.C. § 401(l)(3)(A); Prop. Treas. Reg. § 1.401(l)-1 *et seq.*

Treatise Reference: Tax Mgmt. (BNA), No. 356, *Qualified Plans—Integration.*

unit benefit plan   A type of defined benefit pension plan under which a participant's benefit is calculated based on a unit of length of service, typically years of service. Thus, a plan that provided participants with a benefit equal to 1 percent of their FINAL AVERAGE COMPENSATION for each YEAR OF SERVICE they performed with the employer would be a unit benefit plan.

See DEFINED BENEFIT PLAN, INTEGRATION (SOCIAL SECURITY).

Treatise Reference: Tax Mgmt. (BNA), No. 351, *Pension Plans—Qualification*, and No. 356, *Qualified Plans—Integration.*

universal life insurance   A type of insurance policy with a pure term life insurance component and an accumulating cash fund. The policyholder pays an initial premium for the term life insurance coverage from which mortality charges and expenses relating to administration of the policy are deducted. The remaining amount is credited to a cash value account that earns interest tax free. Policyholders can borrow or withdraw funds from the cash value account. Policyholders generally can choose a level death benefit equal to the face amount of the policy or an increasing death benefit equal to the initial face amount plus the policy's cash value. Universal life insurance differs from traditional life insurance because: (1) there is an explicit separation of policy into two parts (the investment fund and the protection element) in the universal policy; (2) the interest feature in universal life is more sensitive to current interest rates and the guaranteed interest rate is generally lower; and (3) the

premiums, cash values, and death benefits are flexible for universal life.

See LIFE INSURANCE CONTRACT, TERM LIFE INSURANCE, WHOLE LIFE INSURANCE.

Statutory and Regulatory Reference: I.R.C. § 101(f) (for pre-1985 policies); §§ 7702 and 7701A (for post-1984 policies).

Treatise Reference: Tax Mgmt. (BNA), No. 111, *Life Insurance;* Tax Mgmt. (BNA) *Financial Planning*, Para. 425, *Insurance Planning* (1991).

unrealized appreciation   An increase in the FAIR MARKET VALUE of an asset on which federal income tax is not currently due because of the operation of the Internal Revenue Code's rules governing the taxability of the asset. In the qualified plan context, this term usually refers to the increase in fair market value of an asset held for a participant's benefit in a plan over its value at the time it was contributed to the plan on which the participant does not yet have to pay federal income tax. The Code provides, in certain circumstances, that the APPRECIATION on employer securities held in a qualified plan on a participant's behalf will not have to be realized (taken into account for tax purposes) until the stock is distributed and/or the participant sells or disposes of it in a taxable transaction.

See LUMP-SUM DISTRIBUTION.

Statutory and Regulatory Reference: I.R.C. § 402(a)(1) and Treas. Reg. § 1.402(a)-1(b) (general rule); I.R.C. § 402(e)(4)(J) (special rule when employer securities are distributed as part of a lump-sum distribution).

Treatise Reference: See Tax Mgmt. (BNA), No. 370, *Qualified Plans—Taxation of Distributions.*

unrelated business income tax (UBIT)
A tax on a tax-exempt organization's income-producing activities, whereby a tax is imposed on unrelated trade or business taxable in-

come, i.e., the organization's gross income from an unrelated trade or business regularly carried on by it, less any deductions that are directly connected with the carrying on of the trade or business. An unrelated trade or business is any trade or business the conduct of which is not substantially related to the organization's exercise or performance of its exempt function (with several exceptions for activities such as a trade or business carried on by volunteers and the selling of merchandise received by the organization as gifts or contributions).

Example: An example of a related activity is a hospital's operation of a cafeteria, parking lot, and gift shop. This contributed to the organization's exempt purpose and therefore did not generate unrelated business taxable income. Rev. Rul. 69-267, 69-268, 69-269, 1969-1 C.B. 160. An example of an unrelated activity is a school's use of its tennis facilities during the summer as a public tennis club. This is an unrelated trade or business and generated unrelated business taxable income. Rev. Rul. 76-402, 1976-2 C.B. 177; Rev. Rul. 80-297, 1980-2 C.B. 196.

Statutory and Regulatory Reference: I.R.C. §§ 511, 512, 513, 514, and 515; Treas. Reg. § 1.513-1 (defining unrelated trade or business); Treas. Reg. § 1.512(a)-1 (exploitation of exempt function; e.g., sale of membership lists).

Case and Other Interpretive Reference: TAM 8706012 (business league will not have UBI even though it owns several taxable subsidiaries that earn unrelated income; separate corporate entities respected so long as subsidiaries have substantial individual business purposes). *See also Suffolk County Patrolmen's Benevolent Association v. Commissioner,* 77 T.C. 1314 (1981), *acq.,* 1984-2 C.B. 2 (income derived from annual vaudeville show not considered UBI; show not conducted with sufficient frequency and continuity or in such a manner as to be regularly carried on); *United States v.*

American Bar Endowment, 477 U.S. 105 (1986); *Hope School v. United States,* 612 F.2d 298 (7th Cir. 1980); *Commissioner v. Groetzinger,* 480 U.S. 23 (1987); *National Collegiate Athletic Association v. Commissioner,* 92 T.C. 456 (1989).

Treatise Reference: Tax Mgmt. (BNA), No. 331, *Trade Associations*; *Employee Benefits Law* 1011-12 (1991).

user fee   A fee charged by a governmental agency (e.g., the IRS) for performing a function on an applicant's behalf. E.g., the IRS charges private letter ruling (PLR) and determination letter applicants a user fee for processing the application on the taxpayer's behalf.

utilization review   A method of health care cost control focused on reviewing the appropriateness and quality of care given to hospitalized patients. Utilization review encompasses several different techniques, for example, preadmission screening and second surgical opinions. Some of the factors considered in the process include a treatment's medical appropriateness (generally determined with reference to practice guidelines which provide parameters of acceptable practice for specific clinical conditions), where the treatment is provided (for example, at a hospital, ambulatory care center, or doctor's office), and the duration of the care (to ensure that it continues no longer than medically necessary). The utilization review process can be prospective (i.e., through preadmission or precertification review), concurrent (at prescribed intervals after the start of a treatment program) or retrospective (e.g, claims review and coverage review). Utilization review is often subject to state regulation.

Statutory and Regulatory Reference: 45 C.F.R. Part 60 (National Practitioner Data Bank Rules); 42 U.S.C. § 1320b-12

(Medicare Act, Federal Outcomes Research Program). Examples of state regulation: MD. HEALTH CODE ANN., §§ 19-1301 *et seq.*; MINN. STAT. 1988, SECTION 72A.20(4a); CAL. CORP. CODE, § 317; MAINE INS. CODE TITLE 24-A, § 2679; LA. REVISED STAT. 22:657(d).

Case and Other Interpretative Reference: Pilot Life Insurance Co. v. Dedeaux, 481 U.S. 41, 8 EB Cases 1409 (1987) (insurance provided through ERISA plan thus common law and state law tort claims preempted by ERISA); *Wickline v. California,* 43 Cal. App. 3d 1630, 239 Cal. Rptr. 810 (1986) (reviewer's liability to patient for harm resulting from prospective or concurrent utilization review); *Sarchett v. Blue Shield,* 43 Cal. 3d 1, 233 Cal. Rptr. 76 (1987) (carrier can perform retrospective medical review and consider medical necessity in reimbursement decisions notwithstanding decisions of treating physicians and patient); *Aetna Life Insurance Co. v. Lavoie,* 550 So. 2d 1050 (Ala. 1987) (bad faith found where payor decided to limit or deny treatment before engaging in sufficient review).

Treatise Reference: See Directory of Practice Parameters; Practice Parameter Update (quarterly), American Medical Association, 535 North Dearborn Street, Chicago, Illinois 60610; *Controlling Costs and Changing Patient Care? The Role of Utilization Management,* Institute of Medicine, Committee on Utilization Management, (Washington: National Academy Press, 1989); Blum, *An Analysis of Legal Liability in Health Care Utilization Review and Case Management,* 26 HOUSTON L. REV. 191 (1989). *See also Employee Benefits Law* 1040 (1991).

V

valuation   Determining the worth of assets, such as property held in a plan's trust account on behalf of participants or beneficiaries. A qualified plan's assets must undergo periodic valuation.

Statutory and Regulatory Reference: ERISA § 302(c)(2)(9); I.R.C. § 412(c)(2)(9); Treas. Reg. § 1.412(c)(2)-1.

Treatise Reference: Tax Mgmt. (BNA), No. 371, *Employee Plans—Deductions, Contributions, and Funding.*

variable annuity   An annuity having features that can vary based on changes in circumstances. One common type of variable annuity is one where the payments to the recipient (the annuitant) will vary in amount based on the investment performance of the funds that underlie the annuity. Another type of variable annuity is one that allows the annuitant to increase or decrease the periodic premium payments.

See ANNUITY.

Statutory and Regulatory Reference: I.R.C. § 72 and the regulations promulgated thereunder.

Treatise Reference: Tax Mgmt. (BNA), No. 134, *Annuities.*

variable life insurance contract   Inflation-hedged life insurance with cash reserves, and to some extent death benefits, fluctuating according to chosen investment vehicles. This life insurance policy is subject to both state law and federal securities laws that require it to include a prospectus following the appropriate SEC format (the policy can only be delivered by an agent licensed under state law and registered with the National Association of Security Dealers (NASD)). A variable life insurance policy is a type of whole life insurance with a guaranteed minimum death benefit predicated upon a fixed premium. Cash value is held in a separate account and invested at policyholder direction among a limited number of funds, for instance, stock funds and money market funds, available from the insurance company. The policyholder assumes the risk of these investments. The contract must provide for the allocation of all or part of the amount received under the contract to an account that is segregated from the general asset accounts and must either provide for the payment of annuities or must be a life insurance contract. If the contract is an annuity contract, the amounts paid in and out of the separate account must reflect the investment return and the market value of that segregated account. If the contract is a life insurance contract, the amount of the death benefit must be adjusted on the basis of the investment return and the market value of the segregated account.

See LIFE INSURANCE CONTRACT.

Statutory and Regulatory Reference: I.R.C. § 817(d), 7702; Treas. Reg. § 1.817-5T.

Treatise Reference: Tax Mgmt. (BNA), *Financial Planning,* Para. 425, *Insurance Planning* (1991).

VEBA (Voluntary Employees' Beneficiary Association) A tax-exempt entity used by employers to self-fund various employee benefits, such as health, disability, death, and severance benefits. The entity must qualify for tax-exempt status and may be organized as any form of association, including a corporation or trust, with nonprofit corporations being the preferred entity. Membership must be voluntary, i.e., employees cannot be forced to join unless there is no detriment to them – they do not have to make any payments. A VEBA functions primarily as a cooperative device for pooling funds and distributing risk in order to provide certain Internal Revenue Service-approved benefits to employees (as well as some nonemployee members). A VEBA must benefit and be controlled by employees (as well as some non-employees such as sole proprietors who have an employment-related common bond with employee/members), and it must have as its purpose the provision of life, sick, accident, or other benefits (such as vacation and unemployment benefits). The VEBA must function to benefit its members, their dependents, and beneficiaries and a VEBA's net earnings cannot inure to the benefit of private shareholders or individuals. After the Deficit Reduction Act of 1984 (DEFRA), Pub. L. No. 98-369, a VEBA is treated as a welfare benefit fund and is subject to the various rules which apply to these funds. As a welfare benefit fund, contributions by employers to a VEBA are deductible only in the tax year when paid and are limited to qualified costs for the year.

See WELFARE BENEFIT FUND, EXEMPT ORGANIZATION, QUALIFIED COSTS.

Statutory and Regulatory Reference: I.R.C. §§ 419, 419A, 501(c)(9), 511-12; Treas. Reg. §§ 54.4976-1T; 1.419-1T and -2T; 1.461(h)-4T; 1.501(c)(9)-1 through -7; 1.505(c)-1T; and 1.512(a)-5T.

Case and Other Interpretive Reference: See GCM 39, 194 (March 15, 1984). *See also Water Quality Association Employees' Benefit Corp. v. United States,* 795 F.2d 1303 (7th Cir. 1986) (geographic locale requirement of Treas. Reg. § 1.501(c)-9 invalid in Seventh Circuit in defining what employees can be members of a VEBA); *Greensboro Pathology Associates v. United States,* 698 F.2d 1196 (Fed. Cir. 1982) (employer's payments of educational benefits through a plan deductible as ordinary and necessary business expense rather than deferred compensation); *Moser v. Commissioner,* U.S.T.C. 3/30/89, 10 EB Cases 2509 (1989) (closely held corporation may deduct $200,000 one-time VEBA contribution where VEBA provided benefits to three employees since benefits provided were commensurate with salaries and ages of members, plan operated in accordance with its terms, assets did not revert to plan sponsors, investments were prudent, and contribution was ordinary and necessary amount to fully fund plan); *American Association of Christian Schools VEBA Welfare Plan v. United States,* 850 F.2d 1150, 10 EB Cases 1006 (11th Cir. 1988) (welfare trust providing insurance benefits to member/employees did not qualify as an I.R.C. § 501(c)(9) VEBA; trust controlled by school association's board of directors and not by board chosen by employees, did not meet employee control requirement, did not meet nondiscrimination requirements).

Treatise Reference: Tax Mgmt. (BNA), No. 395, *Section 501(c)(9) and Self-Funded Employee Benefits; Employee Benefits Law* 1015-23 (1991).

vesting The process whereby accrued benefits under a plan become NONFOR-FEITABLE to the participant.

Benefits under qualified plans that are attributable to employee contributions must always be 100 percent vested. Benefits attributable to employer contributions must vest at least as rapidly as under one of two statutory schedules: five-year cliff vesting or seven-year graded vesting. Top-heavy plans must satisfy one of two accelerated vesting schedules: three-year cliff vesting or six-year graded vesting.

See QUALIFIED RETIREMENT PLAN, TOP-HEAVY.

Statutory and Regulatory Reference: See ERISA § 203(a)(2); I.R.C. § 411(a); Treas. Reg. § 1.411(a)-3 (reflecting pre-Tax Reform Act of 1986 law); Treas. Reg. § 1.411(a)-3T (reflecting post-TRA 1986 law). *See also* I.R.C. § 416(b) and Treas. Reg. § 1.416-1, Q&A V-1 *et seq* (top-heavy vesting rules).

Case and Other Interpretive Reference: Quality Brands Inc. v. Commissioner, 67 T.C. 167 (1976) (reallocation of forfeitures under defined contribution plan to accounts of remaining participants based on the relative level of their account balances is permissible under the vesting rules so long as it does not discriminate in operation). *See* Rev. Rul. 76-47, 1976-1 C.B. 109 (conversion factors for allocating accrued benefits under a defined benefit plan where NORMAL RETIREMENT AGE is not age 65 between employee contributions and employer contributions for vesting purposes). In Rev. Rul. 76-259, 1976-2 C.B. 111, the IRS ruled that a defined contribution plan that does not provide an uncon-ditional contribution allocation to the account of a participant who has completed 1,000 hours of service in a computation period does not automatically violate the VESTING rules, but may result in DISCRIMINATION under I.R.C. § 401(a)(4)). *See also* Rev. Rul. 81-10, 1981-1 C.B. 172 (profit-sharing plan will not be disqualified due to provision that reallocates forfeitures from the accounts of terminating participants among the accounts of the remaining participants based on their respective account balances); Rev. Rul. 81-211, 1981-2 C.B. 99 (plan that provides that participants' employer-derived benefits will become nonforfeitable on a date that occurs after normal retirement age causes plan to fail to satisfy the I.R.C. § 411(a) vesting rules); Rev. Rul. 85-31, 1985-1 C.B. 153 (plan may forfeit the amount in excess of that which is statutorily required to be vested upon an employee's being discharged for cause, provided that such forfeitures do not result in discrimination prohibited by I.R.C. § 401(a)(4)); Rev. Rul. 89-53, 1989-1 C.B. 116 (profit-sharing plan fails to qualify where, during first PLAN YEAR, the plan did not specifically require that employees' rights to benefits became nonforfeitable upon the complete discontinuance of contributions).

Treatise Reference: See Tax Mgmt. (BNA), No. 351, *Pension Plans—Qualification,* and No. 353, *Owner-Dominated Plans—Top-Heavy and H.R. 10 Plans; see also Employee Benefits Law* 105-17 (1991).

Voluntary Employees' Beneficiary Association *See* VEBA.

W

waived funding deficiency   A permission granted by the IRS to the sponsor of a qualified pension plan subject to the Internal Revenue Code's minimum funding standard whereby, instead of contributing the funds needed to meet that standard for the current PLAN YEAR, the plan is allowed spread out FUNDING payments in installments over a period of 15 years. The IRS will grant a waiver if certain financial distress criteria apply, such as declining profits in the employer's industry.

See   EXTENSION OF AMORTIZATION PERIODS, MINIMUM FUNDING STANDARD, FUNDING STANDARD ACCOUNT.

Statutory and Regulatory Reference: See ERISA § 303(d)(1), I.R.C. § 412(d)(4). *See also* ERISA §§ 303(e), 304(c), and I.R.C. § 412(f)(4) (notice requirements); ERISA § 304(b) and I.R.C. § 412(f) (bar on benefit increases during a period when a waiver of the minimum funding standard is in effect); ERISA § 306 and I.R.C. § 412(f)(3) (security requirements).

Treatise Reference: *See* Tax Mgmt. (BNA), No. 371, *Employee Plans—Deductions, Contributions, and Funding.*

welfare benefit fund (WBF)   A fund set up as part of a plan of an employer and through which the employer provides welfare benefits to employees or their beneficiaries. For purposes of a welfare benefit fund, welfare benefits are any benefits other than a benefit to which I.R.C. §§ 83(h), 404, or 404A applies. The fund can be any organization described in I.R.C. § 501(c)(7)(9)(17), or (20), and any account held for an employer by any person, to the extent provided in regulations. Note that employer contributions to a separate bank account of the employer, a subsidiary, or to another related party are not considered contributions to a fund. Contributions made by employers to WFBs are only deductible if a deduction is permitted under some other Code section, and only in the taxable year paid and subject to qualified cost limitations. Employees exclude payments only to the extent the amounts are excludable under another Code section and include benefits in income when paid by the trust.

Statutory and Regulatory Reference: See I.R.C. §§ 83(h), 419, 419A, 501(c), 511-12, 4976; Treas. Reg. §§ 1.419-1T (Q&A-3), 419A-1T and -2T.

Case and Other Interpretive Reference: See IRS Announcement 86-45, I.R.B. 1986-15 (clarifying treatment of experience-rated insurance contracts under the welfare benefit fund rules).

Treatise Reference: See Tax Mgmt. (BNA), No. 395, *Section 501(c)(9) and Self-Funded*

Employee Welfare Benefits; Employee Benefits Law 944-1061 (1991).

welfare benefit plan   Programs through which employers provide benefits such as medical, surgical, or hospital care, disability payments, life insurance, severance pay, and vacations (all of which are not compensation arrangements).

Statutory and Regulatory Reference: ERISA § 3(1)(definition).

Treatise Reference: See Tax Mgmt. (BNA), No. 395, *Section 501(c)(9) and Self-Funded Employee Welfare Benefits; Employee Benefits Law* 944-1061 (1991).

welfare plan   *See* EMPLOYEE WELFARE BENEFIT PLAN, EMPLOYEE BENEFIT PLAN, WELFARE BENEFIT FUND.

whole life insurance   A type of cash value insurance coverage that is traditionally a single financial instrument rather than a combination of term insurance with a cash savings account, designed to provide protection for the life of the insured. The insurer charges a fixed premium based on mortality charges, partially prefunded; expense charges, for example, commissions and administration expenses; and investment experience. The insurer guarantees fixed death benefit and cash values that can be borrowed or withdrawn. Any amount borrowed reduces the face value of the policy until it is repaid. Any amount withdrawn from the cash value reduces the cash value and the death benefit, and the death benefit cannot be restored without supplementing basic coverage through a rider or paid-up additions. If the insurer's investments did well, the policy paid dividends that could be recognized by the policyholder as cash, paid-up additions to the policy, additional term insurance, additions to the cash value, or reduced premiums. A level premium whole life contract is a policy in which the premiums payments remain constant. These contracts are also referred to a straight life policies. Graduated payment whole life contracts are designed to appeal to younger purchasers and the early premiums are substantially less than the later premiums. These policies are also referred to as modified life policies.

See LIFE INSURANCE CONTRACT, PS 58 RATES, TERM INSURANCE, WHOLE LIFE INSURANCE.

Statutory and Regulatory Reference: I.R.C. §§ 72, 264 and the regulations promulgated thereunder.

Treatise Reference: Tax Mgmt. (BNA), *Financial Planning,* Para. 425, *Insurance Planning* (1991).

window plan/window benefit   A provision in a qualified defined benefit plan under which, if employees retire early, e.g., before normal retirement age, the employees will receive additional benefits over and above the amount they would be entitled to receive based on their attained age and service at the time of separation from employment. Window benefits are used to provide employees an incentive to retire early.

See DEFINED BENEFIT PLAN, NORMAL RETIREMENT AGE.

Statutory and Regulatory Reference: I.R.C. §§ 401(a), 411(a) and the regulations promulgated thereunder.

Treatise Reference: See generally Tax Mgmt. (BNA), No. 351, *Pension Plans—Qualification.*

withdrawal liability (multiemployer plans)   The liability of a contributing employer to a qualified multiemployer defined benefit plan to make contributions necessary to fund benefits of employees before it may cease contributing to the plan. Plans subject to the Multiemployer Pension Plan Amendments Act of 1980 (MPPAA),

Pub. L. No. 96-364, impose liabilities on contributing employers upon a complete or partial withdrawal of the employer from the plan, rather than on plan TERMINATION, as is the case for multiple and single-employer plans.

MPPAA removed multiemployer plans from the termination insurance system that governs single and multiple employer plans and substituted a system that imposes liability for certain unfunded vested benefits when an employer partially or totally withdraws from a multiemployer plan.

ERISA § 4201(a) provides that a complete withdrawal has occurred either when there is a permanent cessation of the employer's contribution obligation or when, despite the fact that the employer literally still has an obligation to make contributions, e.g., under the collective bargaining agreement, the employer no longer has operations that are covered by the plan. ERISA § 4204 also treats certain employer asset sales as a withdrawal, but creates an exception for arm's-length sales where the buyer assumes the seller's contribution obligation and the buyer either purchases a bond or places in escrow sufficient funds to cover the seller's contribution obligation for one year. This bond or escrow account must be maintained for five years after the asset sale. It insures the plan should the buyer withdraw or default on its contribution obligation. For purposes of this rule, ERISA § 4204(b)(1) attributes the seller's contribution history to the buyer.

A partial withdrawal will also give rise to withdrawal liability. A partial withdrawal will occur when there is a 70 percent decline in the employer's contribution base units (CBUs) (the units on which an employer's contribution obligation is calculated, such as work days) over a three-year period. The CBUs in this period are compared with the employer's average contribution obligation in its two highest years of the five years preceding the three-year period being tested. *See* ERISA § 4001(11). Under ERISA § 4202(a)(2), the

closing of an employer facility or the termination of a collective bargaining agreement can also give rise to partial withdrawal liability.

ERISA contains various special rules for those industries that calculate partial withdrawals differently. Further, any multiemployer plan may choose among several methods of determining withdrawal liability. These rules are discussed below.

Under the presumptive rule of ERISA § 4211(b)(3), annual changes in unfunded vested benefits (UVBs) are allocated ratably to employers based on each employer's share of UVBs during the current year and the immediately preceding four years, with a reduction in each employer's share of five percent for each passing year, i.e., 20-year amortization. Different rules apply to employers that were in the plan in plan years ending before April 29, 1980, and those that were not. Further, under the presumptive rule, when an employer becomes unable to pay its share of UVBs, its share is reallocated to employers remaining in the plan.

Instead of using the presumptive rule, which will apply if the plan does not specify an alternative, a plan may use certain statutory alternative rules. Under the first alternative rule of ERISA § 4211(c)(2), pre-1980 UVBs are allocated in the same manner as they are under the presumptive rule. Post-1980 UVBs are allocated to employers in a block, but not, however, on a year-by-year basis. Thus, this rule is less favorable to new employers entering the plan than the presumptive rule. Under the second alternative method of ERISA § 4211(c)(3), no distinction is made between pre- and post- 1980 UVBs. Thus, this rule is even less favorable to new entrants than the first alternative, although it is comparatively easy to administer. A plan might wish to use the first or second alternative methods where attracting new employers is not a significant concern.

The third alternative method is known as the attributable rule. As its name suggests, this rule attempts to trace each employer's obligation to the service performed by its employees under the plan. Where such service cannot be traced, each employer is allocated a share of this unattributable liability. The attributable rule promotes fairness in dividing liability among employers, but is the most complex to administer.

Note that an employer's liability for a partial withdrawal is a proportionate share of the liability that it would have incurred had it totally withdrawn. When a partially withdrawing employer resumes its prior level of contributions, ERISA § 4208 provides that partial liability will be reduced (abated) for subsequent years. A *de minimis* rule allows small employers to escape partial withdrawal liability. Further, under ERISA § 4210, a plan may adopt a free look rule, which allows an employer to enter the plan and withdraw within six years without incurring withdrawal liability. This rule has the effect of encouraging new employers to enter the plan. Under the 20-year cap of ERISA § 4219, an employer's withdrawal liability obligation is limited to payments over 20 years unless a mass withdrawal, as defined in ERISA § 4219(c)(1)(D), took place. Other special restrictions on partial withdrawal liability apply for pre-April 28, 1980, partial withdrawals, insolvent employers, cases of liability of employers to multiple plans, and successive withdrawals.

When a withdrawal occurs from a multiemployer plan, ERISA § 4219 requires the plan sponsor to notify the employer within a reasonable time of the amount of liability and provide a schedule for its payment. The employer may request a review of this determination before payments begin. Payments are made based on the number of contribution base units in the average year of the three highest years in the previous 10 years, multiplied by the employer's highest contribution rate within the 10-year period. The payments are made in equal annual installments and are subject to the 20-year cap. *See* ERISA § 4243(b)(1).

See COMPLETE WITHDRAWAL DEFINED BENEFIT PLAN, MPPAA (MULTIEMPLOYER PENSION PLAN AMENDMENTS ACT OF 1980), MULTIEMPLOYER PLAN, PARTIAL WITHDRAWAL.

Statutory and Regulatory Reference: ERISA § 4201 *et seq.*

Treatise Reference: See Tax Mgmt. (BNA), No. 359, *Multiemployer Plans — Special Rules. See also Employee Benefits Law* 742-840 (1991); D. McGill & D. Grubbs, Jr., *Fundamentals of Private Pensions* 618 (6th ed. 1989.

workers' compensation Amounts provided by state laws allowing for disability income, rehabilitation benefits, and lump-sum payments for certain injuries or disabilities arising out of and in the course of an individual's employment. Disability benefits generally are expressed as a fraction of the injured worker's weekly wages and may be payable for a maximum number of weeks, or in some cases for life, depending on the nature of the injury. To be excludable from gross income, workers' compensation benefits must be mandated by statute and must constitute compensation for an occupational sickness or injury. The exclusion generally is available to a disabled employee or to the dependents of a disabled employee.

Statutory and Regulatory Reference: I.R.C. § 104; Treas. Reg. § 1.104-1.

Case and Other Interpretive Reference: See Rev. Rul. 72-400, 1972-2 C.B. 75 and Rev. Rul. 77-235, 1977-2 C.B. 45 (exclusion available to dependents of disabled employee); Rev. Rul. 57-399, 1957-2 C.B. 101; Rev. Rul. 56-83, 1956-1 C.B. 79 (payments received from private employer's plan without statutory mandate not excludable). *See also Golden v. Commissioner*, 30 T.C.M. 691 (1971)(payments not excludable where there was failure to prove a disability was job-related).

Treatise Reference: Insurance and Risk Management for Business and Government, A Desktop Manual (Washington: BURAFF Publications, The Bureau of National Affairs, Inc., 1989) (guide to state, federal, and Canadian laws); J. V. Nackley, *Primer on Workers' Compensation* (1989); Larson, *Workers' Compensation Law* (1952 and suppl.).

working condition fringe benefits   Any employer-provided property or services that, if paid for by the employee, would be deductible by the employee under I.R.C. § 162 (as a business expense) or § 167 (as depreciation) assuming substantiation requirements are met and ignoring the 2 percent floor on miscellaneous itemized deductions under I.R.C. § 67. Employees may exclude the value of these benefits from income. Employer-provided parking on or near the business premises, use of company cars, and certain security services are some examples of working condition fringes.

Example: Assume that in response to several death threats on the life of A, Company X's president, Company X establishes an overall security program for A, including an alarm system at A's home and guards at A's workplace, the use of a vehicle that is specially equipped with alarms and bulletproofing and a body guard/driver. Assume that A is driven for both personal and business reasons in the company-supplied vehicle. Assume also that but for bona fide business security reasons, these benefits would not have been supplied to the president. With respect to the transportation provided for security reasons, A may exclude as a working condition fringe the value of the special security features of the vehicle and the value attributable to the bodyguard/driver. A must include in income the value of the availability of the vehicle for personal use.

Statutory and Regulatory Reference: I.R.C. §§ 132(a)(3), 132(d), 162, and 167(a); Treas. Reg. § 1.132-5.

Treatise Reference: Tax Mgmt. (BNA), No. 394, *Employee Fringe Benefits*; *Employee Benefits Law* 982-84 (1991).

Y

year of service A 12-consecutive-month computation period under a qualified plan in which an employee performs enough hours of service to be credited with a year of service under the plan. In general, a qualified plan cannot require a participant to complete more than 1,000 hours of service in a computation period before crediting him or her with a year of service for participation or VESTING purposes. A slightly less stringent standard applies to service for purposes of benefit accrual, under which an employee with 1,000 hours must be given at least credit for a partial year of service. Since this is a minimum standard, a plan may elect to require a lesser number of hours than the statutory requirement.

See EQUIVALENCY, HOUR OF SERVICE.

Statutory and Regulatory Reference: ERISA § 202(a)(3) and I.R.C. § 410(a)(3)(A) (participation); ERISA § 204(b)(4) and I.R.C. § 411(b)(4) (benefit accrual); ERISA § 203(b)(2), I.R.C. § 411(a)(5) (vesting), and 29 C.F.R. § 2530 *et seq.*

Treatise Reference: Tax Mgmt. (BNA), No. 351, *Pension Plans—Qualification*; *Employee Benefits Law* 107-11 (1991).

Z

ZEBRA plan *See* ZERO BALANCE REIM-BURSEMENT ACCOUNT PLAN.

zero balance reimbursement account plan A pre-January 1985 cafeteria plan that provided for reimbursement of uninsured medical and dental expenses as well as dependent care expenses without establishing a FLEXIBLE SPENDING ACCOUNT. Reimbursements generally were made on payday, with a corresponding reduction in the employee's paycheck, and no balance accumulated in any accounts.

See CAFETERIA PLAN.

Statutory and Regulatory Reference: See Pub. L. No. 98-369 (DEFRA); I.R.C. § 531(b)(5); *see also* I.R.C. § 125(a) and Treas. Reg. § 1.125-1.

Treatise Reference: Tax Mgmt. (BNA), No. 397, *Cafeteria Plans*.

About the Authors

VIRGINIA L. BRIGGS, ESQ., received a BA from the University of Delaware in English and in Anthropology with a concentration in linguistics. She received her J.D. from Cornell Law School and currently is pursuing a Master of Laws in Taxation at Georgetown University Law Center. As Research and Development Manager of BNA's Reference Guide Development Unit, Ms. Briggs directs the development of new reference products in the business and human resources area, including compensation and benefits related products. Ms. Briggs has published numerous articles on taxation and employee benefits issues and has co-authored BNA's *Retirement & Welfare Benefit Plans* and the *Federal Taxation of Employee Benefits* portfolio in BNA's Corporate Practice Series.

MICHAEL G. KUSHNER, ESQ., received his J.D. from the University of Virginia and his LL.M. in Taxation from George Washington University. As a tax law analyst for Tax Management Inc. in the area of ERISA and compensation planning, he analyzes developments and trends for a variety of practioner-oriented publications. He is an adjunct professor at Dickinson Law School and has taught in the Certified Employee Benefits Program at Georgetown University. He is the author of *ERISA; Qualified Retirement Plans and Employee Benefits,* published by The Bureau of National Affairs, Inc. Mr. Kushner practices law in the ERISA area in Washington, D.C.

MICHAEL J. SCHINBACK, ESQ., received his J.D. from Boston University School of Law and his LL.M. in Taxation from George Washington University. Until his recent reassignment as the Assistant Managing Editor—International Taxation, he was the Assistant Managing Editor (Editorial) for Tax Management Inc. In that capacity, he oversaw the work of attorneys and accountants in analyzing developments in all areas of federal income, estate, and gift tax, and coordinated the editing and updating of Tax Management's tax services and periodicals, including the compensation planning portfolios and the Tax Management Compensation Planning Journal. He has taught as an Adjunct Professor at the Dickinson School of Law, and is the author of several articles on federal taxation that have appeared in the *Tax Management Weekly Report* and the *Tax Management Financial Planning Journal.*